GRACIA & GENTIL:
Hymn Stories
Have Lessons for Us Today
Volume II

MUGERWA Paul
Church Elder, Education Director & Music Evangelist
Author: Hymn stories & Contemporary Lifestyles
SDA Church Najjanankumbi District

E-mail: tatagracia2007@gmail.com / asantecap@gmail.com
+256 782 640448

GRACIA & GENTIL: Hymn Stories Have Lessons for Us Today

Copyright @ 2016 Mabira International Publishers Ltd
P.O Box 36750 Kampala

All Rights Reserved.

No part of this publication may be reproduced or distributed in any form or by any media, or stored in a database or retrieval system without the prior written permission of the author or publisher.

ISBN: 9789970532025

Concept Editor: Pr. Dr. Ikechukwu Michael Oluikpe
Production Editor: Rev. Dr. Kiwanuka Emmanuel
Principal Contributors: Mugerwa Paul and Rebecca Nakisozi Mugerwa,
P.O Box 36750 Kampala
+256 782640448   tatagracia2007@gmail.com

Layout Design & Cover page Design: *Wakabi Joe* (Geneprint Limited)

Publisher: Mabira International Publishers

Content: Music/ Church Hymns; Personal Development; Worship & Spiritual; Inspirational; Devotional; Christian Historical Context; Theology.

DETAILED TABLE OF CONTENTS

ACKNOWLEDGEMENTS .... *i*
EDITORIAL TEAM .... *iii*
DEDICATION .... *iii*
PREFACE .... *iv*
FOREWORD .... *vi*

PRAISE SONGS:

1. MY MAKER & MY KING 1
   (Gwe Eyanunula nebaza Ekisa kyo)
   Lest We Forget (The Sin of Forgetting) 2
2. BLESSED ASSURANCE 4
   (Gwe Yesu Oli Wange Ddala)
   This is my Story (Allen's Inspirational Life) 5
3. BURDENS ARE LIFTED AT CALVARY 7
   Burdens Can Bring Blessings
4. ONWARD CHRISTIAN SOLDIERS 10
   (Kale Ggye Lya Yesu, Mugolokoke)
   Discipline & Diligence for the Christian Life 11
   The Lion Courageous & Bold 12
5. SUNSHINE IN MY SOUL TODAY 13
   Victory in Jesus (The Book of Philippians) 15
6. THE GREAT PHYSICIAN 17
   (Omusawo Alikumpi)
   Who is Jesus 18
7. WHEN WE ALL GET TO HEAVEN 20
   Higher Attitude Leads to Higher Altitude 21

8.	O FOR A THOUSAND TONGUES TO SING	23
	(Bonna Basute Mukama)	
	Your Words as a Personal Brand	24
9.	WE'RE MATCHING TO ZION....................................	25
	(Come We that Love the Lord)	
	(Ffe Abaagala Yesu)	
	Importance of Singing in the Bible	27
	Model Christian Music Ministry	28
10.	I AM SO GLAD THAT JESUS LOVES ME	29
	(Nsanyukira Ekigambo Kino)	
	Wisdom for a Loving Marriage	30
11.	THERE SHALL BE SHOWERS OF BLESSINGS.........	33
	The Time Zone of Your Blessings	33
12.	I WILL SING OF JESUS' LOVE	35
	(Nyimba Okwagala Kwe)	
	Writing on Sand and Stone	36
13.	WHAT A FELLOWSHIP	37
	(Leaning on the Everlasting Arms)	
	(Nsanyukira Obulamu Bwange)	
	My Tanzanian Escapades Along Mt. Kilimanjaro	38
14.	MARVELOUS GRACE OF OUR LOVING GOD	40
	The Parable that was not Completed	40
15.	PRECIOUS SAVIOR, THOU HAST SAVED ME	42
	(Yesu Mulokozi Wange)	
	The Vision of Mission	42

CHRISTIAN LIVING SONGS:

16.	O LET ME WALK WITH THEE	44
	(Kantambule Nawe Yesu)	
	Understanding Our Mission Call	45

17.	FACE TO FACE WITH CHRIST	46
	(Mulokozi Ndimulaba)	
	The Apocalyptic Church of 'Philadelphia'	47
18.	FILL MY CUP CUP LORD	50
	Jesus & the Samaritan Woman	51
19.	I NEED THEE EVERY HOUR	53
	(Nkwetaga Bulijjo)	
	The Cheetah & Leopard Relationship: Our Complete Dependence on God	55
20.	SWEET HOUR OF PRAYER	60
	(Ky'Ekiseera Ky'okusaba)	
	Prayer with Others in the Process	57
	The Indispensable Power of Unity	59
21.	TAKE THE WORLD ANG GIVE ME JESUS	60
	(Twala Ensi Ompe Yesu)	
	Fundamentals of Social Development	61
22.	TAKE TIME TO BE HOLY	63
	(Nonyanga Mukama Mu kusaba)	
	Great Quotes on Prayer	64
23.	TURN YOUR EYES UPON JESUS	66
	The Beauty in Deep & Self-Study	67
24.	WHEN THE ROLL IS CALLED UP YONDER	69
	(Bwebayita Amanya Nange Ndibawo)	
	Balance Sheet of Life	70
25.	TELL IT TO JESUS	72
	(Gw'omunafu Azitoweredwa)	
	God Knows Everything	73
26.	SITTING AT THE FEET OF JESUS	75
	(Bwentuula Awali Ebigere)	
	The Old Professor & His Former Students	76

27.	I WOULD RATHER HAVE JESUS	77
	How Mighty is your God?	78
28.	TRUST & OBEY (When We Walk with the Lord)	80
	(Bwetuba ne Yesu)	
	Are We Walking Alone?	81
29.	LORD, I WANT TO BE A CHRISTIAN	83
	Genuine Christian Living	84
30.	O FOR A FAITH	86
	(Mpa Okukkiriza Okunene)	
	Problems: God's Blessing Wrappers	87
31.	WORK, FOR THE NIGHT IS COMING	89
	(Yesu Mukama Wange)	
	The Stanford University Story	90
32.	HEIR OF THE KINGDOM	92
	(Gwe Omwana wa Yesu)	
	The Message to the Dead	92
33.	O FOR THE FLAME OF LIVING FIRE	95
	(Tuwe Omuliro ogwo)	
	The Quest for Own Balloon	96
34.	I WILL FOLLOW THEE, MY SAVIOR	97
	(Nakugoberera Yesu)	
	The Story of Japanese with Fish	97
35.	CALLED TO THE FEAST BY THE KING	100
	(Ffe Twayitibwa Ku Mbaga ye)	
	The Great Disappointment at the Feast	101
36.	ANGRY WORDS, OH LET THEM NEVER	102
	(Buli Kigambo Ekibi)	
	Fight the Right Battle	103
37.	WE HAVE THIS HOPE	105
	(Tulina Esssubi)	
	The Two Prisoners in a Foreign Land	106

DISCIPLESHIP SONGS:

38. ANYWHERE WITH JESUS 109
    (Buli wantu Wonna)
    Can a Christian Drink Alcohol? 111
39. JOY TO THE WORLD 112
    (Tusanyuka Yesu Ajja)
    My Daughter's Favourite Psalm 98 113
40. LET HIM IN (There's a Stranger at the Door) 115
    (Yesu Ali ku Luggi)
    Steve Job's Last Words 116
41. SWEET BY AND BY (There's a Land) 118
    (Waliwo Ensi Enungi Ennyo)
    Life's Points (Change How you Approach your Life) 120
42. THERE'LL BE NO DARK VALLEYS 121
    (Essanyu n'Eddembe Tulifuna)
    The Beauty in Dark Valleys (Failure) 122
43. WHEN HE COMETH 124
    (Bwalijja Mukama Waffe)
    Resource Mobilization in Ministry 125
44. REDEEMED, HOW I LOVE TO PROCLAIM IT 128
    (Nsanyuka Okuyimba nti Yesu)
    Redemption: God's Faithfulness 129
45. SHALL WE GATHER AT THE RIVER 131
    (Mu Kibuga kya Katonda)
    Elderly: Appreciating this Divine Privilege 132
46. THERE'S A GATE AJAR FOR ME 135
    (Waliwo Oluggi Oluggule)
    Christ's Evangelistic Methodology 136
47. GIVE ME THE BIBLE 138
    (Mpa Ekitabo Ekitukuvu Ennyo)
    Centre of Influence 139

48.	WATCHMEN ON THE WALL OF ZION	140
	(Mwe Abakuumi Ba Sayuni)	
	Watch and Hold Fast	141
49.	ON JORDAN'S STORMY BANKS	144
	(Nsinzira ku Yoludaani)	
	The Biblical Pilgrimage	146
50.	HOW FAR FROM HOME?	147
	(Kiseera Ki Ekisigadde?)	
	Success in Perspective	148
51.	NOT I BUT CHRIST	149
	Sinze Naye Kristo Alabikenga)	
	Jesus Christ, in Perspective	149
	The Vision of Self	150
52.	WONDERFUL WORDS OF LIFE	151
	(Netaaga Okuwulira)	
	Christian Education (Holistic Perspective)	152
53.	PASS ME NOT O GENTLE SAVIOR	154
	(Beera Mu Ffe, Ayi Yesu)	
	Called By His Name	155
54.	ASK NOT TO BE EXCUSED	157
	(Tewewolereza Mulimu Munene)	
	The 16 Things Mentally Strong People Do	158
55.	COME TO THE SAVIOR MAKE NODELAY	159
	(Mujje Eri Yesu Temulwawo)	
	Making Bad People Good	160
56.	LOVINGLY, TENDERLY CALLING	162
	(Omusumba Omulungi Akuyita Leero)	
	Psalms 23 Redefined	162
57.	IT MAY BE AT MORN	164
	(Oba Ekiseera Kirituuka ku Nkya)	
	Music Basics	165

WORSHIP SONGS:

58. A SHELTER IN THE TIME OF STORM 167
    (Mukama Lwe Lwazi Lwaffe)
    Escape from Trouble (Kendu Bay to Kisumu) 168
59. SAFELY THROUGH ANOTHER WEEK 170
    (Yesu Atutusiza ku Sabiiti Endala)
    Theory of Competitive Advantage 171
60. AMAZING LOVE: AND CAN IT BE 172
    Forgiven: Paid By the King 173
61. GUIDE ME, O THOU GREAT JEHOVAH 174
    (Yakuwa Omutukuvu)
    The FAMILY: Earthly Guide to Responsibility 175
62. JESUS, THOU HAST PROMISED 176
    (Yesu Wasubiza Ffe Abantu Bo)
    The Mission Gist of the Church 177
63. TO GOD BE THE GLORY 179
    (Mu maaso ga Yesu)
    The Vision of God 180
64. O DAY OF REST & GLADNESS 182
    (Olunaku Lw'essanyu n'Emirembe)
    The Two Weeks of Creation 183
65. WE'LL BUILD ON THE ROCK 185
    (Tulizimba ku Lwazi Kristo)
    The Lessons from the Hen 186
66. GREAT IS THY FAITHFULNESS 187
    Showing Sympathy 188
    Social Capital 190

EXTRAORDINARY OCCASION SONGS:

67.	ABIDE WITH ME	**189**
	(Beera Nange)	
	Alexander the Great's Death Wishes (Gist of Time)	**190**
68.	I AM COMING TO THE CROSS	**192**
	(Njija Ku Musalaba)	
	Growing in Grace	**193**
69.	O PERFECT LOVE	**194**
	(Ggwe Okwagala Kunene)	
	Marriage: Making Your Spouse the Rarest Thing	**195**

BENEDICTION & DOXOLOGY SONGS: **196**

70.	BLEST BE THE TIE THAT BINDS	**196**
	(Balina Omukisa)	
	Disappointment: Surviving the Aftermaths	**197**
71.	LORD, DISMISS US WITH THY BLESSINGS	**200**
	(Katonda Tuslibule Nno)	
	The Blind man who Gathered an Antelope	**200**
72.	TREAD SOFTLY	**202**
	(Sirika, Sirika, Mukama Wali)	
	Lest We Forget II	**203**

BIBLIOGRAPHY & REFERENCE SECTION **206**

BOOK REVIEWS

The Hebrew Psalter was by no means an isolated literary phenomenon but a posture of intensely religious activities as reflected in their attitudes in a wide variety of extant literature which included epic poetry, hymns, penitential psalms, prayers, incantations, thanksgivings, and petitions addressed to Yahweh. Putting it differently, the Psalms of the Hebrews must be considered suigeneris since they constituted the supreme example of religious devotion and served as effective vehicle for the propagation of truths unfolded in the process of divine revelation. Simply put, the Bible says that Praise God with shouts of joy, all people! Sing to the glory of his name; offer him glorious praise (66:1-2). Elsewhere, Sing a new song to the Lord; praise him in the assembly of his faithful people (149:1)! This book is just about that. Let us do just that in our Christian experience for ever more.

Prof. REUBEN T. MUGERWA,
Formerly DVC – Academics & Professor Emeritus of Biblical Theology
Bugema University & Seventh-Day Adventist Church

I am happy to pen this foreword to Mr. Paul Mugerwa 2nd volume on Hymns. Hymns in particular and music in general are an indispensable part of the public worship and witness of the church. This 2nd volume on this subject is, just like the first, a timely and valuable contribution to this area of the church's life and ministry. Although hymns are, in fact, an invaluable treasure of the church, they are not as widely appreciated as they ought to be. Even in liturgical church traditions, which have traditionally used them, the power and appeal of hymns is gradually waning. Partly because of the cumulative effect of universal factors such as culture and the passage of time. However, even after one takes these universal factors into account, two other reasons are key to why a broad section of the church today does not appreciate hymns.

The first reason, is what I call 'spirit of this age' which can be described as humanistic and intrinsically opposed to genuine, godly spirituality. This, I believe, is the spirit the Apostle Paul is warning against in his letter to Timothy (1Timothy 4:1-5). In our generation this spirit manifests in a trend of general value preferences and appetites which are focused on what is entertaining and pleasurable to human senses and, if possible, what produces or guarantees happiness. One cannot help but wonder whether the catchy three-chord tunes or choruses which dominate much of the worship in our church services today are not in some way a symptom of the way the church has accommodated her practice to the spirit of the age. It is worth noting the chief characteristics of these choruses: they are easy to sing and dance to; they carry a positive, light-hearted message designed to help us feel good about ourselves.

The second reason is a portent mixture of ignorance on the one hand, and spiritual bigotry (pride) on the other. The ignorance stems from a woeful lack of historical knowledge of the spiritual roots, heritage, and pilgrimage of the church—the struggles, joys, agonies, tragedies, triumphs, and wisdom of the saints who have gone before us. Blinded by our ignorance we are unable to recognize that hymns preserve the spiritual heritage of the church in a special living form. This ignorance separates us from the spiritual resources that would otherwise nourish and encourage us in our own struggles today. The spiritual bigotry, on the other hand, stems from misplaced sense of spiritual superiority that leads some to despise hymns and the liturgical church traditions that use hymns. Those who hold this position tend to dismiss hymns altogether as unspiritual, carnal, dry—the product of human efforts to worship God without the help and/or unction of the Holy Spirit. It is sad to note that, primarily because of this false and baseless perception, the church in our generation has deprived itself of the benefits of the spiritual resources which God has given the church through the hymns.

The issues that contribute to the general lack of appreciation of hymns, discussed above, all serve to highlight both the value and necessity Mugerwa's 2nd volume for the church today. In my view, the value of this book consists in four things:

- First, it provides knowledge that helps to dispel the ignorance and spiritual bigotry that impoverishes believers by keeping them from discovering the power of hymns
- Second, it brings hymns to life by highlighting the general historical circumstances surrounding them, but most especially by telling the personal stories from which the hymns originally arose
- Third, it demonstrate that hymns are, not the carnal human attempts to worship God but, in fact, the fruit of the encounter between the human spirit and God's gracious work in Christ as mediated by Holy Spirit who is at work in the world and human hearts
- Fourth, it shows that hymns are a multilayered spiritual resource which, to name a few include: testimonies to God's mercy, faithfulness, and grace towards those who believe; confessions of sin, failure, and weakness, and a plea for forgiveness; declarations of faith, confidence, and commitment to God;

and, a celebrations of God's love, power, goodness, and wisdom throughout the ages.

For these reasons, and even more, I commend Mr. Mugerwa's book as a resource that can be used in different ways: by the individual, as devotional guide that facilitates personal worship and prayer; by a pastor as a tool to educate church members about the hymns and spiritual heritage of the church; by any group, as study guide on the subject of music and church worship; and not least, by theological colleges, as a resource for courses on church music and worship. No matter who uses it, individual or group, this book will educate and deepen one's appreciation of hymns along with the worship tradition and heritage of the church.

PHILIP M. WANDAWA PhD.
Principal, Kampala Evangelical School of Theology
Baptist Church Leader & Professor

A must read for every Christian and more especially those in Ministry. Brother Paul accords the reader a clear view of the circumstances that shaped the thoughts that brought forth the great hymns we love to sing. This background provides the readers with a fresh recognition of their Christian heritage and hence they are able to return to their present situations with a tremendous Spiritual Knowledge.

Pr. BITAMAZIRE NICHOLAS
Theologian, AIIAS (Philippines)
Chaplain, Lakeside College

"Reading Scriptures ignite in us interest to know more about God's promises for His people. Singing Scripture is a call to worship which brings about transformation. A new song is about one's testimony of God's goodness. Reading through this well-articulated and assembled book will help you to appreciate God's love, His faithfulness, and open your heart to worship Him in spirit and in truth, John 4:24."

SIMON PETER MUKHAMA,
General Secretary/ CEO, The Bible Society of Uganda

Whereas singing hymns in all congregations globally is next to preaching and Bible study;

And whereas hymn books have been considered secondary to Bibles in the hand of any Christian worshipper across cultures, nature and place of worship; and where as many preachers, evangelists, pastors, elders, Bible instructors and church music leaders can exegetically endeavour to make the word of God 'living and powerful' (Heb. 4:12) in the hearts of worshippers;

Very few of these ministries of God can, in reality, make live these BELOVED HYMNS and meaningful in the hearts of those who sing them in worship services. The lack of the historical background of their original composers has always been a barrier to worshippers from experiencing those spiritual, devotional, confessional and theological appreciation of these inspired oracles. Thus, this causes a failure to having a spiritual fellowship with the experiences of the composers in similar situations of our contemporary Christian lifestyles. As a Pastor (with more than 36 years in ministry), I strongly commend the invaluable work by Elder Mugerwa Paul in writing such a very wonderful and precious book, "Gracia & Gentil: Hymn Stories Have Lessons for Us Today". I do hereby unreservedly consider as a fundamental and imperative tool in the hands of all modern Gospel ministers and music leaders, both in Christian churches and homes. Let everyone get a copy of the Book, read it and be blessed with it!

SEMBUSI JOSEPH
Senior Pastor & District Leader, SDA Church Najjanankumbi District;
Ministerial Head, Kampala Zone of the SDA Church;
Senior Member, Ministerial Council of Central Uganda Conference of the SDA Church.

As a church music professional, composer and trainer, I would gladly wish to appeal to all Christians, church choirs and singing groups to make this vital and resourceful Book a must-have for personal and corporate use in various ways of their musical career. We thank God for Elder Mugerwa's unique ministry in authoring this all-time invaluable manual that will go a long way in incentivizing and facilitating our worship and devotional services through music.

SAABWE MOSES
Music Professional Trainer & Composer
Managing Director, Sound Huts Studios

"For generations musicians have composed songs that have impacted or influenced society at large. It is one thing to sing and another to know the background and song content. A phrase can have several meanings when interpreted by two or more minds. The question is how one catches the meaning or original meaning of the original phrase makes a difference. This is what Mugerwa has done to alert the church regarding the songs we cherish in worship today. He has taken the time to take us back to the mind and experiences of the composers. His work assists contemporary man to identify with the message of the song(s). Why? Music is vital in the Christian life, and its impact for good or bad in the church is immeasurable.

As you read you will notice the historical context of each song. One of the reasons of studying history is to appreciate what the Lord has been doing through his people. The book you have in your hands is a fruit of such reflection on the side of the author for his love for music and recapture the meaning of song(s). He has attempted to study different songs and the authors' times and experiences. Many Christians have a difficulty of relating to the songs they sing. The effects of music on the human soul can set the stage for many things mentally and spiritually. Music can be used to change our state of mind or for mere entertainment. The church should be aware of the impact that music has on believers and act accordingly. Therefore we should monitor what we allow ourselves and our children to listen to. Remember that what we listen to will affect us.

Christian songs are intended to communicate God's Word through music. Songs have words connected into phrases to bring meaning and meaning is application. In a world where people are just enjoying the rhythms, we need a book like this to help us step back and reflect on the songs we sing. My prayer is that by bringing these songs to light, you will endeavor to sing within the context of the original composers."

EMMANUEL KIWANUKA (Rev. Dr.)
Principal, Westminster Christian Institute Uganda
Presbyterian Church leader & Professor

Borrowing from the Hebraic tradition of psalmody, latter Christian music composers and musicians derived their songs and hymns from their faith experiences with God and the community. Apart from their melodious distinctiveness, and the universal application of the lyrics, the respective backgrounds of these hymns make them more relevant and more applicable to our present day situations. Mr. Paul Mugerwa's noble efforts help to liven our corporate worship and personal devotional experiences as these hymns, their lyrics, and history unite to connect and lift our hearts both horizontally and vertically. This books is a must read for the worshipper, worship leaders, music leaders, music lovers, preachers and any believer looking for a deeper and higher experience in Christian music.

MOSES MAKA NDIMUKIKA, PhD
Professor of Old Testament Exegesis and Theology.
Director, Bugema University, Kampala Campus.

Relating the experience of hymn writers, the hymn stories and scripture goes a long way in enriching bible study and worship. This book adds to the desired literature about hymns for people who enjoy reading Christian literature and preachers who would wish to use hymn stories as reference for their sermons. Whereas all the hymns considered in this book are for authors from Europe and America, it is my humble prayer that the author of this book will also take interest in the original composition of our time here in Uganda. May God bless you the reader of this book and the author for this creative work.

Elder DANIEL WASSWA
Musician, Composer & Music Presenter
Managing Director, Talanta Studios

Dear preachers, choristers and church leaders, try this out for yourself and you will be amazed at the results. Give to your congregation a hymnal background and unpack the scriptural truths and vitamins embedded therein and I assure you that their faces will be shining with joy and even the hunger to learn more. I write this from my own 'every Sunday' experience.

By the time you actually sing the hymn, many will have been set free to sing with a meaningful reflective expression. Here, at last, is the resource we have been waiting for. It is high time we saw Ephesians 5:19 living in our households and church congregations. Thank you Mr. Mugerwa for obeying the Lord by doing a vital job well.

STEVEN OGWANG
Music Evangelist & Global Missionary
Pentecostal Church Hymnologist & Director, Living Sounds Choir Ministries.

As a church and worship leader for a couple of years in the Seventh-Day Adventist Church, I have come to appreciate music as a medium through which God's eternal truths shine, and a reflection of what any church and society believes about God, His nature, and His revelation for the present life and their future destiny. This resourceful Book by Mr. Mugerwa (a scholar, church leader and music evangelist) has served to better my understanding of the psalms, church hymns and gospel songs that have been used for centuries. This Book perfectly links the biographical information of the composer, to the events that occasioned a song's composition, to the biblical background of each hymn, and most importantly, blessing us with the life application resources for our contemporary Christian lifestyles. I gladly and unreservedly recommend this Book to any church minister, musicians, devoted Christian and any reader to enjoy its invaluable resources.

ESTHER WAISWA (Mrs.)
Director, Music, Youth & Children
Seventh-Day Adventist Church, Uganda Union Mission

This resourceful Book attempts to make the knowledge of the beloved hymns available to the ordinary reader and musicians. There are probably not many songs that have appealed to the youth and/or elderly congregations of believers like hymns such as, "I Surrender All" which have seen many mortal beings submit their lives to Christ. These songs are so remarkable in bringing unity in worship congregations across the Christian community as they continue to reason with the grieved and those souls seeking after God, giving them a more valid and joyous experience of the Christian life.

What benefit can we reap from these hymns if we don't the meaning and background of these psalms, hymns and gospel songs explained to us? This Book is so timely in the way of helping any reader to make deeper sense of the beautiful lyrics of these timeless hymns of the Church and thus have a more fruitful, rewarding and life changing worship experience.

Elder LUGGYA BENON
Public Evangelist & Music Enthusiast
Managing Director, Maganjo Grain Millers Ltd

The power of music cannot be overstated. And the power of good music, Gospel music is enormous. "There are few means more effective for fixing His [God's] words in the memory than repeating them in song. And such song has wonderful power. It has power to subdue rude and uncultivated natures; power to quicken thought and awaken sympathy, to promote harmony of action, and to banish the gloom and foreboding that destroy courage and weaken effort." Education 167. Music for centuries has been a source of comfort, courage and celebration of God's goodness for His people. This is because each piece of a psalm or hymn has a story, which the faithful can relate to. This book by Mr. Mugerwa lifts the curtain as it were behind some favorite hymns and helps us to relive these stories.

I find this book "Gracia and Gentil: Hymn Stories" inspiring and riveting. The author goes beyond narrating the stories behind the hymns to spiritual lessons derived from these stories. This is not so with many "stories behind the hymns" out there. The book is a great contribution to meaningful singing in our churches and beyond. The joy in worship is attained when one goes beyond formalism to finding meaning in worship and music forms an integral part of worship. This work will greatly enhance our worship services. On a personal level the book will revitalize our journey of faith as we find "a cloud of witnesses" that have trod the path we are on, sharing our experiences as found the stories behind the hymns. May we find encouragement on our pilgrimage as we read this book. That is my prayer

ODEK RABACH, PhD
Dean, Faculty of Theology & Religious Studies
Adventist University of Eastern Africa (Baraton, Kenya)

I am so excited about the publication of "Gracia & Gentil: Hymn Stories Have Lessons for Us Today". Paul Mugerwa brings a new dimension to congregational worship and praise through "Gracia & Gentil: Hymn Stories Have Lessons for Us Today". When the community of believers arise to sing and fellowship in hymns, psalms and spiritual songs, the richness of the background of the hymn brings the heart of the gospel and the beauty of Jesus Christ to minister in a memorable way to each other, giving the singer hope and faith. The 66 hymns in "Gracia & Gentil: Hymn Stories Have Lessons for Us Today", unites our hearts with the mind of Christ, which inspired the original authors and made practically alive by Paul Mugerwa's modern day life experiences. His testimonies grip our hearts to turn our eyes upon Jesus and not on ourselves, to continue speaking to one another in psalms, hymns and songs of the Spirit (Ephesian 5:19). May this "Gracia & Gentil: Hymn Stories Have Lessons for Us Today" become a treasure to all congregation gatherings of this generation until the appearing of our LORD Jesus Christ.

NGAITE MGENI, PhD
Country Director, ADRA Rwanda

Each page of this beautiful book reflects balanced and holistic approach to singing that is grounded in spiritual values. In this book the Author has produced our evidence-based spiritual applications from the Bible that embraces not just music but also spiritual nourishment. I pray that readers will be inspired by its straightforward lessons from songs and they will come to realize that music is part of worship which envigorouse spiritual affairs.

Pr. DAVID MADUHU MAKOYE
Executive Secretary
Northern Tanzania Union Conference

"This book exposes the rich heritage and tradition of many well-known Christian hymns and gospel songs. It reminds believers in Jesus Christ, regardless of their denomination, of what they share in common from the Bible: Divine Creation, salvation by grace through faith, the Second Coming of Jesus, Resurrection into Eternal life, Heaven and the New Earth. May each reader discover a more enriching worship experience, both personally and congregationally, through thoughtful reflection on and practice of the themes and lessons behind these gospel songs and hymns revealed in this book."

IKECHUKWU OLIUKPE MICHAEL, PhD
Professor of Theology & New Testament
Philippines

This guide makes us traverse the hymns and their background as we make meaning out of them. What struck me even more was how he tries to show worship and praise experiences in music and how worthwhile it is when we sing hymns in different places and occasions. The let-it-all-hang-out honesty made his writing not only accessible, but relatable, for beneath all the monsters and aliens and fanciful stories were recognizable human characters and emotions are attached therein.

Christians have been introduced, sometimes painfully, to more variety in church music than ever before, and we are still learning music appreciation from younger generations. The same is true of this current collection. You may not have been any of the people who populate this guide, but I expect you have known versions of them. You may not have lived these experiences, but I am certain you will recognize them: the painful choice; the longed-for love; the yearning for rest; the joyful moments and the like.

Therefore this edition contains collection of uplifting, informative stories behind your favorite hymns that can warm your heart and revitalize your worship. Perfect for devotions, sermon demonstrations, bulletin inserts, and introducing congregational hymns, each hymn story includes information about the author, composer, the experiences and scriptural basis. For music there is need to reflect and recognizing that followers of Jesus can worship God with various musical tastes. To know the hymns of the Church is to know something of the spiritual strivings and achievements of the people of God throughout the centuries.

Thus I recommend forth this guide with the earnest prayer that it may inspire many hearts to sing with greater devotion the praises of Him who redeemed us with His blood. For you, I hope reading it and sharing it will be as well a nourishing experience.

OBBOKO MARK, PhD
Pastor & Professor of Higher Education

Entant que charge de la Jeunesse et la musique et President sortant de la Mission de l Eglise Adventiste du Septieme au Burundi, je voudrais affirmer et confirmer que la musique est une partie de la priere.

Ce livre sera un outil de travail pour la gloire de Dieu. Il a ete confectionne avec le plan de Dieu pour faciliter a tout le monde a adorer Dieu par les cants et les Psaumes.

Pr. NDABADUGITSE SAMSON

Charge de la Jeunesse et de la Musique
dans la Mission de l Eglise Adventiste du
Septieme jour au Burundi

As a former President and currently Director in charge of Youth & Music – Burundi Union Mission of the Seventh-Day Adventist Church, I would wish to affirm and emphasize that music is an integral part of prayer. This Book will serve as an invaluable instrument and manual for glorifying God. It has been conceived with the worship of God in mind, to facilitate everybody's quest of worshipping God through Psalms and Hymns.

Pr. NDABADUGITSE SAMSON

Director, Youth & Music
Seventh-Day Adventist Church, Burundi Union Mission

Living a life of praise is not only the most enjoyable way to live, but it's also one of the most powerful ways to change your life. Praise isn't like the caboose that just follows what happens, but it's more like the engine of a train that makes things happen. Your faith isn't complete without praise. The book you are holding is all about praising God, praying to God with full of thanks giving. The use of music in worship, praise, and in helping to manifest the power and presence of God is entirely scriptural. Music was a frequent accompaniment to the prophets in the Old Testament. And here is one verse where the power of God came on Elisha as the musician played his harp. 2Ki 3:15 "Now get me a musician. As the musician played his harp, the power of the LORD came on Elisha."

Music has enormous power to engage the emotions, and the Bible resounds with praise and thanks to God through music. In the Old Testament music played a number of different roles, including assisting in the memorization of God's truth and in reminding God's people of their sinfulness and salvation. In the New Testament God's people gather together to express their praise to him and to build one another up in the faith. A rich variety of music that is in harmony with the ministry of God's word is a significant part of the life of the church and points towards the role of music in our praise of God in heaven.

Elder MATHIAS EGID MAVANZA (B.COM, MBA (FINANCE)
Music Enthusiast & Presenter on Morning Star TV
Internal Auditor, South Tanzania Union Mission

As a lover of Hymns, this is one of the best and timely publications! I have personally been blessed with every song and reasons that prompted the composer to meditate and note down each Hymn. I honestly confess that I have been singing some Hymns without much insight and understanding! With "Hymn Stories Have Lessons for Us Today" you will be encouraged, challenged, and provoked to read the story of every song and why it was composed. It is my sincere appeal to you not to miss a copy for yourself, your church and your family.

Pr PAUL GIRIMBE
Executive secretary, Ranen Conference.
SDA Church Kenya

Entant que charge de la Jeunesse et la musique et President sortant de la Mission de l Eglise Adventiste du Septieme au Burundi,je voudrais affirmer et confirmer que la musique est une partie de la priere.
Ce livre sera un outil de travail pour la gloire de Dieu.Il a ete confectionne avec le plan de Dieu pour faciliter a tout le monde a adorer Dieu par les cants et les Psaumes.

Pasteur Ndabadugitse Samson
Charge de la Jeunesse et de la Musique
dans la Mission de l Eglise Adventiste du
Septieme jour au Burundi

ACKNOWLEDGEMENTS

Notwithstanding the efforts of a couple of people (theologians, scholars, music professionals and evangelists, church and worship leaders), in a resourceful and timely book of this size that is not only a devotional, inspirational but also a historical, errors can't be avoided. Any error you come across is the responsibility of Mugerwa Paul. Among the many reviewers and contributors is my lovely wife, Mrs. Rebecca Nakisozi Mugerwa, Co-author and whose fixes and suggestions make the book more outstanding and readable than it otherwise would have been; and my parents (Mr & Mrs. Paul & Ritah Ssali). My dear brothers and sisters: Steven, Tracy, Vicky, Sanyu, Jenipher, Paul, etc have furnished me with all spiritual, moral, financial and intellectual support to complete this publication.

Frankly, I was fortunate to have the following outstanding Reviewers of this book, whose support, counsels and contributions were exceedingly invaluable:

Pr. Dr. Blasious Ruguri (President, East-Central African Division (ECD) of the SDA Church)

Prof. Dr. Nathaniel M. Walembe (Formerly, Executive Secretary – ECD of the SDA Church)

Bishop (Pr.) Kajoba Samuel (President, Central Uganda Conference of SDA Church)

Prof. Reuben T. Mugerwa, DVC – Academics: Bugema University.

Pr. Daudi Makoye (Executive Secretary, Northern Tanzania Union of the SDA Church)

Pr. Paul Girimbe (Executive Secretary, Ranen Conference of SDA Church – Kenya)

Pr. Dr. Wandawa Philip (Baptist Theologian & Principal, Kamapala Evangelical Sch. of Theology)

Rev. Dr. Emmanuel Kiwanuka (Presbyterian Theologian & Principal, Westminster Theological Sch

Rev. Dr. Mary Kinoti Kathambi (Methodist Theologian & DVC-Academics, Kenya Methodist Univ

Rev. Robert Mayes (Lutheran Theologian & expert Hymnologist, USA)

Pr. Mugabi Peter (General Secretary, Baptist Union of Uganda)

Pr. Ndabadugitse Samson (formerly, President of Burundian Mission of the SDA Church)
Mr. Mukhama Simon Peter (General Secretary/ CEO: The Bible Society of Uganda)
Rev. Samuel Muwonge (Mission Coordinator, Namirembe Diocese – Anglican Church of Uganda)
Dr. Ngamije Jean (VC, University of Lay-Adventists Kigali)
Prof. Peter Ensor (Dean, Theology & Religious Studies – Kenya Methodist University)
Dr. Rabach Odek (Dean, Faculty of Theology – Baraton, Kenya)
Dr. Ngaite Mgeni (Country Director, ADRA-Rwanda)
Pr. Dr. Maka Moses Ndimukika (Prof. Theology & Director, Bugema University – Kampala)
Pr. Dr. Bwambale Simon (Prof. of Theology, Caribbean Islands)
Dr. Ikechukwu Michael Oluikpe, (Prof. Theiology 'New Testament' – Philippines).
Dr. Rosette Kabuye, (Dean, Graduate School – Bugema University)
Pr. Dr. Oboko Mark (Professor in Education & Pastor, Bugema University)
Mr. Kiyingi Elijah, University Secretary: Ndejje University.
Mrs. Esther Waiswa (Director, Music & Youth – Uganda Union of the SDA Church)
Mr. Ogwang Steven (Pentecostal Hymnologist & Director, Living Sounds Choir)
Pr. Sembusi Joseph (Senior Pastor & District Leader, SDA Church Najjankumbi District)
Pr. Bitamazire Nicholas (Theologian from AIIAS, Philippines)
Rev. John Wilson Wabwire (Retired, Bunamwaya-Kamanya Anglican Church)
Eld. Kamanga Gilbert (National Director, World Vision Uganda).
Eld. Kabuye Stephen, Head Elder SDA Church Najjanankumbi & Mayor Emeritus.
Eld. Luggya Benon (Popular Evangelist & MD, Maganjo Grain Millers)
Eld. Mavanza Mathias (Music Presenter on Morning Star TV – Tanzania)
Eld. (Eng.) Jonathan Muwonge.
Eld. (Eng.) Mangeni Solomon, Swansea University – UK

Eld. (Eng.) Kawooya Abraham Byandala
Eld. Daniel Wasswa (Musician & Director, Talanta Studios)
Eld. Kasozi Gideon (Musician & Director, CMMS Studios)
Mr. Ssaabwe Moses (Music Professional & Director, Sound Huts Studios)

EDITORIAL TEAM
Pr. Dr. Ikechukwu Michael Oluikpe (Prof.- New Testament)
Rev. Dr. Emmanuel Kiwanuka (Prof. Biblical Languages)

DEDICATION

This publication is dedicated to:
My lovely children- Namuli Gracia Ritah and Katumba Gentil Reuben.

PREFACE
Study Aids with a Practical Focus
This publication has been simplified for the reader so as to get the best out of its practical life and devotional resources for daily life. There are six classifications of the hymn and gospel songs background stories depend on their broad categories; and the book has been organised along those classifications for simplicity purposes, including:

i) Praise Songs:
These songs talk about God's miracles; His workings through our daily lives; our response to His goodness by shouting and dancing to praise Him. Simply put, responding to what God has done for us or seen us through.

ii) Worship Songs:
These songs express and manifest God's glory; creative power; His holiness. Simply put, singing about "who/ what God is".

iii) Discipleship Songs:
These songs are about evangelism (the good news about Christ- life, resurrection, redemption, divine ministry in heaven, etc). They focus on Christianity; inviting/ mobilizing fallen humanity to Christ.

iv) Christian Living & Virtues Songs:
These songs are in the themes of: prayer, dedication, pleading, judgment, family life, etc. Most of them are played with a low tempo that implies thoughtfulness and a calm ambiance for spiritual needs.

v) Extraordinary Occasions Songs:
These songs are used on special/ unique ceremonies for the church, these include: baptism, weddings, funerals, offerings, Holy Communion, and when dedicating either children or church ministers.

vi) Benedictions & Doxologies Songs:
These songs are aimed at: wishing/ bidding farewell to God's people with blessings; in a special way glorying God's protection, providence and faithfulness toward His people. Doxologies are songs of praise.

Lay-Out of the Texts (Songs)
Each song is organised in the following way:
a) It begins with a simple biography of the author(s).

b) It is followed by the circumstances that occasioned his/her composition of the song in question.

c) Then, it is by a "devotional" in the form of Scriptures that either inspired his/her composition or that are in line with the song's spiritual resources (theology).

d) Finally, the text is wound up with the life application lessons from the song that we need to draw from: the author's biography; the circumstances of the song's composition; and the Scriptural resources of the song.

Key to Abbreviations of Hymn Books & Bible Versions:
CH - Church Hymnal
SDAH - Seventh-Day Adventist Hymnal
A & M - Oresmus Hymnal: Hymns Ancient & Modern 1875 – 1924
NLT - New Living Translation (Life Application Study Bible) @ 2007
NKJV - New King James Version

NB: Luganda (local language) Titles refer to hymn titles in the SDA Church's Luganda hymnal called *"Enyimba za Kristo"*

In reference to my writing of this master-piece, I would happily love to use George Orwell's rationale for authorship. He said, "Putting aside the need to earn a living; there are four great motives for writing:

'Sheer egoism'- the desire to seem clever, to be talked about or even remembered after death, etc.

'Aesthetic enthusiasm'- the desire to share an experience which one feels is valuable and ought not to be missed. (Such as my musical experience that I feel worth sharing).

'Historical impulse' – the desire to find out true facts about something and store them up for posterity. (Hence, unearthing stories behind the glorious hymns about our Eternal God).

'Political purpose' – the desire to push the world in a certain direction. (By impressing on my readership the beauty & overwhelming experiences of hymn writers, the authors' and other world personalities that can guide our spiritual & physical lives).

FOREWORD

In this generation, the role of music in worship is undervalued; we just sing anything and anyhow without paying attention to the message in the songs. We thank God because this Book is in line with the words of the Psalmist, "For God is the King of all the earth; sing praises with understanding" – Psalms 47:7 (NKJV). This resourceful Book provides us with knowledge and insights about the psalms, hymns and gospel songs we sing so as to praise with understanding. May the pages of this Book guide your singing and your heart as you sing for the Lord!

Bishop (Pastor) SAMUEL KAJOBA
Executive Director,
Central Uganda Conference of the SDA Church

As a church administrator and a leader of worship for many years, with deep interest in the role music plays in Christian worship, I feel greatly honored to have been asked to write a Foreword to GRACIA & GENTIL: Hymn Stories Have Lessons for Us Today Volume II. My acceptance to carry out the task was dictated by two reasons: The first one is the fact that I was impressed by the passion the author has towards singing with understanding. I was further moved by his interest to make a contribution in the area of church music. Thus I felt obliged to support him in his fervent desire to help worshippers of all denominations to appreciate the fact that every song that is sung has a story that led to it being written, and that those stories have lessons which contemporary Christians should learn. But this can only be if such a lesson has been pointed out to the worshipper, which the author has ably done.

The second reason is due to my strong belief that the book fills what I consider to be a missing link in the understanding of worship music. Many of us sing and listen to songs because we enjoy the music and sometimes the song content appeals to us, but we never think of relating the song to the circumstances that led to it being written. In this book however, the author clearly indicates that when relating the circumstances that led to the writing of the hymn, singing will take on a different dimension and this is one of the objectives that the author hopes the book will achieve.

As one reads the book, one appreciates the fact that the author has ably indicated that singing is worshiping. It is not something that one does to occupy time before worship begins. That being the case, the choice of songs should be relevant to the occasion and the sermon.

Another useful aspect of the book is the way the author relates the hymn author's experience to our daily challenges. He suggests that if the various authors had succumbed to the feelings that come with suffering, loss or misfortune, we would not have the songs/hymns that we have today. The message is clear that in life, we should always look beyond the present circumstances. In some situations, the author's condition in the case of those who were forced by circumstances to remain indisposed provided an opportunity for them to be creative and indeed the Spirit of God was with them and today we are beneficiaries of the fruits of their creativities. Nick Vujicic was right when he said, "I'm officially disabled, but I'm truly enabled because of my lack of limbs. My unique challenges have opened up unique opportunities to reach so many in need." The story of the song writers confirm what Hellen Keller said, "Your success and happiness lie in in you. Resolve to keep happy, and your joy and you shall form an invincible host against difficulties."

The book lists seventy two hymns and songs. This then means that there are an equal number or more lessons to learn. I therefore commend the author for assembling this resource and I recommend it to every Christian worshipper especially those who organize and lead worship. The selection of songs for a particular worship service should be deliberate and purposeful. Many hymn books list songs in groups according to the meaning. This should help worship organizers to select songs/hymns, which are relevant to the worship service and message.

NATHANIEL MUMBERE WALEMBA, *PhD (Professor of Theology)*
Retired Executive Secretary,
East-Central Africa Division of Seventh-day Adventists

WHY READ THE HYMN STORIES BOOK?
Why does every congregation, household and institution need this tool in worship and general lifestyle?

Bacchiocchi et al (2000) argues that music is like a glass prism through which God's eternal truths shine, and music breaks this light into a spectrum of many beautiful facts. Thus, the psalms, hymns and gospel songs sung during any church and Christian service express what a church believes about God, His nature, and His revelation for our present life and future destiny. Music defines the nature of the worship experience by revealing the manner, participants, facilitators, and object of true worship. Throughout Christian history, the production of music has been largely influenced by the evolution of the understanding of God. This has since then seen a progressive and historical shift from the transcendental understanding (God beyond us) in the medieval era, to the immanental conception (God for us) in the 16th Century reformation, to the "God within us" perception from the 17th Century to the present day music concepts.

This Book serves as a guide. Just like a Bible study guide facilitates our study of the Bible, this book serves as a guide to singing hymns and gospel songs and encourages the readers to live out the messages in their lyrics on a daily basis
If Christians are to sing, it should not be done out of formality but should be done deliberately in truth and spirit (John 4:23); some people normally say "lets sing as we wait for others to assemble or enter then we shall begin the worship program". That is very wrong, blasphemous and really relegates this music resource to something of a pastime, less formal and even less spiritual.

In fact, in this generation there is a need for more worship services for only singing as God's worshippers; many more than preaching, praying sessions or even development project issues in Christian gatherings. The example of Paul and Silas praying and singing hymns to God in prison (Acts 16:25) is a challenge to contemporary Christians who live freely without persecution and imprisonment.

This resource will serve to enliven our Christian worship and praise experiences in music which will consequently contribute to bring back our youth to churches since they always enjoy a spirited worship environment.

Appreciating this Christian music resource will serve as a reminder of the historical heritage handed down to us by our fore fathers, which is worth upholding, in the wake and/or in the face of the contemporary secularized noisy "Christian" music. This can serve to stimulate a rebirth of real Christian music and lifestyle in this world where virtually everyone and/or everything seem to have lost the true identity and guidance due to simplistic modernism. In fact, it is high time that each Christian household should have at least a small keyboard or musical instrument to add flavor to our music.

There is a popular saying that, "When you teach, you hold", implying that the Christian church should teach its members to identify themselves with the original inspired music setting. This will serve to inculcate spiritual and other crucial life values that are required of people who profess to be Christians and come from Christian households and communities. This is why every Christian household, congregation and institution needs this book.

1. MY MAKER AND MY KING (C.H 71)

1) My Maker and My King, To Thee my all I owe;
Thy Sovereign bounty is the spring, Whence all my blessings flow;
Thy Sovereign bounty is the spring, Whence all my blessings flow.

2) The creature of Thy hand, On Thee alone I live;
My God, Thy benefits demand, More praise than I can give;
My God, Thy benefits demand, More praise than I can give.

3) Lord, what can I impart when all is Thine before?
Thy love demands a thankful heart; The gift, alas! How poor.
Thy love demands a thankful heart; The gift, alas! How poor.

4) O! let Thy grace inspire, My soul with strength divine;
Let every word and each desire, And all my days be Thine;
Let every word and each desire, And all my days be Thine

This praise song was composed by Anne Steele (1717 – 1778) in 1760 under the title "God My Creator and Benefactor". Born in the countryside around Southampton, England, her father was a timber merchant who also was an unsalaried Baptist minister. She was the first major woman hymn writer in the memorable past. It is said that she suffered an accident in childhood that left her a lifelong invalid, and she experienced extreme sorrow when her fiancé was drowned on the eve of their wedding (a horrible experience/ story that is related to another hymn writer called John Scrivens of 'What a Friend We have in Jesus' – who lost two fiancées in life as he was nearing his wedding ceremonies). Anne was devoutly consecrated to God. Although she wrote poetry from her childhood onward, she did not publish until others persuaded her to do so in 1760, resulting in two volumes, and in all, she wrote 144 hymns, 34 psalms, and 30 short poems, using the pen name Theodosia.

This song comes from the Baptist Church background and so, it is significantly affected by such theological orientations (most of which are shared by many Christian faiths across the board). This song comes at a time when the world has forsaken God and they largely despise even the fact that God, from His gracious love, purposed to create the world, and humanity in a special way. They have deliberated resolved to forget

God the creator and have heeded to fables and concoctions like the evolutionistic theory of creation as devised and propagated by among others Charles Darwin (whose theory actually begun in the mid-19th Century but has since then significantly infiltrated the whole world – religion, politics, education, etc; and has been indirectly, and at times, deliberately embraced by Billions of people globally).

Music is a ministry, and according to the Oxford English Dictionary, 'ministry' is the active practice and education of the minister of a particular religion or faith. This term is believed to have been initially used in religious system or leadership before it was adopted by the political system and leadership. Unfortunately, ever since it crossed to politics, the meaning has been largely twisted (negative connotation) to selfishness and personal interest. Nonetheless, the term 'minister' primarily meant 'servant'; to minister is not a rank but a call to serve, offer oneself and sacrifice one's life for others' good. This is premised on the fact that that our lives belong to God and also that the church is God's initiative and creation, which were actually both redeemed by Jesus' blood. Thus, it is our special privilege to be called "God's servants" – but neither life nor the church belongs to us, we are simply ministers of the gospel in our various categories including music. We ought to be humble, reverent and glorify God, but above all, acknowledge Him as 'our Maker, Benefactor and King' as Anne Steele penned these fundamental truths in 1760 (more than 250 years ago). In ministry, there is: a call, evangelism, prayer life, healing, reconciliation, and welfare of the people.

Lest We Forget II (The sin of forgetting)
Jeremiah 6:16 "This is what the Lord says, 'Stop at the crossroads and look around. Ask for the old, godly way, and walk in it. Travel its paths, and you will find rest for your souls. But you reply, No, that's not the road we want".

The right path for living has been marked out by God and the only way to find peace and rest for our souls is to walk on God's path. Prophet Jeremiah is also believed to have been the author of the Book of "Lamentations". This was a time when the kingdom of Israel had stooped so low spiritually; they had embraced and accommodated homosexuality, idolatry, and all kinds of evil against God but also against humanity.

A popular story is told of an old man who had 3 dogs (allegedly believed that one dog had attained a university degree, another had a diploma, and the third one had a certificate; that's quite strange and absolutely outlandish!). It is said that whenever a guest would come to this household, this Mzee (Swahili term for 'old man') would ask him how many days the guest was planning to stay at this household. In case the guest would declare that he would stay for 3 days, then the host (Mzee) would take him to his comrades/ dogs to inform them of the guest's request or proposal to stay for three (3) days so that they could accommodate his stay and treat him well during those definite days that he has requested for. During those agreed days, these comrades would shower him with the best hospitality and protection that he needs; but the problem would only arise when the guest (by any chance or misfortune) he forgets that his days were done and that the contract expired. These guys would pretend that they had never seen him in their lives, and that he is either dangerous, irresponsible because he doesn't stick to his words or that he needs to have a mental checkup to establish whether his head is okay. They would treat him in the rudest manner possible in a bid to remind him that there is nothing as bad as forgetting and/or not being consistent to what one says.

If mere dogs can resolve to be consistent in what they have been instructed to religiously uphold, then a human being who was created to be a rational can desist from forgetting and from being inconsistent in life. Let us disregard evolutionists and determine not to forget our 'Maker and our King'.

2. BLESSED ASSURANCE

1) Blessed assurance, Jesus is mine!
O what a foretaste of glory divine!
Heir of salvation, purchase of God,
Born of His Spirit, washed in His blood.

Refrain
This is my story, this is my song,
Praising my Savior, all the day long;
This is my story, this is my song,
Praising my Savior, all the day long.

2) Perfect submission, perfect delight,
Visions of rapture now burst on my sight;
Angels descending bring from above
Echoes of mercy, whispers of love.

3) Perfect submission, all is at rest
I in my Savior am happy and blest,
Watching and waiting, looking above,
Filled with His goodness, lost in His love.

This hymn was uniquely composed by two prolific hymn writers. The first is Fanny J. Crosby (1820 -1915), she was born in Putnam County, New York, and at just six weeks she lost eyesight due to the incompetence of a village doctor. Nevertheless, she is known to have written at least 9,000 hymns. The other writer was Phoebe Palmer Knapp (1839 – 1908), daughter to evangelists and musicians Walter and Phoebe Palmer. Young Phoebe (whose husband for identity purposes was John Knapp) was a great musician and hymn writer who produced at least 500 hymns in her lifetime.

One day, this younger Phoebe combined her talents with those of Fanny Crosby in the writing of a hymn; Mrs. Knapp composed a melody, and played it over to Fanny Crosby a couple of times on the piano. Phoebe then asked Crosby what it said, and she instantly replied Blessed Assurance." In just a few minutes, Fanny Crosby supplied the words for the now popular and inspirational song.

Records have it that this hymn was used in an unusual way by the British troops during the Boer War as a instrument of enlivening the army given its allusion to the term 'Blessed Assurance' that has a lot of significance. Assurance includes a full confidence, and freedom from doubt and fear, it's the other side of trust, or faith. This represents an out-flowing attitude of putting our faith in something or someone. And when we trust in God, the Spirit of God brings an inward assurance that our trust is well founded.

Let's capitalize on "Confidence", which in Latin is composed of two words: "con" meaning 'with' (just like in Spanish); and also "fides" which means 'faith'. To throw more light on the word "faith" – whose main root in Hebrew is 'amn' from which the popular term "amen" is derived that signifies continuity, belief, trust, absolute certainty, constancy, reliability, and unwavering and solid commitment that can also be found and premised on Christ. This implies that much as we live in a world filled with uncertainty but also unreliable and inconsistent human beings, we have all reasons to have confidence and trust God's absolute certainty and constancy as reflected in His character and His word.

The term assurance means to be fully persuaded; all this is premised and wrapped up in the declaration of Crosby that "Jesus is mine" which is a possessive first person pronoun indicating ownership or strong relationship. The phrase "this is my story" has a lot of significance and implications – one of which reveals that everyone has a life story to tell about one's relationship with Christ; but also that this life story should be inspirational to other people on earth.

Scripture – Psalms 57:7 (NLT) "My heart is confident in you, O God; my heart is confident. No wonder I can sing your praises". David's firm faith (assurance and confidence) in God contrasted sharply with his enemies' loud lying and boasting. When confronted with verbal attacks, the best defense is simply to be quiet and praise God, realizing that our confidence is in His love and faithfulness. Hence, in times of suffering (just like the life story I narrate here below), a Christian should not turn inward to self-pity or outward to revenge, but turn upward to God.

This is my Story (Allen Natukunda's Life)
This is a true story of my close friend, and one time business partner whose life was quickly ended by a reckless car cleaner just at the verge of her beginning her dream career/job.
It was in early 2012 when I first met Allen, and I don't believe that our meeting was a coincidence but God's design that would see us friends until her premature death in 2016. Having come to visit her elder sister who was a fellow

lecturer at Bugema University, given my background in foreign languages (particularly French and Spanish), my colleague introduced me to her sister who had just come from Cuba where she had completed her Bachelor's degree in Spanish Literature & Diplomacy (after a whole five years of intensive study). Our relationship picked up quickly since we both spoke French and Spanish languages, and so, she shared with me lots of her past experiences including having been the leader of Ugandan students in Cuban universities that one time earned her a prestigious meeting with the President of Uganda when he had gone to meet his Cuban counterpart. It is said that the president had since then promised to consider offering her a job placement as soon as she completes and returns to Uganda. As time flies, she soon completed, and her together with other connected relatives, began to hunt for the President through all possible ways so as to claim the promise for a job. Unfortunately, the pursuit took more than six years, then in 2nd quarter of 2016 through the grace of God, she got applied to Ministry of Foreign Affairs which required her to undergo specialized training for a couple of months, which she successfully did and highly passed. After having been placed in one juicy position (Diplomacy & scholarship in relationship to some Asian countries), she had even signed her contract and ready to begin her employment that same week. She had to go one prestigious hotel in Kampala to finalize other formalities of her new assignment in a bid to begin her dream job that she had anticipated for close to a decade. Around the same time, a Spanish couple had come to Uganda to visit the country's beauties including the gorillas. So, as they wound up their deliberations so that she can quickly rush to the said hotel, gorgeously dressed for the occasion, one reckless car washer had unofficially stole the car from the washing bay. This young man rammed into my dear friend along with the Spanish couple, just minutes to officially commencing her job, and soon this would not only end my beloved friend's life but also her brilliant and decorated life story that had served as a great inspiration to many of us.

The inspiration to appreciate and also write about this beautiful hymn was borne from such tragic happening, and as we were agonizing during the funeral mass in Kampala, the Reverend who officiated the occasion chose this resourceful hymn. He emphasized that "everyone has a life story but, despite everything, we should all keep our blessed assurance that Jesus is ours". My friend's story reminds us of the realities of death in this mortal world and our only assurance in Christ's victory over sin and death.

3. BURDENS ARE LIFTED AT CALVARY (C.H 432)

1)   *Days are filled with sorrow and care,*
       Hearts are lonely and drear;
       Burdens are lifted at Calvary, Jesus is very near.

Chorus
Burdens are lifted at Calvary, Calvary, Calvary,
Burdens are lifted at Calvary, Jesus is very near.

2)   *Cast your care on Jesus today,*
       Leave your worry and fear.
       Burdens are lifted at Calvary, Jesus is very near.

3)   *Troubled soul, the Savior can see,*
       Ev'ry heartache and tear.
       Burdens are lifted at Calvary, Jesus is very near.

This song is one of the most recent and 20th Century compositions that have found a place in many Christian hymn books and competing in prominence with other golden and classic hymns of the Christian church. It was composed by Pastor John MacFarlane Moore (1925 –till date); born in Kirkintilloch, Scotland. He first pursued a career in electrical engineering in his early years. At the age of 15 years, having become a dedicated Christian and heavily involved in soul-wining, he decided to switch to ministry studying at the Evangelical Baptist Fellowship Bible College. After serving in various churches and positions, he was elected national President of Fellowship of Evangelical Baptist Churches in Canada. Pastor Moore composed more than 150 songs and conducted Bible conferences and evangelistic crusades each year, but this particular hymn is the best known of all the hymns he wrote in his life.

In 1952, then a young pastor John Moore visited a critically ill sailor in a Glasgow hospital. After chatting with him a few minutes, he checked in his bag for a tract he might leave with him, and what came to hand was a little summary of John Bunyan's classic story, The Pilgrim's Progress. On the front was a picture of Pilgrim coming to the cross with an enormous sack tied to his back, and Pastor Moore explained how the weight of sin rolled off Pilgrim's back at the cross. He asked the sailor, "And do you feel that kind of burden on your heart today?" The young man nodded, with tears running down his cheeks. The pastor prayed with him, and was privileged to lead him to faith in Christ that day. Later on, a remarkable smile of peace and assurance lit up his face. Back home, John M. Moore could not get the thrill of the experience out of his mind. "His burden is lifted!" he said to himself. And later in the night while sitting at the fireside, he took a piece of paper and pen, and wrote the words and music for a song which, he reports, just seemed to flow from his pen.

The word "burden" speaks of many things: a load that is carried, a wearying weight, an affliction, an obligation of some kind, something that holds us down or holds us back. In life, there are frankly different kinds of burdens (especially in the Christian life), some of which are spiritual like the burden of sin, challenges of Christian ministry, but others are carnal and bodily like disease, quest for decent life, among others. But beyond all the other burdens of life, how much more is it necessary for us to recognize our Savior as the supreme 'Burden Bearer', bearing the weight of all our sins on the cross of Calvary.

Though John Moore's original inspiration for his song was to lead a burdened sinner to the Savior, his song makes a wider application to all the burdens that we battle with in life

This same quest led King Solomon to write some of the most remarkable and historical words about our daily toil, "What has man for all his labour, and for the striving of his heart with which he has toiled under the sun? For all his days are sorrowful, and his work burdensome; even in the night his heart takes no rest. This also is vanity" (Ecc. 2:22-23).

Burdens can Bring Blessings

Sometimes, to succeed in life one needs Enemies!!!
One needs people who will mock him/her so that he can run to God;
One needs folks who will try to intimidate him so that he can be courageous;
One ought to have people who will say 'NO" so that one can learn how to be independent in life and do things by oneself;
One needs people who will disappoint him so that one can put all one's trust in God alone;
One needs people who will work towards him losing that job, so that one can start his own business;
One needs people who will sell one's 'Joseph' so that one can get to 'Egypt and become a Prime Minister' in a strange country of captivity.

One needs a cruel landlord, so that one won't be too comfortable in someone else's house then one can builddown house on time.

But sometimes, when we are disappointed, we feel very bad and we tend to remain on that spot. Not knowing that the end-point of disappointment is the beginning of one's accomplishment. Being able to understand this, "that every disappointment comes with a blessing"; however, it is not everyone that partakes in this blessing that this illustration is referring to. One can hardly see a new open door while he is still putting all attention, time, resources, and energies to force the closed door to open. All disappointments come with attached blessing; and so, when it comes, we need to ask God to open our eyes to see the new blessing that he has for us!

4. ONWARD CHRISTIAN SOLDIERS (C.H 566)

1) Onward, Christian soldiers, marching as to war,
With the cross of Jesus going on before.
Christ, the royal Master, leads against the foe;
Forward into battle see His banners go!

Refrain
Onward, Christian soldiers, marching as to war,
With the cross of Jesus going on before.

2) At the sign of triumph Satan's host doth flee;
On then, Christian soldiers, on to victory!
Hell's foundations quiver at the shout of praise;
Brothers lift your voices, loud your anthems raise.

3) Like a mighty army moves the church of God;
Brothers, we are treading where the saints have trod.
We are not divided, all one body we,
One in hope and doctrine, one in charity.

4) What the saints established that I hold for true.
What the saints believèd, that I believe too.
Long as earth endureth, men the faith will hold,
Kingdoms, nations, empires, in destruction rolled.

5) Crowns and thrones may perish, kingdoms rise and wane,
But the church of Jesus constant will remain.
Gates of hell can never gainst that church prevail;
We have Christ's own promise, and that cannot fail.

6) Onward then, ye people, join our happy throng,
Blend with ours your voices in the triumph song.
Glory, laud and honor unto Christ the King,
This through countless ages men and angels sing.

This military-like hymn was composed by an Anglican clergyman, Sabine Baring-Gould (1834 - 1924); born in Devon, he was also a hagiographer, antiquarian, novelist and eclectic scholar. His bibliography consists of more than 1240 publications, though this list continues to grow even up to the present, these included subjects like: religion and theology, travel, folklore and mythology, history, fiction, and also collected sermons. Though he was regarded as one of the top ten novelists, he is largely remembered for two hymns that are still in common use today: "Onward, Christian Soldiers' and 'Now the Day is Over".

Sabine Baring-Gould's life is a story in itself, with his unconventional childhood, his marriage to a mill-girl half his age and his dedication to antiquarian pursuits alongside his life as proprietor and priest of a small Devonshire village. He was an early archaeologist, respected for his work on Dartmoor, in Cornwall, in Wales and in France. He was also a folklorist, but he regarded his greatest achievement to be his collection of songs, most of them heard from singers in Devon and Cornwall. Besides his writing he re-created the twin hearts of his beloved parish of Lew Trenchard - his home, Lew House and the beautiful little church of St Peter, Lewtrenchard.

The Bible says enough about Christian warfare to assure us that this and other such songs in our hymnody are quite appropriate. This rhymes well with the apostle's counsels to young Timothy, "You therefore must endure hardship as a good soldier of Jesus Christ. No one engaged in warfare entangles himself with the affairs of this life, that he may please him who enlisted him as a soldier" (II Tim. 2:3-4). Paul's testimony, near the end of his life, was, "I have fought the good fight" (II Tim. 4:7). It was a battle that he exhorted others to join. "This charge I commit to you, son Timothy, according to the prophecies previously made concerning you, that by them you may wage the good warfare" (I Tim. 1:18).

Discipline and Diligence for the Christian Life

Scripture – 2 Timothy 2:3-6; 14-16. Paul uses comparisons with soldiers, athletes and farmers (all key professions in human survival) who must discipline themselves and be able to sacrifice to achieve the results they want (3-6):

a) Like Soldiers, we must give up worldly security and pleasure but endure rigorous training and discipline. My dad was in the army, and so this was how they were trained to interface the world, which eventually becomes their discipline.

b) Like Athletes, we must train hard and follow the rules in a given sporting activity. I have been an athlete (given the fact that I come from such a background – with my dad (Coach Paul Ssali) having been the goalkeeper of Uganda Cranes in 1978 when our national team played the Africa Cup of Nations, and reached the finals with Ghana). By the way, since then it was not until this year, January 2017 in Gabon, that we appeared again after 38 years of trying and training hard. I have been a player of football, table tennis, but especially basketball at a higher level – we have been trained to follow rules and focus on attaining the crown of victory.

c) Like Farmers, we must work extremely hard and be patient but keep going despite suffering because of the thought of victory, the vision of winning, and the hope of harvest. I have been partly involved in agriculture and I do appreciate the hard-work and patience in the whole process.

In verse 2, Paul emphasizes that when we suffer (sacrifice ourselves), we share in the common experience of those who have been suffering for generations for the gospel's sake. All the martyrs, missionaries and pioneers who had to face all that we are facing now. Let's have the same courage, commitment and willingness to renounce worldly pleasure in order to serve God. Can you face the challenge?

Then, in verses 14-16, Paul urged Timothy to remind believers not to argue over unimportant details or having foolish discussions because such are confusing, useless and harmful. This is because God will examine what kind of workers we have been for him; we should build our lives on His word, and build His word into our lives. It alone tells us how to live for him and serve him. Consistent and diligent study of the word is vital, otherwise we may be soothed into neglecting God and our true purpose for living. We should hold a tool (instrument of work) in one hand; and a weapon (word of God) in the other hand.

The Lion (Courageous and Boldness)
In the jungle, if we are to look for the biggest animal….Elephant
In the wilderness, if we are to search for the tallest animal…..Giraffe
In the forest, if we are to look for the wisest animal…..Fox
In the bush, if we are to hunt for the fastest animal……Cheetahs
Among all these wonderful qualities mentioned, where is the Lion in the picture, yet, we've grown saying that the Lion is the king of the jungle, even without being the best in any of the above qualities. But this is what is quite fascinating about the Lion:

The Lion is courageous, very bold and always ready to face any mountains, any challenges, and any barriers that cross his path regardless of how big they are. The Lion walks with confidence, it dares anything and it is never afraid; it believes that it is unstoppable, and it is a risk-taker. The lion believes that any animal is food for him; and that any opportunity is worth giving a trial and never allows it slip from his hands; it has charisma.

In other words, one doesn't need to be the fastest, wisest, smartest or generally accepted to achieve your dream; but all one needs is courage, boldness, willingness to try, faith to believe in possibilities, and also believing in your God-given capabilities. This same courage and boldness is a huge requirement for real Christians who are disciplined and diligent in their Master's service.

5. SUNSHINE IN MY SOUL (SDAH 384)

1) There is sunshine in my soul today,
   More glorious and bright
   Than glows in any earthly sky,
   For Jesus is my Light.

Refrain
O there's sunshine, blessèd sunshine,
When the peaceful, happy moments roll;
When Jesus shows His smiling face,
There is sunshine in the soul.

2) There is music in my soul today,
   A carol to my King,
   And Jesus, listening, can hear
   The songs I cannot sing.

3) There is springtime in my soul today,
   For, when the Lord is near,
   The dove of peace sings in my heart,
   The flowers of grace appear.

4) There is gladness in my soul today,
   And hope and praise and love,
   For blessings which He gives me now,
   For joys "laid up" above.

This hymn was composed by Eliza Edmunds Hewitt (1851 – 1920); born and lived her entire life in the city of Philadelphia where she was a public school teacher for a couple of years.

In 1887, this hymn was written and the words are intimately connected to a personal experience of Eliza. While she was a public school teacher, something happened one dreadful day. She had attempted to correct a rebellious student, but when she turned away he struck her across the back with a heavy slate, severely injuring her spine. Suddenly, her whole life changed. She never fully recovered from the damage done, she was often bedridden for long periods, and had trouble getting around for the rest of her days. In the immediate aftermath of the attack, she was placed in a body cast for six long months. Her painful confinement could have been a breeding ground for depression and bitter cynicism, but it wasn't.

This reminds me of a similar experience while I was still also a teacher in a public secondary school called Ndejje Senior Secondary School, (some seven years back, I was a very young man about 26 years old). A rebellious and poorly-brought child refused to take my instructions and he resolved to wrestle me while I was teaching, and it was really a nasty experience because despite the fact that I could easily beat him up, his fellow classmates found it very unbecoming and weird of him that they attacked him, no sooner had he begun the fight, up to the point of throwing him out of the class.

In reference to Eliza's situation, there is a common saying that behind the clouds, the sun is always shining but that may not be much comfort to a life that is overcome with dark clouds of pain and trouble. Had it been you, could you possibly avoid being overwhelmed by despair, when buried in a flood of disaster? How possible could it have been for you to find some semblance of sunshine in the storm? This hymn is a life story of Eliza Hewitt who had put her faith in the Lord Jesus Christ, and He eventually sustained her all through this nasty scenario. The One whom the prophet Malachi calls "the Sun of Righteousness" (Mal. 4:2) had entered her life and brought the radiance of His love.

Six months after her back injury, the body cast was removed, and she was later able to take her first faltering steps outside. Eliza went for a short walk in Fairmount Park in Philadelphia. She loved the beauty of nature, particularly flowers; it was such a delight to feel the breeze again, and the warm sunshine. Though brief, it was an energizing outing, and this experience inspired her to write a song she called "Sunshine in My Soul". In it she applies the excitement of stepping out into the sunshine to the joy she found in fellowship with Christ. It is pertinent to note that the light is used in Scripture as a symbol of truth and purity but it also depicts the abundant life the Lord can give to those who trust in Him.

After several years, her physical condition improved somewhat, and she served as a Sunday School Superintendent, for several decades, at the Northern Home for Friendless Children, and later at the Calvin Presbyterian Church. Miss Hewitt was also a regular contributor to Sunday School Helps.

Eliza Hewitt was the good friend of another prolific hymn writer, Fanny Crosby and, like her friend, she concentrated on that ministry. Though hindered from moving about, she began writing gospel songs, and eventually produced many hundreds of them. Some of these were written under the pen name Lidie H. Edmunds. Brightly joyous songs of faith and hope, they include: "More About Jesus"; "My Faith Has Found a Resting Place"; "Since the Fullness of His Love Came In"; "Singing I Go"; "Sing the Wondrous Love of Jesus"; and "Stepping in the Light".

Eliza's experience vividly reminds me of another warrior of faith the Apostle Paul (with whom I incidentally share the remarkable name 'Paul'). This guy had his share of troubles in life, but the most outstanding element is that he tested the two extremes of life – being the persecutor, influential figure, wealthy background and extraordinarily schooled but also the other end that he happily chose of becoming the persecuted, fugitive in life, prone to poverty and destitution. But despite this latter kind of painful life that he chose as result of the beauty in knowing Christ, he overcame and excelled in everything – thanks to his faith in Christ that procured him victory.

Victory in Jesus (The Book of Philippians)

Philippians 4:13 was his flagship statement in his life of toil. This is arguably the only epistle that Paul utilizes to give more clarification about himself (his profile) than in any other of his epistle. Below is a key snapshot of this Epistle, which have crucial lessons for us today:

Acts 6:9ff – this will give you the glimpses into the history and/or background information about Philippe as a region. Paul writes to the Philippians found in Macedonia, a peaceful and obedient church unlike other peers at the time. Worth noting is that Paul never condemned nor scolded them in anywhere of his writings but largely wrote in appreciation and expression of joy for the church there.

Philippians 1:1 – 3, the church had grown in grace and it was blessed with a strong leadership, with people from diverse background (Cosmopolitan).

Philippians 1:21, Paul asserts that, "To me, being alive is Christ, and dying is a gain...."

Philippians 3:7-8, recounting his past and the vain glory he used to enjoy before receiving Christ, Paul ironically affirms that, "But all that was profit/ valuable to me, I realized that it was a loss for Christ …… for the excellence of the knowledge of Christ Jesus my Lord for whom I count them as rubbish........"

Philippians 3:12-14, "Not that I have achieved all …….but I press on that I may lay hold of that for which Christ Jesus has also laid hold of me…………. forgetting those things which are behind me and reaching forward to those things which are ahead…………"

Philippians 4:11ff, "Lest I talk for need but I learnt that in all situations to be content……"

NB: Philippians 1:15ff, "Some indeed preach Christ from envy and strife, and some also from goodwill….. Self-ambition, what then? Only that in every way, whether in pretense or in truth. Christ's message is preached……….." I personally used to be pained and/or infuriated by guys in the form of "pastors, men of God, apostles, bishops, etc" who claim to be preaching and talking about God's goodness but simply to find their way in other people's pockets or resources but not for the benefit of the kingdom of God. These guys have really mastered the art of manipulating, convincing and swaying innocent believers in a bid to make them sentimentally offer and 'sow' whatever they have supposedly for furthering the mission of Christ. But after reading Philippians 1:15, I can realize that even Christ permits that this happens since whether they preach Christ for their own benefit or for the increase of the kingdom of God 'either way, the word of God is preached, proclaimed and dispersed' and the Bible says that His word can't go in vain without harvesting any soul.

Philippians 4:13, "I can do everything in Christ who empowers me"
Philippians 3: "Our home is in heaven, where we are waiting our Lord………"

6. THE GREAT PHYSICIAN (SDAH 254)

1) The great Physician now is near,
The sympathizing Jesus;
He speaks the drooping heart to cheer,
Oh! hear the voice of Jesus.

Chorus
Sweetest note in seraph song,
Sweetest name on mortal tongue;
Sweetest carol ever sung,
Jesus, blessèd Jesus.

2) All glory to the dying Lamb!,
I now believe in Jesus;
I love the blessed Savior's name ,
I love the name of Jesus.

4) And when He comes to bring the crown,
The crown of life and glory,
Then by His side we will sit down,
And tell redemption's story.

This wonderful hymn was composed by a Methodist minister, William Hunter (1811 – 1877). He was born in Ireland but his family emigrated to U.S.A when he was 6 years old. Later in life, he was ordained as a minister in the Methodist church, but he did a couple of other remarkable things in life including teaching Hebrew at Allegheny College, and editing a variety of religious periodicals. Despite the fact that he authored more than 125 hymns, this particular hymn is the only one that is still in popular use now, and it was initially called "Christ, the Physician".

In 1859, there was a serious railway accident in the US, many people lost their lives. Medical reports believe that many more might have died, except for timely efforts of five medical doctors who had been on the train. The invaluable intervention of these physicians during this awful happening was the inspiration for this song.

Physicians are mentioned a number of times in the Word of God. When the Lord Jesus was criticized by the Pharisees for eating with tax collectors and "sinners," He responded pointedly, "Those who are well have no need of a physician, but those who are sick. I did not come to call the righteous, but sinners, to repentance (Mk. 2:17).

Hardly can one find Christ in the Scriptures being described as "the great Physician", despite the fact that the largest part of His ministry was connected to healing. On the other hand, William Hunter's phrase has become proverbial, and is still used more than a century and a half after the song was composed. Rather than focusing on the physical miracles of Christ, Hunter speaks of Him as One who brings sympathy and cheer to the troubled soul, and forgiveness of sins and peace with God to the sinner. He rejoices that through Christ we can look forward to a home in "that bright world above," there to worship around the throne.

Christ's methods of healing were so comprehensive and systemic; unlike the contemporary worldly physicians who are highly limited in their medical interventions and/or healing capacities given their professional orientations and specialties such as opticians, cardiologists, general medics, dentists, pediatricians, gynecologists, orthopedics, etc. Whenever Jesus would resolve to heal a person, He would heal all elements of unhealthiness – physical, mental, emotional and spiritual so that such a person can be comprehensively and systemically healed to praise and serve the Lord. Nonetheless, that healing would not make someone immune from further illness and ultimately death, because of the simple instruction and/or contract that, "When you sin, you will surely die". This is why, even those who were healed by Christ Himself, including Lazarus later had to succumb to this temporary death. Nonetheless, it is imperative to note that Jesus offers life beyond this physical death, and so, we have all reasons to count on him as our greatest physician. To better appreciate who Christ is, and how some analysts perceived him in relation to worldly professions, below is the examination:

Who is Jesus?
In Chemistry, He turned water into wine;
In Biology, He was born without the normal conception;
In Physics, He disapproved the law of gravity when he ascended into heaven;
In Economics, He disapproved the law of diminishing return by feeding 5000 men (not counting women and children) with two fishes and five loaves of bread;
In Medicine, He cured the sick and the blind without administering a single dose of drugs or at times using dust and saliva;
In History, He is the beginning and the end, but also the architect of creation;
In Government, He said that he is the wonderful Counselor and Prince of peace;

In Religion, He said that no one comes to the Father except through him; He is the greatest Man in history, he had no servants yet he was called Master. With no university degree but he was called the greatest Teacher of all time; he had no physical medicines, yet the world called him the greatest Healer that history has ever produced. Without an army, kings feared him; no military battles yet he conquered the world. I feel so honored to serve such a Leader who lives today and loves us so much. This absolutely makes Him the greatest Physician the world has ever witnessed since His healing capacity by far exceed physical, emotional, psychological, spiritual and any other kind of sickness and/or infirmity. And so, His being close to me means the world to me!

7. WHEN WE ALL GET TO HEAVEN (SDAH 633)

1)   Sing the wondrous love of Jesus,
       Sing His mercy and His grace.
       In the mansions bright and blessèd
       He'll prepare for us a place.

Chorus
When we all get to heaven,
What a day of rejoicing that will be!
When we all see Jesus,
We'll sing and shout the victory!

3)   Let us then be true and faithful,   4)   Onward to the prize before us!
       Trusting, serving every day;   Soon His beauty we'll behold;
       Just one glimpse of Him in glory   Soon the pearly gates will open;
       Will the toils of life repay.   We shall tread the streets of gold.

This hymn was composed by Eliza Edmunds Hewitt (1851 – 1920). She was born and lived her entire life in the city of Philadelphia where she was a public school teacher for a couple of years.

In 1887, this hymn was written and the words are intimately connected to a personal experience of Eliza. While she was a public school teacher, something happened one dreadful day. She had attempted to correct a rebellious student, but when she turned away he struck her across the back with a heavy slate, severely injuring her spine. Suddenly, her whole life changed since she never fully recovered from the damage done. She was often bedridden for long periods, and had trouble getting around for the rest of her days. In the immediate aftermath of the attack, she was placed in a body cast for six long months. Her painful confinement could have been a breeding ground for depression and bitter cynicism, but it wasn't.

After several years, her physical condition improved somewhat, and she served as a Sunday School Superintendent, for several decades, at the Northern Home for Friendless Children, and later at the Calvin Presbyterian Church. Miss Hewitt was also a regular contributor to Sunday School Helps.

This is one of those simple gospel songs that contains some encouraging and challenging Bible truth. It begins with a joyous celebration of the promises of the Lord Jesus in John 14:2-3…

As the song flows, Eliza Hewitt deals with a couple of related themes: she reminds us that, though this life for the Christian may include suffering and sorrow, that will all be over when we go to our heavenly home. These thoughts surely encouraged her, in her long and painful suffering (from a back injury). This is enhanced by Paul's admonitions in Romans 8:18 that "I consider that the sufferings of this present time are not worthy to be compared with the glory which shall be revealed in us".

Stanza 3 and 4, Hewitt seems to be in harmony with the Pauline writings in Philippians 3:13ff "Brethren, I do not count myself to have apprehended [attained what is expected of me]; but one thing I do, forgetting those things which are behind and reaching forward to those things which are ahead, I press toward the goal for the prize of the upward call of God in Christ Jesus." Some scholars see this as a reference to the heavenly rewards Christians will receive at the judgment seat of Christ. Others see the upward summons of Christ itself to be the prize–as though it will be an indication that the individual's life work has been completed successfully. As we ponder about what really affects our capacity to attain the heavenly prize that our Lord Jesus Christ will crown us when we get to heaven, we ought to address and/or appreciate the fundamentals of our success even in this mortal life.

Higher Attitude Leads to Higher Altitude: *Prophet Elisha and King Joash*
An inspirational account is given in 2 Kings 13:14-19 (NLT) "When Prophet Elisha was in his last illness, King Jehoash of Israel visited him and wept over him………. Then, Elisha told him, 'Get a bow and some arrows'………Put your hand on the bow'…'Open that eastern window'………'Shoot' …..This is the Lord's arrow, an arrow of victory over Aram, for you will completely conquer the Arameans at Aphek'..". This story reveals how God, through His servant Elisha had given King Jehoash an opportunity to widen the scope of his victory and blessing in his reign over Israel. And this would be manifested in the number of arrows that Jehoash would shoot (all signifying victories over his adversaries). Unfortunately, Jehoash chose to shoot just three arrows (due to either sheerly despising God's capacity or not really trusting/taking God at His word or even just being unserious about crucial matters of life). This saw Elisha lament and also feel so sorry for Jehoash's failure to grab God's blessings

in plenty, and possibly challenging God by putting his attitude quite high in a bid to heighten his altitude (success) by God's grace. Jehoash assumed the throne in 798 B.C; at that time the king of Judah, Joash, was nearing the end of his reign (Joash and Jehoash are two forms of the same name). While Joash of Judah began as a good king, Jehoash of Israel was evil but both reigned at approximately the same time. Elisha was highly regarded for his prophetic powers and miracles on Israel's behalf, since he had been given a double portion of Elijah's prophetic power. Jehoash feared Elisha's death because he attributed the nation's well-being to Elisha rather than to God – which reveals Jehoash's spiritual deficiency. When Jehoash was told to strike the ground with the arrow, he did it only halfheartedly; and as a result, Elisha told him that the victory and/or blessings in all his initiatives would be incomplete since he had set very lower goals and expectations of God's capacities and potentialities. This, in itself, is equivalent to sin because he despised God, underrated his providence yet receiving the full benefits of God's plans for our lives requires us to receive and obey His commands fully. If we don't follow God's instructions fully, we should never be surprised of not enjoying his full benefits and blessings. Thus, as we set our annual goals (be they – spiritual, personal, business, church, ministerial, family, and otherwise), we should never be tempted to underestimate God's capacity and generosity by setting low and simplistic goals because that is a direct attack on His person and goodness to His beloved children. Simply put, our attitude towards God's providence but also towards life significantly determines our ultimate altitude (how far we can achieve) in life. But above all, we should understand that in all we do in this life, heaven should be our ultimate altitude (goal) because without this in mind, everything we do simply amount to what King Solomon referred to as "vanity and pursuing the wind".

8. O FOR A THOUSAND TONGUES TO SING
(SDAH 250   A & M 522)

1) O for a thousand tongues to sing
My great Redeemer's praise,
The glories of my God and King,
The triumphs of His grace!.

2) My gracious Master and my God,
Assist me to proclaim,
To spread through all the earth abroad
The honors of Thy name.

3) Jesus! the name that charms our fears,
That bids our sorrows cease;
'Tis music in the sinner's ears,
'Tis life, and health, and peace.

4) He breaks the power of canceled sin,
He sets the prisoner free;
His blood can make the foulest clean,
His blood availed for me.

5) Hear Him, ye deaf; His praise, ye dumb,
Your loosened tongues employ;
Ye blind, behold your Savior come,
And leap, ye lame, for joy.

This hymn was composed by Charles Wesley (1701 – 1788), who was born in Lincolnshire by an Anglican village priest who had 18 children. Wesley, his brother and George Whitefield, along with some other Christians founded the "Holy Club" which adopted habits of methodical study, prayer, devotions and fasting. These practices were needed besides attending communion services regularly and practicing charitable works. The adherence to such strict rules and regular methods gave rise to the denominational name "Methodists". He led a very controversial life in ministry to the point that once he was forbade from preaching due to his theological views, which saw him along with his brother John Wesley become itinerant preachers across England, Scotland and Wales. Charles Wesley, as a prolific writer, was credited with more than 6,500 hymns. It is also believed that even on his deathbed, he dictated a hymn just minutes to his death. His songs largely appealed to the spiritually starved, pointing them to the enjoyment of a renewed life, hope and faith in the Scriptures.

When Charles Wesley was converted, he had been ill in bed for some time, and the fear of death had often come into his mind. On Sunday, May 21, 1738, his brother and some friends came in and sang a hymn. After they went out he prayed alone and decided to write a hymn to commemorate this event. The result was an 18 stanza long poem, and the seventh verse, which says, "O for a thousand tongues to sing" has become the first verse of the shorter hymn well known today. These words of the hymn title are most likely from Peter Bohler who said, "Had I a thousand tongues, I would praise Him with them all." Bohler had taught the Wesley brothers about true evangelical Christianity and led a renewal in their lives.

On the contrary, it is said that, Charles Wesley usually celebrated each anniversary of his birthday by writing a hymn of praise to God. Little wonder, therefore, that the first anniversary of his conversion, his spiritual birthday, should be celebrated by one of the most helpful hymns in use among Christian churches.

Your Words as a Personal Brand

Matthew 12:35 "A good man's speech reveals the rich treasures within him. An evil-hearted man is filled with venom, and his speech reveals it" (The Living Bible).

Your words are your brand…..not just your business brand but what announces to the world each and every day your character and integrity. Every time one opens up his/her mouth or put something in writing, this ought to be kept in mind.

The most important part of one's life is actually the ability to use words; words define one's life, and words define one's values; they define one's personality. A person is no better his words, nor greater than his words. The character of one's words is the character of one's personality; and one's life is the expression, manifestation and the reflection of one's words. It doesn't take long to know who you are; all it would require is for someone to talk for a few minutes – this is because one's words can locate him and tell one's intentions. The words that I'm referring to are not just those that are spoken but even those that are not spoken (even silence speaks volumes). There is popular saying that, "The tongue has no bones, but is strong enough to break a heart. So be careful with your words". The bottom line is that one's words are his/her brand, and the way one expresses oneself matters a lot ; nothing is more important than the integrity of one's words, and the way one expresses them. So, may we be noted for praising and honoring God with our words and tongues as the hymn implicitly encourages us to do.

9. WE'RE MARCHING TO ZION (SDAH 422)

1) Come, we that love the Lord,
And let our joys be known;
Join in a song with sweet accord,
Join in a song with sweet accord
And thus surround the throne,
And thus surround the throne.

3) The hill of Zion yields,
A thousand sacred sweets
Before we reach the heav'nly field,
Before we reach the heav'nly field
Or walk the golden streets,
Or walk the golden streets.

Chorus
We're marching to Zion,
Beautiful, beautiful Zion;
We're marching upward to Zion,
The beautiful city of God.

2) Let those refuse to sing,
Who never knew our God;
But children of the heav'nly King,
But children of the heav'nly King,
May speak their joys abroad,
May speak their joys abroad.

4) Then let our songs abound,
And every tear be dry;
We're marching thro' Immanuel's ground,
We're marching thro' Immanuel's ground,
To fairer worlds on high,
To fairer worlds on high.

This revolutionary hymn was composed by the well-known Isaac Watts (1674 – 1748); born to Dissenting parents - people who refused to accept the authority and practices of the Church of England. Given his Non-conformist religious background and stance, he was denied admission to a university – which required all prospective students to sign allegiance to the 39 Articles of the Church of England. This saw him pursue ministry in a Nonconformist academy in Stoke Newington, London between 1690 to 1692; later on, as he awaited to be appointed as church minister, he was at home for slightly more than two years, and during this period he wrote the largest part of his hymns that he published in Hymns and Spiritual Songs in 1709.

As a boy, he sang hymns outside prison walls to encourage his father, who had been arrested for his non-conformist beliefs. Isaac showed promise as a poet at a very young age. As he grew, he became increasingly unhappy with the hymns that he sang in church each week. At age of 18, Watts complained to his father (a deacon in the Independent church at Southampton) of the poor quality of the psalms that were sung in church services, then his father suggested to him to compose better songs for church services instead of always complaining about the old-fashioned existing hymns.

During the 17th and 18th Centuries, a huge controversy erupted amongst many congregations on whether parishioners should sing psalms or hymns in the church services! Isaac Watts was the life-long champion of the 'humanly composed' hymn while the majority of the English-speaking churches insisted on the traditional psalm settings. Records have it that even tempers frequently flared, and some churches actually split in the heat of this decidedly unharmonious musical conflict. In some churches a compromise was reached; the psalm setting would be sung in the early part of the service with a hymn used at the close of the service, during which time the parishioners could leave or simply refuse to sing.

This Isaac Watts' composition of Come, We That Love the LORD was absolutely written in part to refute his critics, who had actually code-named his hymns "Watts' Whims", as well as to provide some indirect spikes for those who refused to sing his hymns: 'Let those refuse to sing who never knew our God; but children of the heavenly Kings may speak their joys abroad.' The hymn first appeared in Watt's Hymns and Spiritual Songs of 1707 and was titled 'Heavenly Joy on Earth'.

How I pray that we always remember the importance of 'psalms and hymns and spiritual songs, singing and making melody in your heart to the LORD' (Ephesians 5:19).

Because Paul knew the importance of Christian music in personal spiritual growth and worship, he often encouraged believers to "be filled with the spirit, addressing one another in psalms and hymns and spiritual songs – singing and making melody to the Lord with all your hearts" (Ephesians 5:18ff). Furthermore, just like Isaac Watts, Paul admonishes his readers, "Let the word of Christ dwell in you richly, teach and admonish one another in all wisdom, and sing psalms and hymns and spiritual songs with thankfulness in your hearts to God" (Colossians 3:16). Much as it is hard to draw a concrete distinction between psalms, hymns and spiritual songs, Bible scholars maintain that these three terms are indicative of various forms of musical compositions used in worship service. They further give the following definitions: Psalms are religious songs that are influenced by the Old Testament scriptures; Hymns would signify newly composed songs of praise directed to Christ; and Spiritual songs refer to unstructured praise songs which the Holy Ghost would place on the lips of the captivated worshipper.

Importance of Singing in the Bible

God's creative and redemptive activities, in the Bible, were accompanied and celebrated by music. This is evidenced by an account during creation in Job 38:7, "the morning stars sang together, and all the sons of God shouted for joy". This is further supported by Luke 2:14, where the heavenly host broke into song at Christ's incarnation. In addition, Revelation 19:1ff also points out that the climax of redemption will witness a great multitude of the redeemed expressing their joy through music.

Given the sacredness of music in the Bible since it is not only for God but also from God, He gave specifications on how to use this sacred instrument is to be used by humanity. Careful attention should be given to these instructions in order to avoid use the ignorant use of music to blaspheme His name as it is in common practice in the contemporary world. Singing should be directed to God, since it is God's gift to the human family. It should also be as inspired by God as His holy word, just like the Psalms, the hymn book used by God's people during the Bible times.

From the genesis of this world, the Bible tells us in Genesis 4:20ff, that Lamech had three sons who incidentally originated three basic professions that are instrumental to human living, including the great aesthetic profession "music". These included: Adah's lineage produced pastoralists (agriculturalists); Jubal's produced instrumentalists (who play musical instrumentals); and Zillah fathered industrialists and/or tool makers (those forgers of instruments of iron and bronze). The implication is that music is a valuable gift provided by God to comprehensively address human needs and also to express gratitude to God right from creation even past redemption but not a casual/ leisure activity as commonly misused now.

Besides, singing was meant for humanity's total existence, a tool for those who intended to live in peace with God through constant praise in their hearts but not limited to the worship experience. This prompted the Psalmist to say in Psalms 146:2, "I will praise the Lord all my life; I will sing praises to my God as long as I live".

Model Christian Music Ministry

During David's reign as King of Israel, in appreciation of the sacredness and importance of this ministry, he resolved to render it a lot more professional in a bid to curb down on the popular and contemporary tendencies of "gambling" in that industry. It was restricted to the Levites, and only men (largely priests and in full-time service) who had to undergo a special examination as a selection method to establish their musical ability. The Hebrews enjoyed a successful music ministry at that time (which can serve as lessons for our modern music ministry) in the following ways:

- Records have it that Levite musicians were mature and musically trained (1 Chronicles 15:22) – emphasizing the importance of musical skills and intensive musical training.
- Musicians had to be prepared spiritually (1 Chronicles 15:12) – set aside, ordained and nurtured for music ministry just like the other priests.
- Besides, musicians were full-time workers, given the detailed preparation and the need to minister in all the sacrificial and godly services.
- These musicians were ministers of music (1 Chronicles 6:31ff) - but not singing artists that are there to entertain people. That is why they had to be trained musically, prepared spiritually, supported financially, and served pastorally.

10. I AM SO GLAD THAT JESUS LOVES ME (C.H 423)

1.   I am so glad that our Father in heav'n,
   Tells of His love in the Book He has giv'n;
   Wonderful things in the Bible I see -
   This is the dearest, that Jesus loves me.

Chorus
I am so glad that Jesus loves me,
Jesus loves me, Jesus loves me,
I am so glad that Jesus loves me,
Jesus loves even me.

2.   Tho I forget Him and wander away,
   Still He doth love me wherever I stray;
   Back to His dear loving arms would I flee
   When I remember that Jesus loves me.

3.   O if there's only one song I can sing
   When in His beauty I see the great King.
   This shall my song in eternity be:
   "O what a wonder that Jesus loves me!"

This popularly known children's hymn was composed by Philip Bliss (1838 – 1876). He was born in July 1838 in Pennsylvania to religious and musical parents. He first saw the piano at the age of 10 years, and he used to work on farms and in lumber camps but he accepted Christ and joined the Baptist church at the age of 12. In 1876, while on a trip back from England to Chicago where he was to sing in Moody's service, a bridge gave way and the train plunged into the icy river below and burst into flames. Reports have it that he had actually survived the fall by escaping through a window but he went back to try to rescue his wife Lucy and both lost their lives in the flames.

This children's favorite hymn was composed in 1870 while Mr. and Mrs. Bliss were at that time living with Major Whittle's family in Chicago. One morning Mrs. Bliss came down to breakfast and said, as she entered the room: ' Last night Mr. Bliss had a tune given to him that I think is going to live and be one of the most useful that he has written. I have been singing it all the morning, and I cannot get it out of my mind.' The narrative continues that she then sang the notes over to the group of believers around. The idea of Bliss, in writing the hymn, was to bring out the truth that the peace and comfort of a Christian are not founded so much upon his love to Christ as upon Christ's love to him, and that to occupy the mind with Christ's love would produce love and consecration. Mr. Paul Bliss testified that this song was suggested to him by hearing the chorus of the hymn, "Oh, how I love Jesus, "repeated very frequently in a meeting which he attended. After joining in the chorus a number of times the thought came to him, "Have I not been singing enough about my poor love for Jesus, and shall I not rather sing of his great love for me?" Under the impulse of this thought he went home and composed this, one of his most popular children's hymns.

Though Bliss' major intention was to instil the love of God in the youngsters he also sought to impress on them the evident reality that Jesus loves even me, as clearly revealed in the Bible (remember that Paul Bliss' ministry was basically focused on the children and youths). I would wish to orient to another type of love "marital relationship". This is especially because it is God who instituted the family relationship, which is premised on love. Unfortunately many youths enter into this sacred institution without fully understanding some simple basics that are so fundamental to healthy marital relationship. And so, below are some marital resources that can bless those already in a formal relationship but also those who are just starting their own so that they can take glimpses into this sacred field.

Wisdom for A Loving Marriage

One of the most remarkable scriptures in the Bible on marital relationship and welfare are in 1 Peter 3:1-7; filled with packed resources for both wives and husbands. It may at times be quite hard to clearly establish who, among Christ's apostles, was officially married or not; but at least all Bible students can absolutely affirm that Apostle Peter was married, and this is why we shall take crucial lessons from his marital experience and resources. In my culture, just like most masculine-dominated (male superiority complex) societies, there are deliberate tendencies of preparing women/girls for marriage institution for quite a long time but neglecting training men/boys as family heads and thus discounting their need for prior-preparation for this life-long profession and/ or institution. Peter, as a senior church leader and experienced family head (husband) strongly cautioned husbands in verse 7 (actually the only counsels for men in the seven verses), 1 Peter 3:7 (NLT), "In the same way, you husbands must give honor to your wives. Treat your wife with understanding as you live together. She may be weaker than you are, but she is your equal partner in God's gift of new life. Treat her as you should so your prayers will not be hindered." According to Apostle Peter, the most important instrument and/or resource that a husband needs to plan, manage and ensure success of his household is understanding. In the English Oxford Dictionary, this is defined as: mental but sometimes emotional process of comprehending and assimilating knowledge; intelligence and/or ability to grasp the full meaning of knowledge; judgment or informed opinion; sympathy and showing compassion. If only a husband can have the above, it would be practically easier for him to efficiently and effectively manage his household, beginning with understanding his wife (who she is, what she wants, her extremes in life, her capacities, but also interpreting her mental processes and words); but also his children and the family resources. A man who honors his wife as a member of a weaker sex will protect, respect, help, and stay with her. He will not expect her to work full-time both at home and outside home; he will lighten her load wherever he can. He will be sensitive to her needs, and he will relate to her with courtesy, consideration, insight and tact. If a man is not considerate and respectful of his wife, his prayers will not be heard, because a living relationship with God is related to and manifested in right relationships with others.

Scripture; Amos 3:3 – "Can two walk together, unless they are agreed?"
A certain author wrote that marriage requires a relationship between these parties: a deaf person and a blind person. Deaf signifies being deaf to all words that are irrelevant to one's marriage – gossip, loose talk and impertinent stories about one's spouse that would be detrimental to a successful marriage relationship. Blind signifies being blind to all other men and women just like the marriage vow goes, that henceforth, one will no longer have his/her eyes wide open in regards to the opposite sex in the context of marital love affairs and undertakings.

To further illustrate the relevance of blindness in marriage, a story is told of a frog which had purposed to climb despite their natural endowment and possibly inability to climb; all the other peers (frogs) pleaded with it not to give a try by climbing but it was to no avail. As they continued to yell at it not to continue, it climbed up to the top of the tree. On wondering how this guy defied nature, and also the pleas from friends, as they tried to interact with it the peers came to realize that this friend of theirs (frog) was Deaf, which is why it couldn't hear discouragements from others

Another commentator said that all those who believe in Socrates' philosophy as regards marriage can't manage marital relationships; because in marriage, it is not healthy to ask the Socrates' questions of: why, what, when, who, and how. By and large, much as marital love is so important in the success of marital and earthly relationships, we especially need to appreciate the fact that divine love (as majorly expressed in this Paul Bliss' song) is so fundamental in the sacred institution of marriage and in all that goes on under the sun.

11. THERE SHALL BE SHOWERS OF BLESSINGS (SDAH 195)

1. "There shall be showers of blessing" -
This is the promise of love;
There shall be seasons refreshing,
Sent from the Savior above.

2. "There shall be showers of blessing" -
Precious reviving again;
Over the hills and the valleys,
Sound of abundance of rain.

Chorus
Showers of blessing,
Showers of blessing we need;
Mercy drops round us are falling,
But for the showers we plead.

3. "There shall be showers of blessing" -
Send them upon us, O Lord;
Grant to us now a refreshing,
Come, and now honor Thy Word.

4. "There shall be showers of blessing" -
O, that today they might fall,
Now as to God we're confessing,
Now as on Jesus we call!

Major Daniel Webster Whittle was born in November 1840 in Massachusetts, but as a young man he moved to Chicago and took on a job as a cashier in Wells Fargo Bank. During the American Civil war, he earned the rank of second lieutenant but after losing his right arm in the battle, he was taken as a prisoner by Confederates. Later, he became a Christian after reading a copy of the New Testament given to him by his mother; and he was thereafter promoted to the rank of Major following the end of the war. Later in life, he met evangelist D. Moody who made him accept godliness that saw him devote his life to winning many souls for God's kingdom. Webster wrote a couple of hymns that were set to music by some of the best musicians of his time such as Philip Bliss, James McGranahan, George Stebbins, etc.

This hymn was basically inspired by God's gracious promise to the children of Israel through prophet Ezekiel around 570 B.C under the title 'The Lord's Covenant of Peace' in Ezekiel 34:26 (NLT) "I will bless my people and their homes around my holy hill. And in the proper season I will send the showers they need. There will be showers of blessing."

The Time Zone of Your Blessing

Uganda is barely two hours ahead of Tanzania, but it doesn't mean that Tanzania is slow, and it doesn't equally mean that Uganda is faster than Tanzania. Both countries are working based on their own "Time Zone".

One person could still be single yet another person got married but had to wait for ten years before bearing a child yet another one simply got a baby within one year after marriage.

Some people graduate at 22 years but wait for a whole five years to get a job; yet another one can graduate at 30 and he/she gets a job at the spot.

Everyone works according to the God-designed "Time Zone". As Christians, we all ought to appreciate this fact in life. God has designed us for a particular purpose that is different from the other person. This is why He allows things to happen at His own time in our lives. Each one's time will come, even though, others might seem to be ahead of yours. There is no need for being envious of others since it is their "time zone". What we all need is to hold on, be strong and stay true to ourselves because all things shall work together for our good.

NB: No one is late……..but each one is in his/her time based on our gracious Lord's Time Zone for our lives.

12. I WILL SING OF JESUS' LOVE (SDAH 183)

It was authored by Franklin Edison Belden (1858 – 1945). He was born at Battle Creek, Michigan, as the eldest of the five children of Stephen Belden and Sarah Harmon (the eldest sister of Ellen Harmon White – the pioneers, along with her husband, James White). Most of his education was at Battle Creek College, but in 1876 he moved, along with father, stepmother, and aunt and uncle (James and Ellen White) to California where he began to compose music. He later moved to Colorado in 1881, where he married Harriet MacDearmon, a woman with musical talent but the couple later moved to Battle Creek. Belden was so talented that he could write a new song within an hour; while the preacher was reading the morning scripture, he would then slip out and write a new hymn based on the text, which he and his wife would stand and sing. After the service he would give a copy to the preacher. By 20 years, Belden was already writing hymns and he wrote several hundred hymns during his lifetime.

In 1888 Frank Belden went to the General Conference session in Minneapolis. Unfortunately, he did not accept the message of righteousness by faith there. Ellen White in Australia, wrote to her nephew to plead with him to accept and believe the doctrine of Righteousness by Faith. While actively writing for the church, he compiled and assisted with others in the following hymnbooks: "Hymns and Tunes" in 1886, "Joyful Greeting for the Sabbath School" in 1888, "Songs of Freedom" in 1891, and "Gospel Song Sheaf" in 1894. Probably the most popular hymnbook ever used in the SDA Church was his "Christ in Song" Book published in 1900.

This song was inspired by Psalms 59:16 (NLT) "But as for me, I will sing about your power. Each morning I will sing with joy about unfailing love. For you have been my refuge, a place of safety when I am in distress". This Psalm was composed by young David under the theme 'Prayer and praise for God's saving help'. He composed it for the choir director, during the time King Saul sent soldiers to watch David's house in a bid to kill him. Throughout this psalm, He describes in ugly details the behavior of his enemies, and conveys his own feelings of terror with desperation and despair that he sees in the lives of those who want to harm him. Nevertheless, in the final accounts, he praises God for being his refuge, a place of safety and a source of unfailing love. David had learnt to turn negative circumstances into reminders of God's faithful presence.

It is very prudent for all Christians to learn to write and/or engrave God's blessings and His redemptive love in our hearts so that as the devil tries to discourage us during hard times in life, we can count our blessings and recall all that our good Lord has done to give us success in life. It is equally good not to magnify and emphasize the challenges we face in life so as to have a happy and healthy physical and spiritual life. We also need to look at the positive side of fellow Christians. A case in point is Franklin Belden who was so instrumental in the SDA Church hymnody but he later left this church due to some misunderstandings. We ought not to condemn and/or demonize him for that decision, however unbecoming many might have interpreted it. But we ought to thank God for the wonderful ministry that the Lord blessed him with during his life time, so as to find reason to rejoice for his contribution to Christian hymnody at large.

Writing on Sand and Stone

A popular story is told of two friends were walking through the desert, and at one point they had an argument. This saw one slap the other one in his face; the one who was slapped was so hurt but without saying a word, he wrote in the sand: "Today, my best friend slapped me in the face". They kept on walking until they found an oasis, where they decided to take a bath. The one who had been slapped got stuck in the mud and started drowning but the friend saved him. After he recovered from the near drowning, he wrote on a stone: "Today, my best friend saved my life". The friend who had slapped and also saved him asked, "After I hurt you, you wrote in the sand and now, you write on a stone, why?" The other friend replied, "When someone hurts us we should write it down in the sand where winds of forgiveness can erase it away. But, when someone does something good for us, we must engrave it in stone where no wind can ever erase it."

It is therefore imperative to learn to write our pains and hurts in the sand, but to carve our benefits in stone. Besides, we ought to value the people we have in life much more than the things we have in our lives. By so doing, we reflect the Savior's love for us in our relationships – which should fully indicate a Christ-like character and also a changed belief system and lifestyle choices.

13. WHAT A FELLOWSHIP (SDAH 469)

1. What a fellowship, what a joy divine,
   Leaning on the everlasting arms!
   What a blessedness, what a peace is mine,
   Leaning on the everlasting arms!

Refrain:
Leaning, leaning,
Safe and secure from all alarms;
Leaning, leaning,
Leaning on the everlasting arms.

2. O how sweet to walk in this pilgrim way,
   Leaning on the everlasting arms!
   O how bright the path grows from day to day,
   Leaning on the everlasting arms!

3. What have I to dread, what have I to fear,
   Leaning on the everlasting arms!
   I have blessed peace with my Lord so near,
   Leaning on the everlasting arms.

This hymn was composed in 1887 by Professor Anthony Johnson Showalter (May 1858 – September 1924). He was born in Virginia and he became a professional. He was known to teach it, produce it and publish about 60 songbooks. Showalter was an elder and music director in the Presbyterian Church for years.

One night, Showalter returned to his temporary housing in Alabama just to find two letters awaiting him, both from his former students in South Carolina. Each letter indicated that the writer had lost his dear wife, outlandishly, both women had died on the same day. Quite touched and confused at the same time, he resolved to refer to the Old Testament in a bid to get words that could console his friends. He later landed on Moses' comforting words to the Children of Israel before he died (actually they are referred to as 'His Blessings to the Israelites before he died') in Deuteronomy 33:27 (NLT) "The Eternal God is your, and His everlasting arms are under you. He drives out the enemy before you; He cries out, 'Destroy them'".

Soon he finished his two letters of reply, then he begun to think of other who might to be troubled, which prompted him to write the words and music of the refrain of this hymn, and sent them to his friend (prolific hymn writer) Elisha

Albright Hoffman (composer of tune of many hymns including "I must Tell Jesus") who lived in Pennsylvania. Elisha wrote three stanzas and sent them back to Showalter who then set them to music and sent it to his two mourning friends but to the whole world which lives in absolute grief ever since we began the awful experience of sin, disease and finally death so that the resources in the hymn can serve as instruments for comforting and pointing us to Christ.

My Tanzanian Escapade near Mt. Kilimanjaro

During my study on, "The East Africa Financial System", as I was traversing from Dar es Salaam to Nairobi, at a place called Mailu Kumi after Segewa towards Korogwe (along Mt. Kilimanjaro), the bus stopped to load some merchandise. I resolved to get out and ease myself in the woods since I had been traveling a long distance. Goons rounded me up alleging that I had committed an awful crime (yet it is common knowledge that in Africa, that is an acceptable practice for those who travel long distance). These guys wanted to devour me and/or lynch me because of their attitude towards foreigners. There was desperation and animosity, so evident on their looks, since they thought that all their woes were as a result of such foreigners. Consequently, they had resolved to extort any money that they could in a bid to get even. Incidentally, by the time I got out of the bus to ease myself I had been into deep bible study and the biblical texts that I was reading were related to what was soon to happen, as if my good Lord was preparing me for the events that would soon unfold. In the midst of the negotiation with these guys to 'pardon me for whatever wrong' I had committed, for every 2 minutes five more guys joined until it became a huge crowd, all on just one foreigner who was struggling with Swahili (since Tanzanian Swahili is quite different from what most East Africans speak). God's intervention came from the bus drivers who later realized that something wrong was happening to their traveler, and as they also tried to intercede for me, but one could hear their disappointment about these bus guys who were 'treacherously defending' the foreigner at the hand of their own. Finally, they asked for a sum of money they wanted and they left very happy since they had gotten back 'what belonged to them' from this foreigner. I really thank God that the worst scenario didn't happen to me that day, given His everlasting arms that protected me.

Moses' song in Deuteronomy declares that God is our refuge, our only true security. How often we entrust our lives to other things – perhaps our own strength, money, career, a noble cause, or a lifelong dream. But our only true refuge is the eternal God, who always holds out His arms to catch us when the shaky supports that we trust collapse and we fall. This is my personal testimony trusting God, but it is the gist in this Showalter-Hoffman hymn that we studying now – which also fits so well with Moses' blessings to the Children of Israel.

14. MARVELOUS GRACE (SDAH 109)

1) *Marvelous grace of our loving Lord, Grace that exceeds our sins and our guilt!*
Yonder on Calvary's mount outpoured, There where the blood of the Lamb was spilt

Chorus
Grace, grace, God's grace, Grace that will pardon and cleanse within;
Grace, grace, God's grace, Grace that is greater than all our sins

Julia Harriette Johnston (1849 – 1919) was born into a Presbyterian minister's family in Salineville, Ohio. Her family later moved to Peoria when she was aged 6 years and her father pastored the First Presbyterian Church in that community for the rest of his life. Records indicate that Julia never married but she also minister also in the same community for more than 50 years in various high positions, including Presidency of the Presbyterian Missionary Society which was founded by her mother. She was blessed to have been the author of various material for children, books, and more than 500 poems that were later set to music by a variety of composers.

This hymn in question was set to music by the legendary Daniel Brink Towner who began his musical career from the apprenticeship of his father but went ahead to study and become a professional in music up to assuming the office of presidency at Moody Bible Institute of Chicago. This saw him train a diversity of American gospel singers, but also writing music for more than 2,000 gospel songs including the now popular: "T rust and Obey", "Anywhere with Jesus", etc.

This hymn seems to have been largely influenced by the Pauline writings in Romans 5:20"..........God's wonderful grace became more abundant……..." It highlights that where sin abounded, the grace of our Merciful Father did much more abound.

The Parable that was not Completed!
Scripture- Luke 13:6ff "The fig tree that was not productive for 3 years".
Jesus told many parables and stories, most of which he completed, apart from this parable in question. This parable talks about the patience of the owner of the garden who gave a fig tree a whole three years without producing until he got fed up of this unproductive tree that he ordered the gardener/ fig dresser to cut it down but the gardener pleaded with the owner to give the tree a lot

more time so that he can give special care to the fig tree by applying manure, watering it and doing all takes so as to render the tree productive. This time that was requested for by the fig dresser was an additional time out of what was allocated to it initially (indefinite in nature) but it would act as the turning point in the life of this fig tree, once it could respond positively to the care of the gardener. This parable was directed to us as fig trees and that indefinite time is what God has given us to prove that we can be productive, lest he cuts us down. This story can only be completed with/by your own story (life story): preferably with, "At last, I was saved by faith and God's marvelous grace". God showed His patience throughout the 3 years period that He gave the fig tree but the additional time requested by the fig dresser is my time to complete the story. This clearly illustrates God's marvelous grace to us the sinners, because He had all the right to cut us down but He graciously resolved to give us some additional time (which is indefinite in nature either subject to one's life span or Christ's return- which are all out of any one's control and/or knowledge).

Verse 8 "the gardener requested for more time, more chance ie another year to give special attention and plenty of fertilizers.

There are four things that God supplies His people/ Church for growth (largely in this supposed additional time before writing them off:

a) Prayer
b) Bible Study
c) Christian Service
d) Worship

In the Old Testament times, a fruitful tree was often used as a symbol of godly living (Psalms 1:3; Jeremiah 17:7,8). Have you been enjoying God's special treatment without giving anything in return?? If so, then respond to the gardener's patient care and begin to bear the fruit that God created you to produce.

15. PRECIOUS SAVIOR, THOU HAST SAVED ME; (C.H 447   SDAH 359)

1. Precious Savior, Thou hast saved me,
   Thine, and only Thine I am;
   Oh! the cleansing blood has reached me!
   Glory, glory, to the Lamb!

Refrain:
Glory, glory, Jesus saves me,
Glory, glory to the Lamb!
Oh! the cleansing blood has reached me!
Glory, glory, to the Lamb!

2. Long my yearning heart was trying
   To enjoy this perfect rest;
   But I gave all trying over;
   Simply trusting, I was blest.

3. Trusting, trusting ev'ry moment;
   Feeling now the blood applied;
   Lying at the cleansing fountain;
   Dwelling in my Savior's side.

4. Consecrated to thy service,
   I will live and die to thee;
   I will witness to thy glory
   Of salvation full and free.

5. Yes, I will stand up for Jesus;
   He has sweetly saved my soul,
   Cleansed me from inbred corruption,
   Sanctified, and made me whole.

This melodious hymn was composed by Louise M. Rousse whose biographical information is basically known by God. All efforts to establish her bio data have only been futile and to no avail, however lengthy they were. Nonetheless, we should be grateful to the Lord of music who at least preserved the hymn for our edification in this generation. The hymn has a central theme of the cleansing blood of Christ, which is a motivation for wide-spread evangelism and winning as many souls for Christ as humanly possible.

Louise glorifies the name of our Savior for His cleansing blood that was shed once for everyone. She further informs that long our yearning heart has been trying to enjoy this perfect rest; but when we give all trying over; and simply trust the Lord, then we shall enjoy all His blessings. Finally, as a stimulus, she energizes us to declare that we shall stand up for Jesus (similar to the George Duffield popular hymn "Stand up! Stand up for Jesus!"), because He has not only sweetly saved our souls but cleansed us from inherited corruption, then sanctified us, and above all, made us whole for His glory and ministry.

The Vision of Mission (Ministry)

Having appreciated the vision of God, and the vision of self in the whole ministerial process, then we ought to comprehensively appreciate the vision of the vastness of mission. This will serve to open our eyes and attention to the global realities in evangelism, as we objectively make use of statistics in our analysis to better understand how huge our job is in spreading the good news of the Kingdom. When we get the vision of God's mission, we shall get the passion to go preaching. To get more practical, according to Wikipedia, Christianity was the largest by end 2012 estimated at 2.2 Billion followers (approx. a third or 31.5%) of the 6.9 Billion people on earth. Islam was in 2nd position with 1.6 Billion (22.3%); Secular/Nonreligious with 1.1 Billion (15.35%); Hinduism with 1 Billion (13.95%).

On the contrary, the Pew Research Center published its reports on statistics in major religions (2016 and even 2017 – as of 6th April 2017). The reports inform that in the next half century ie 2015 – 2060, Christianity's long reign as the world's largest religion may come to an end. Of the projected 32% growth in the world population, Muslims are expected to increase by 70% from 1.8 Billion in 2015 to nearly 3 Billion in 2060 leading to 31.1%. In 2015, Muslims accounted for 24.1% of the global population, an increase of close to 2% from 2012 statistics. This has a lot of implication to the Christianity community and church at large – which should preoccupy their strategic decisions and perspective.

Besides, as if that is not enough, in the 18th and 19th Centuries when Europeans came to Africa, they referred to Africa as a sleeping giant and fertile ground for many enterprises include Christianity and mission. But now, with the drastic growth in secularism, relativism (relativizing every Biblical doctrine), and atheism; Europe has been relegated to a dying giant as regards godliness and Christianity in particular. This will definitely require the intervention of Africa, and possibly the Americas to revive true godliness and the thirst for genuine Christianity in Europe.

All these realities render Louise's hymn very pertinent and imperative in this 21st Century. That is why, in Stanza 4, she affirms that since we are consecrated to God's service, we ought to live and die to Him; we must witness to His glory of salvation full and free.

16. O LET ME WALK WITH THEE (C.H 395)

1) O let me walk with Thee my God, As Enoch walked in days of old;
Place Thou my trembling hand in Thine, And sweet communion with me hold;
Even though the path I may not see, Yet Jesus let me walk with Thee

2) I cannot dare not walk alone, The tempest rages in the sky;
A thousand snares beset my feet, A thousand foes are lurking nigh;
Still Thou the raging of the sea, O Master! Let me walk with Thee.

3) If I may rest my hand in Thine, I'll count the joys of earth but loss;
And firmly bravely journey on; I'll bear the banner of the cross;
Till Zion's glorious gates I see; Yet Savior let me walk with Thee

In a unique way, both the author and the composer of this hymn were Seventh-day Adventists. This hymn was composed by Lillian Dale Avery-Stuttle (1855-1933) who was a student at Battle Creek College, Michigan, in the late 1870s and become an editorial worker. Out of her deep devotion and faith she authored many beautiful poems and several books. Records indicate that she expected to be one of those alive and faithful at Jesus' second coming, and who, like Enoch, would be translated that he should not see death (Heb. 11:5). The spiritual resources of this hymn are based on Genesis 5:24, "And Enoch walked with God," and it is believed that among all her various hymn compositions, this song was her own favorite despite many being no more in common use today. Besides, the composer of the hymn tune 'Morton' was called Edwin Barnes (1864 – 1930), he was a guru in music in the SDA Church at Battle Creek College and the whole of USA. In fact, in 1920 the Hillsdale College in Michigan conferred on him the honorary Doctorate of Music, thanks to his outstanding service in the music industry. This hymn is filled with SDA theological outlook, which is in line with the biblical truth.

Enoch fully appreciated and/or understood God's call for an obedient and dedicated life to ministry, this helped him to completely understand his mission call not until God saw that he was too good to remain here on earth just like Elijah. This was the fervent prayer of Lillian Dale to walk with God all through this troubled this life – which should equally be a personal prayer for anyone living in these last days of this mortal world's history.

Understanding Our Mission Call

When Prophet Elijah was inspired by God to go and call Elisha into ministry, there is a lot that went on:

Elisha was coming from a commercial background; his father was a commercial agriculturalist, with more than seven oxen, of which Elisha had been given one for himself. His family would produce on large scale (oxen can be likened to present day tractors in modern agriculture).

Elijah had his own team of workers and he was really dedicated and diligent in his trade, just like any godly person would be. When Elijah arrived at Elisha's farm, he simply threw at him a priestly scurf (garment) without even saying a word (in that era, it seems it was indicative of a special vocation from God for priesthood/ ministry). Elisha understood it and tried to plead with Elijah to give him some time to inform his father and maybe prepare himself for the divine calling; but Elijah simply showed him that it is up to him to make a rational decision, as he just moved on for his other mission initiatives. What Elisha did, was to resolve to slaughter his ox (tractor/ commercial machine), later using the yoke (which is normally fixed on the ox for cultivating) built using wooden material; he roasted the ox (beef) using this firewood and made a feast (serving it to his servants) as an indicator that the farming business is fully destroyed and now he has embraced another profession – the priestly ministry (or being a Prophet) with Elijah. Incidentally, since then, his job was to carry Elijah's bag/ suit case wherever he would go for mission causes. This, he efficiently performed until Elijah officially handed over to him before going alive to heaven.

17. FACE TO FACE (C.H 545)

1) Face to face with Christ, my Savior,
Face to face - what will it be,
When with rapture I behold Him,
Jesus Christ Who died for me?

Chorus
Face to face I shall behold Him,
Far beyond the starry sky;
Face to face in all His glory,
I shall see Him by and by!

2) Only faintly now I see Him,
With the darkling veil between,
But a blessed day is coming,
When His glory shall be seen.

3) What rejoicing in His presence,
When are banished grief and pain;
When the crooked ways are straightened,
And the dark things shall be plain.

4) Face to face! O blissful moment!
Face to face - to see and know;
Face to face with my Redeemer,
Jesus Christ Who loves me so.

This beautiful hymn is one of my all-time favorites, composed by two hymn writers, both being inspired by absolutely different circumstances and also in different geographical locations. These were Grant Colfax Tullar (1869 – 1950), a minister of the Methodist Episcopal Church and public evangelist born in Connecticut; and Carrie Ellis Beck (1855 – 1934), a committed Presbyterian who wrote verses for religious periodicals and composed at least 1,500 hymn texts. Rev. Grant Colfax Tullar was named after the then President of the U.S (Grant Colfax). He was converted at 19 years at a Methodist Camp meeting, and since then he was so instrumental in the Christian music industry ranging from a song leader for prominent Evangelists, to establishing music publishing house, to writing and/or editing hymnals and gospel songbooks. This hymn was inspired by both Methodist and Presbyterian backgrounds

Records have it that one day when staying in a home of fellow minister Charles Mead in New Jersey while assisting in an evangelistic campaign this beautiful song was composed. During a series of busy evangelistic meetings in 1898, several faithful and committed workers were gathered in a pastor's home to get a refreshment between sessions, including Grant Tullar. It was during a meal, Tullar loved eating jelly so much, and so there was just small quantity left for him; once given to him the small remaining portion, Tullar responded, "So, this is all for me". Suddenly, the last three words registered in his mind as a theme for a gospel song, he left the idea of jelly and went straight to the piano and began composing words and music under "All for me the Saviour suffered, All for me He bled and died". The pastor encouraged him to sing the hymn during that evening service but Tullar didn't believe the song was good enough.

The following day Tullar received a letter from Carrie Beck, who would write poetry as she sat rocking one of her five children and she wrote more than 2000 poems during her lifetime. Beck was tone deaf, but several of her poems were set to music by various musicians. In her letter to Tullar, Beck had asked him to compose a tune for a poem she had recently written. The meter and sentiment of the poem fit the melody Tullar had written the night before. And this was absolutely the working of the Lord who had brought together writer and musician; words and music to produce a song that was destined for eternal popularity and a blessing to generations globally across Christendom.

It is worth noting that Carrie Ellis' original word was "darkling," meaning obscure and vaguely threatening which is a good word for our earthly perspective in which we view and/or analyze our God but also issues in this mortal life. The phrase "Face to Face" is indicative of a deep and cordial relationship between two parties interfacing each other, visible to one another, and close to one another; with ability to communicate directly, rather than through an intermediary.

Besides, our anticipation of heaven involves many things as highlighted in the song, among which are: dwelling places especially prepared for us by the Lord Jesus, the banishing of pain and sorrow and death, and a reunion with saved loved ones who died. But chief among the joys of heaven will surely be seeing our Savior, face to face, in all His glory. This kind of interaction expressed in the hymn is centered on Christ's love for His people (hence the inspiring words that prompted Tullar to conceive the song, "All for me the Savior suffered, All for me He bled and died"). But also Ellis Beck's poem was premised on love for Christ and the over-anticipation of His soon return so as to joyfully fellowship with His redeemed in glory.

The Apocalyptic Church of 'Philadelphia'
Scripture – Revelation 3:7-13 (NLT) "……………..They will acknowledge that you are the ones I love………………."
I truly love this name possibly because it is the name of my church family in my local church but also the meaning of the name is so packed with value and

significance. And maybe the fact that in the contemporary world, there still exists a physical place region called Philadelphia (USA), I would truly love to visit this place in the U.S.A so as to try to compare it with the feature of the biblical Philadelphia.

Philadelphia – meant "brotherly love" (philo – love, and adelphos – brother). This is believed to have been the time of great awakening in the 18th and 19th Century. This period saw the start of missionary work, whereby missionaries were sent out to continents like Africa, but also other parts of Asia like China, etc. In this time, the Millerite and the Advent movement came on the world stage. In the biblical times, this city was founded by the citizens of Pergamum, and built as a frontier area and gateway to the central plateau of Asia Minor. Residents chased away barbarian cultures from the region and brought in Greek culture and language. This is arguably the current day city of Alashehir, at the foot of the mountain leading to Anatolia. It is believed that the place is geographically along a fault line, prone to earthquakes, hence no wonder, Jesus promises them to be pillars in His Father's temple and never to be shaken again. This community worshipped Dyniosus (god of noise) worshipped through drinking alcohol, sex and other crude rites; these pagans exerted a lot of stress on the small group of believers in the city in the first century. Given their being few in numbers, and hence very weak in the face of the majority pagans, it would only require the brotherly love and clinging onto the word of God, but also patience that would keep the church afloat a sea of scorn and general bullying. This is one of the two letters out of the seven that Jesus has no reproof/ complaint on, and the other is Smyrna. This church has little strength but Christ introduces himself to them as the one holding the key of David; they have an open door before them, they have the word of his patience; but above all, they have a crown already in store for them (a distinct exception since in all the other letters, the churches are to attain the crown later on, but for Philadelphia, their job is not to lose the crown given the fact that they already have it).

In fact, it is believed that for some major Protestant movements, like the Advent movement, started in the Philadelphia time period; this was after the great disappointment in the mid-1840s, which saw a small group remain – weak and disappointed but remained steadfast in prayer and study of the word. It took brotherly love to keep the small group together.

In this era, it would take the same Philadelphian spirit to awaken the brotherly love among Christians since the love of many is growing cold. Selfishness and worldly lust are progressively separating brothers and sisters. If we are not vigilant, our crown may go and our over-anticipation for His glorious return will be in vain. All that will be replaced with people's opinions just like in the Laodicea church, and this will ultimately see our privileges as the Remnants of the Lord go away. By the way, it is imperative to note that the word, "Love" is believed to be found more than 700 times in the Bible – which alludes to how pivotal 'Love' is to human relationships.

18. FILL MY CUP, LORD (C.H 493)

1) Like the woman at the well, I was seeking
For things that could not satisfy;
And then I heard my Savior speaking:
"Draw from my well that never shall run dry."

Chorus
Fill my cup, Lord, I lift it up Lord
Come and quench this thirsting of my soul.
Bread of heaven feed me till I want no more.
Fill my cup, fill it up and make me whole.

2) There are millions in this world who are craving
The pleasure earthly things afford;
But none can match the wondrous treasure
That I find in Jesus Christ, my Lord.

3) So my brother if the things this world gave you
Leave hungers that won't pass away;
My blessed Lord will come and save you
If you kneel to Him and humbly pray.

This hymn was composed by Richard Blanchard Eugene (1925 – 2004); born in China of missionary parents but on return to the United States, they lived in Indiana, then North Carolina. Blanchard trained for ministry and he served as a pastor in the United Methodist denomination for forty years in Georgia and Florida.

Later in life, he was attacked by a severe lung condition which required two surgeries, leaving him with only one third of the normal lung capacity. But in spite of physical limitations, the pastor continued to serve the Lord, even launching a television ministry in the Miami area. He also wrote numerous songs and, interestingly, a musical about Francis of Assisi. Fill My Cup, published in 1959, is by far his best known song.

In 1959 this hymn's writing came about in an unusual way. Pastor Blanchard was waiting for the arrival of a couple for marriage counseling but they were late for the appointment. Never was he even a little irritated, the pastor sat down at the piano to spend time while the minutes went by and it was then that the idea for a gospel song came to him. He said, "When I was not in the mood to be used of God, God was in the mood to use me."

The song is based on the Lord's encounter with a Samaritan woman at Jacob's well, in a place called Sychar in John. 4:5-42; she was indeed searching for something better in her life like for happiness, for meaning, for contentment. But so far she'd been looking in all the wrong places. Scriptures have it that she had been married five times, and currently living with a sixth man yet she was about to find the answer to her lifelong quest. Having come to draw water from the well for her daily needs, the Lord Jesus used that water to start a conversation about spiritual things.

Christ began by asking for a drink, which was in itself very unusual, given that Jews have no dealings with the Samaritans yet they all descended from Abraham (and were once one kingdom during David and Solomon's reigns), but later the two groups became absolutely hostile to one another.

In the contemporary world, people have tried numerous things in a bid to satisfy their longing and/or find fulfilment as the song points out. These ways include: academic pursuit, amassing wealth, charitable works, political power, self-aggrandizement, self-denial, joining associations and clubs, but also turning into ardent fans of football and theatre. But among all these, none can match the endless treasures that we can find in Jesus Christ our Lord – since Christ gives real peace and satisfaction unlike the cosmetic and temporal happiness that worldly things provide.

Jesus and the Samaritan Woman

It was a Jewish culture for men, having got fed up of their wives, and backed by the traditional law of Moses, that empowered them to simply divorce them through writing a letter to the wife justifying the divorce due to any issue as trivial as not cooking well or no longer being attractive to the man. These guys had developed a tradition of going to the well in a bid to get a suitor/new prospective wife; it is said that they would camp near the well and sit on stones within the vicinity to trap any young girls/ladies. Whenever a man could call upon a young lady and she responds positively (since they also knew the custom), and then after having asked for water, the lady happily grants the man's request; this guy would hastily write a divorce letter. This would facilitate the man's desire to take on a new wife; and this would continue as long as men wanted the vice – women had been dehumanized and relegated to this level for a long time.

When Christ found this Samaritan woman at the well alone and asked her for water, not only did His apostles (when they returned), disciples and spectators (who came later on) wonder but also the woman herself stood in surprise – could Christ also be making an advance for relationship/ proposing to the Samaritan woman?? Despite the historical and generational animosity (hatred) that existed between the children of Israel and the Samaritans from Prophets Ezra and Nehemiah's time. This had absolutely ruled out any practical interactions (and possibly any initiatives for reconciliations) between these two rival societies. But Christ wanted to use this opportunity to make the Samaritan woman and her whole community (Samaria was a hated mixed race) but also his disciples learn from this making good use of this 'old and faulty' custom of the Hebrews. He wanted to give them a unique living water that would never run dry and that would eternally quench the world's thirst. Fortunately, Jesus succeeded in offering them this living water through the medium of the Samaritan woman (who despite being just a woman, and of despicable social status – given her marital history). She drew multitudes to Christ and made her community request Christ to stay/keep around for some days as He shares with them this living water that quenches the thirst for eternity.

19. I NEED THEE EVERY HOUR (C.H 573)

1)   I need Thee every hour, most gracious Lord;
        No tender voice like Thine can peace afford.

Refrain
I need Thee, O I need Thee;
Every hour I need Thee;
O bless me now, my Savior,
I come to Thee.

2)   I need Thee every hour, stay Thou nearby;
        Temptations lose their power when Thou art nigh.

3)   I need Thee every hour, in joy or pain;
        Come quickly and abide, or life is in vain.

4)   I need Thee every hour; teach me Thy will;
        And Thy rich promises in me fulfill.

5)   I need Thee every hour, most Holy One;
        O make me Thine indeed, Thou blessed Son.

This hymn was composed by Annie Sherwood Hawks (1836 – 1918). She was born in New York and is believed to have authored 400 hymns, many of which are not in popular use today but this particular song stands out among all of them.

Hawks was a member of the Baptist church in Brooklyn, New York; her pastor Robert Lowry (1826 – 1899) could encourage her to write hymns basically for Sunday worship services. But in 1872, following an atmosphere of love and joy in the midst of her routine household duties, she experienced a sense of nearness to God, which prompted her to compose this beautiful song. Then, her pastor Robert Lowry provided the words for the refrain and the tune as well Initially, this hymn was headed by John 15:5, "Without Me you can do nothing." This text that inspired the song composition is found in what is at times called the Upper Room Discourse, the Lord's teaching passed on to His disciples, just hours before He was crucified. Jesus compares Himself to a grape vine (vs. 1), and His disciples to branches of the vine (vs. 5). It is from the vine that the branches receive life and nourishment, enabling them to bear fruit. In the same way, it is as we remain in intimate fellowship with the Lord that His people are equipped and energized to bear spiritual fruit. This is also the basis for effective prayer (vs. 7), since it is how our desires are conformed to His will (cf. I Jn. 5:14).

This hymn actually led to the composition of another popular hymn by Major D.W Whittle called "Moment by Moment", which came in opposition to Sherwood's plea of simply being in need of God every hour. It emphasized that we need God every moment due to this tempting, troublesome and challenging world that we live in. But also there is a strong request in the chorus that everyone ought to claim for oneself "O bless me now, my Savior, I come to Thee" – whereby we need God's blessing every now and then.

The Cheetah and Leopard Relationship: *Our Complete Dependence on God*
A popular real life story is told of two members of the cat family (animal kingdom) – the cheetah and the leopard. According to English Oxford Dictionary, a cheetah is a distinct member of the cat family slightly smaller than the leopard but with longer limbs and a smaller head – native to Africa & arguably the fastest terrestrial animal. It is believed that these two 'cousins' have always maintained a cordial and intimate relationship based on survival and/or dependence of one to another. Both animals are carnivores (animals that eat meat as the main diet). It is said that they normally move together simply because when the leopard hunts its prey, its interest is largely sucking blood from the victim and in most cases leaves the corpse (dead body) there, yet for the cheetah which is not as strong as the leopard is basically interested in the corpse. So, right after the leopard sucks the blood of the victim, then the cheetah has gotten food without much hustling. This has led to a significant and dependent relationship between these two cat family cousins – the cheetah's survival squarely depending on the goodness and/or existence of the leopard.

Actually, in my Kiganda culture (arguably, one of the historically and even currently most sophisticated and streamlined societies in Sub-Saharan Africa), our ancestors took keen interest in the symbiotic relationship between these two cousins. This saw the creation of a whole clan under the totem (locally called 'Omuziro') branded after the cheetah (locally called 'Akasimba') and also the related cultural symbol for those in that clan is the leopard (locally called 'Engo'). Besides, the cultural slogan for the members of that clan is literally translated, "I steadily walk along with my elder cousin, I steadily walk with my elder cousin" as being uttered by the cheetah. Then, the leopard angrily barks, "Keep quiet! Keep quiet!" And this barking is aimed at stopping the cheetah from warning prospective victims/ prey of the arrival and/or presence of the predator so that they can run away for their lives.

This intimate relationship reminds me of the Hebrews during their exodus from the Egyptian bondage passing through a scorching sunshine in the desert filled with deadly societies. They truly needed God every hour so that they could survive all those adversities, and that is why the gracious Lord sent them a cloud (protection from the consuming sunshine) which was, in fact, only covering them and giving relief and assurance that the Almighty Creator and their Savior was always with them during the hardships. This gave the Hebrews morale to move on and face any challenges head on because the One who they need 'every hour' had given them assurance of His Omnipresence, and in particular, His personal protection over them. What they needed to acknowledge was that, just like the cheetah fully appreciates that its survival squarely based on the goodness of the leopard, the Hebrews survival (and ours as well) is premised on who God is and what He can do for us. This calls us to fully understand God's nature and character so that we can have peace in Him and the all-time confidence that He is always available to save His beloved children.

20. SWEET HOUR OF PRAYER (SDAH 478)

1) Sweet hour of prayer! sweet hour of prayer!
That calls me from a world of care,
And bids me at my Father's throne
Make all my wants and wishes known.
In seasons of distress and grief,
My soul has often found relief
And oft escaped the tempter's snare
By thy return, sweet hour of prayer!

2) Sweet hour of prayer! sweet hour of prayer!
The joys I feel, the bliss I share,
Of those whose anxious spirits burn
With strong desires for thy return!
With such I hasten to the place
Where God my Saviour shows His face,
And gladly take my station there,
And wait for thee, sweet hour of prayer!

4) Sweet hour of prayer! sweet hour of prayer!
May I thy consolation share,
Till, from Mount Pisgah's lofty height,
I view my home and take my flight:
This robe of flesh I'll drop and rise
To seize the everlasting prize;
And shout, while passing through the air,
"Farewell, farewell, sweet hour of prayer!"

This consecration and prayer hymn was composed by William Walford (1772 – 1850). Historians believe that Walford was an elderly and blind man, who owned a small novelty shop in Coleshire, England. Day by day, he would sit in the chimney corner, carving and polishing pieces of bone to make shoe horns and other useful items for sale. As he worked, he would commune with the Lord in prayer, sometimes putting together thoughts to be shared in church the following Sunday.

Records indicate that Walford had no formal education but the Lord had given him an amazing memory, because he knew much of the Bible by heart, and was sometimes called upon to speak. When he stepped into the pulpit, the blind preacher was able to quote Scripture passages word for word, giving chapter and verse, with hardly a slip.

One day in 1842, an American clergyman named Tom Salmon visited Mr. Walford's little shop. Apparently, the old man talked with him about the theme of prayer, and the delight he took in fellowship with the Lord. Then he asked Pastor Salmon if he could write down some lines of verse he had composed. Wondering how his composition would be received by listeners, he would occasionally ask Pastor Salmon during the process, seemingly uncertain as to the worth of his creation. Little did he know that his poem would become the beloved hymn Sweet Hour of Prayer (one of the best known and best loved hymns on prayer); thanks to a beautiful tune that was written by William Bradbury years later.

This consecration hymn may perhaps compete for prominence with "What a Friend We Have in Jesus" as regards beloved hymn on prayer. The occasion of prayer is described as a "sweet hour" which is evidently indicative of something that is pleasant, agreeable, enchanting and delightful; but it can also signify respected, indicating that the hour of prayer is esteemed and held in high honor. So much is said about prayer in the Word of God that it's almost impossible even to summarize it. In the Gospels we have Christ's example of both private and public prayer, and His instruction on prayer, which includes a pattern prayer (Matt. 6:5-13). Christ assures His listeners that our heavenly Father gives good things to those who ask Him for them (Matt. 7:11). He further teaches that faith is the means by which we can claim heaven's resources (Matt. 21:22), according to God's will (cf. I Jn. 5:14.

Prayer with Others in the Process

A popular story is told of a young boy who lived with his deaf grandfather, he was used to praying aloud in his room. One day, a guest visited and as his praying culture, he really needed a new bicycle and so he took to his room for prayers. He begun to pray so loud as usual, this time round he prayed to God for a blue bicycle from Walmart (market), then the guest got concerned about why the boy was praying so aloud and he scolded him trying to teach him manners when praying. The boy informed him that he was praying so aloud because his grandfather was deaf and yet it would be this same grandfather that God had to use so as to procure this blue bicycle that the boy wanted. Simply put, God will not ascend from heaven to get this boy a bicycle but He will someone (just as He has always been using people in our lives for whatever we ask for) to get him what he wanted, and so, he had to shout in a bid to make the grandfather hear his plea and accept to be used by God in this initiative. This brings in an element of collectiveness and unity during the process of prayer, be it personal or corporate.

The Indispensable Power of Unity (linked to Prayers)

A popular story is told of a teacher who, in a bid to emphasize the importance of unity, gave his students an assignment/homework; this required students to bring a symbol of their religious beliefs and/or orientations to class the following lesson but also to explain its significance. The following lesson, students from diverse religious backgrounds brought their symbols, including the following:

a)   One Catholic brought a rosary, which alludes to Christ's death on the cross;

b)   One American boy brought a cap/hat, which indicates capacity to hold and/or arrest all dreams;

c)   One brought food, signifying that food in her culture/religion means a lot of good things in life;

d)   One brought sea shells, signifying a lot in her culture;

e)   One brought the bible, alluding to God's holy word;

f)   Among other personal symbols from a variety of students; but he later informed them that in Christianity, despite the many symbols as humanly possible, there must be unity of purpose, and this unity ought to be built on Christ the originator of His church.

By the way, to better illustrate the significance of the term "Unity", let me expound on this acronym so that we can better appreciate its package in depth:

UNITY

a)   'U' stands for Uplift. This means that all our families and churches should lift up Christ in whatever we do, but also help lift up other people in the due course. This uplifting can be revealed in the process of prayer given our trust and dependence on God.

b)   'N' stands for Need. This implies that working together arises from need, and God wants us to respond to societal needs wherever we can. These needs are the petitions that we direct to God so that He can use us to efficiently address society challenges.

c) 'I' stands for Integrity. This alludes to righteousness of Christ (John 17:19); and integrity can be defined as the state of being complete on the part of humanity. It is Christ's righteousness that is the basis and focus of our prayers.

d) 'T' refers to Trust. Wherever there is integrity, then trust follows; we ought to put our trust in Christ but also render ourselves trustworthy.

e) 'Y' refers to Yielding. This means accepting to be used by God, and acknowledging that Christ is our Master. This will help us to accept to minister to others but also accept the inconvenience in a way of ministering to other people's needs.

21. TAKE THE WORLD, BUT GIVE ME JESUS (SDAH 329)

1)   Take the world, but give me Jesus,
        All its joys are but a name;
        But His love abideth ever,
        Through eternal years the same.

Chorus
Oh, the height and depth of mercy!
Oh, the length and breadth of love!
Oh, the fullness of redemption,
Pledge of endless life above!

3)   Take the world, but give me Jesus,
        Let me view His constant smile;
        Then throughout my pilgrim journey
        Light will cheer me all the while.

This dedication hymn was composed by Frances Jane 'Fanny' Crosby (1820 – 1915); a daughter of John and Mercy Crosby, was born in Southeast, Putnam County, New York. She became blind at the age of six weeks from maltreatment of her eyes during a spell of sickness. When she was eight years old she moved with her parents to Ridgefield, the family remaining there four years. At the age of fifteen she entered the New York Institution for the Blind, where she received a good education. She became a teacher in the institution in 1847, and continued her work until 1858; she taught English grammar, rhetoric and American history.

This was the great developing period in her life. During the vacations of 1852 and 1853, spent at North Reading, she wrote the words to many songs for Dr. George F. Root, then the teacher of music at the blind institution. While teaching at the institution she met Presidents Yan Buren and Tyler, Hon. Henry Clay, Governor Wm. H. Seward, General Winfield Scott, and other distinguished characters of American history. Miss Fanny Crosby had the honor of being the first woman whose voice was heard publicly in the Senate Chamber at Washington. She read a poem there on one occasion. In addition to the thousands of hymns that she has written (about eight thousand poems in all), many of which have not been set to music, she has published four volumes of verses. The first was issued in 1844 and was entitled "The Blind Girl, and Other Poems", a second volume,

"Monterey, and Other Poems", followed in 1849, and the third, "A Wreath of Columbia's Flowers", in 1858.

It is believed that though these show the poetic bent of her mind, they had little to do with her world-wide fame. It is as a writer of Sunday-school songs and gospel hymns that she is known wherever the English language is spoken, and, in fact, wherever any other language is heard.

Fanny was married in 1858, to Alex. Van Alstyne, who was also a scholar in the same institution in which she was educated. She began to write Sunday-school hymns for Wm. B. Bradbury in 1864, and since then she supported herself by writing hymns; she resided in New York City nearly all her life. Her hymns have been in great demand and have been used by many of the most popular composers

Many of Fanny Crosby's gospels songs were inspired by things that happened to her, or conversations she had, during her long life. For this particular hymn, Fanny was talking to one of her neighbors, who complained bitterly of his poverty. "If I had wealth I would be able to do just what I wish to do; and I would be able to make an appearance in the world." Fanny replied, "Well, take the world, but give me Jesus." She later turned that comment into the present song. These words also seem to draw upon the penetrating statement of the Lord Jesus, "What will it profit a man if he gains the whole world, and loses his own soul? Or what will a man give in exchange for his soul?" (Mk. 8:36-37).

"Take the world, but give me Jesus." This statement is largely inspired by the fact that, the pleasures and treasures of this world are soon going to pass away but "His love abideth ever" (Jn. 13:1; Rev. 1:5). As the Lord told the people of Israel, "I have loved you with an everlasting love" (Jer. 31:3).

Fundamentals of Social Development

In the secular worldly context, materialism (wealth and the love of it) have destroyed all social structures and fabrics to the point that everything including one's valuable opinion in society is viewed in the perspective of how huge his/her earthly possessions are. This has only escalated to aggravated corruption, social indifference and self-centeredness, and outright neglect of the crucial fundamentals which are at the heart of sustainable societies (social development). All these are basically indicators of the fact that people (including many Christians) have deliberately resolved to take the world and its materialistic tendencies in exchange for Jesus – the foundation of all social values and selflessness.

One Oriental scholar once remarked that, "If you want to destroy the civilization of a nation, there are three ways: destroy family structure; destroy education; and, lower their role models and references". In a bid to destroy the family – undermine the role of Mothers so that they feel ashamed of being housewives. For when a conscious mother disappears, a dedicated teacher disappears and there is a downfall of role models who would teach the youngsters crucial values in life. Besides, to destroy education, one simply needs to give no importance to Teachers (as it is so commonplace now in many countries), and lower their place in society so that students can despise them (as it is evidently done now). Furthermore, to lower the role models, the world should undermine the church ministers and Scholars, and doubt them until no one listens to them or follows them. This is now so prevalent, whereby now people are following sentimental and unscientific counsels from whom ever calls oneself an authority in different fields not based on inspiration, professionalism and possibly research but populist views, emotions and hearsays. Simply because this guy has access to the Media, and he/she is either highly connected and/or relatively wealthy. These guys have led numerous unfortunate people make irrational decisions that have adversely affected their lives in all life domains such as: spiritual, financial, health, marital, career, and others. Personally, I'm a financial economists but when I hear the financial counsels that many folks give, one can't help but feel very bad yet these guys claim to be authorities in a field where they don't have any element of professionalism.

Simply put, taking the world and giving me Jesus signifies choosing the best thing that the world can offer, since King Solomon was inspired to write that 'the fear of God is the beginning of wisdom'. And we all know that when God blesses you with wisdom, then He has practically given you everything – just like King Solomon who ended up with wisdom, wealth, dominion, and popularity simply after asking for wisdom.

22. TAKE TIME TO BE HOLY (SDAH 500)

1) Take time to be holy, speak oft with thy Lord;
Abide in Him always, and feed on His Word.
Make friends of God's children; Help those who are weak;
Forgetting in nothing His blessing to seek.

2) Take time to be holy, the world rushes on;
Spend much time in secret with Jesus alone;
By looking to Jesus, like Him thou shalt be;
Thy friends in thy conduct His likeness shall see.

3) Take time to be holy, let Him be thy Guide,
And run not before Him, whatever betide;
In joy or in sorrow, still follow thy Lord,
And, looking to Jesus, still trust in His Word.

4) Take time to be holy, be calm in thy soul;
Each tho't and each motive beneath His control;
Thus led by His Spirit to fountains of love,
Thou soon shalt be fitted for service above.

This sanctification prayer hymn was composed by William Dunn Longstaff (1822 – 1894). He was a rich man who used his wealth to benefit others, including providing funds for the renovation of the church building, and acting as treasurer of the congregation.

Longstaff heard Dr. Griffith John, a missionary to China, use the interesting phrase, "Take time to be holy," while speaking at a conference in England. The same evening, Longstaff wrote a poem on the theme which he handed to gospel musician George Coles Stebbins (1846 – 1945), and he composed a tune to suit it, producing the hymn "Take Time to Be Holy". It presents an important truth that God requires us to dedicate a consistency of time with the Lord and in His Word, and the daily application of the truths we learn. This is because it takes time to build meaningful relationships, and it also takes time to develop a holy character.

But the hymn by Longstaff deals not with our eternal standing in Christ, but with our daily conduct. Then, as to our state in daily experience, we have a responsibility to "put on the Lord Jesus Christ, and make no provision for the flesh to fulfil its lusts" (Rom. 13:14; cf. Eph. 4:22-24).

In a world where everything is viewed in the glasses/ perspective of relativism (relativizing) on anything including holiness, it can only require the Holy Word of God to be our own measure/ yardstick of holiness. This is because, all the human metrics are so faulty and corrupted that they would only lead to more perversion. But, by beholding and taking time with God through Bible study, prayer and godly living, we can emulate Christ's holiness and make it our own. Research has shown that our behavior and decisions are a function of and/or reveal what we invest our time in. If it is fellowship with God, then one will bear the fruits of the Spirit, but if the investment is in worldly cares, then the results will be the fruits of the body and ungodliness. Below are the fundamentals of and possibly rationale for investing in prayer as a way of taking time to be holy:

Great Quotes on Prayer

a) Jesus Christ "But this kind doesn't go out except by prayer and fasting" (Mark 9:29).

b) S.D Gordon "The greatest thing that anyone can do for God or man is pray"

c) John Wesley "Prayer is where the action is"

d) Paul Billheimer "Satan doesn't care how many people read about prayer if only he can keep them from praying"

e) Corrie Boom "Don't pray when you feel like it, have an appointment with the Lord and keep it. A man is powerful on his knees"

f) William Cowper "Satan trembles when he sees the weakest Christian on his knees"

g) Charles Spurgeon "I would rather teach one man to pray than ten men to preach"

h) Andrew Murray "The man who mobilizes the Christian church to pray will get the greatest contribution to world evangelization in history"

i) Oswald Chambers "We have to pray with your eyes on God, not on the difficulties".

j) Andross M E "There is no other activity in life so important as that of prayer. Every other activity depends upon prayer for its best efficiency.

k) John Bunyan "He who runs from God in the morning will scarcely find Him the rest of the day"

l) Taylor James Hudson "I have seen many men work without praying, though I have never seen any good come outside of it; but I have never seen a man pray without working"

m) Bounds E M "Prayer is not learned in a classroom but in the closet"

n) Andrew Murray "We must begin to believe that God, in the mystery of prayer, has entrusted us with a force that can move the Heavenly world, and can bring its power down on earth".

o) Mother Theresa "Prayer is not asking, but putting oneself in the hands of God, at His disposition, and listening to His voice in the depth of our hearts"

p) C.S Lewis "Relying on God has to begin all over again everyday as if nothing had yet been done"

q) Rick Warren "The more you pray, the less you panic. The more you worship, the less you worry. You will feel more patience and less pressured"

r) Martin Luther "I have so much to do that I shall spend the first three hours in prayer"

s) Oswald Chamber "Prayer doesn't fit us for the greater work; prayer is the greater work"

t) D.L Moody "He who kneels the most, stands the best"

u) Prayer is an exchange service – man gives over his worries or problems to Jesus, then He gives His peace that surpasses human understanding.

v) Ellen G. White "Prayer is the opening of the heart to God as to a friend. Not to make known to God what we are, but in order to enable us to receive Him. Hence, prayer doesn't bring God down to us but brings us up to Him".

w) Hasel M. Frank "Prayer doesn't change God; it changes us, because we are brought into the life-changing presence of God".

By the way, it is worth noting that the term "prayer" is believed to be found more than 350 times in the Bible, which shows its significance and imperativeness in our daily lives.

23. TURN YOUR EYES UPON JESUS (SDAH 290)

1) O soul, are you weary and troubled?
    No light in the darkness you see?
    There's a light for a look at the Savior,
    And life more abundant and free!

Refrain
Turn your eyes upon Jesus,
Look full in His wonderful face,
And the things of earth will grow strangely dim,
In the light of His glory and grace.

2) Through death into life everlasting
    He passed, and we follow Him there;
    Over us sin no more hath dominion—
    For more than conquerors we are!

3) His Word shall not fail you—He promised;
    Believe Him, and all will be well:
    Then go to a world that is dying,
    His perfect salvation to tell!

This lovely hymn was composed by Helen Howarth Lemmel (1863 – 1961), who was born in England to a Methodist clergyman and brought to America as a child, where she spent the remainder of her life. Records have it that she was a gifted soloist, who gave concerts in many churches, and taught voice for a time at Moody Bible Institute; and later for three years she was a music critic for the Seattle Post-Intelligencer. Besides that, Helen authored close to 500 hymns.

In 1918, Helen Lemmel was given a tract by a visiting missionary, the leaflet was entitled "Focused," and in it was this exhortation: "So then, turn your eyes upon Him (Christ). Look full into His face and you will find that the things of earth will acquire a strange new dimness." She was captivated by those words, and she says, "I stood still. And singing in my soul and spirit was the chorus, with not one conscious moment of putting word to word to make rhyme, or note to note to make melody." It is said that the three stanzas of the song were added later the same week.

When it comes to faith in God, words such as 'look' are sometimes used. In that case, there's no physical sight involved unless we take it to include the act of reading about Him in the Word of God. God says, "Look (Turn) to Me and be saved, all you ends of the earth" (Isa. 45:22), and we know that it's speaking of an attitude of surrender, trust and utter dependency.

John the Baptist cried to the multitudes, "Behold! The Lamb of God" but even so, we need to be "looking unto Jesus, the author and finisher of our faith." This implies a thoughtful concentration. Christians are also to be "looking for the blessed hope and glorious appearing of our great God and Saviour Jesus Christ" (Tit. 2:13), when we shall indeed see the Saviour, face to face in all His glory.

The Beauty in Deep and Self-Study

Beholding and turning our eyes upon Jesus for all the challenges and desperation we face in this world can be very tricky if we don't seek to appreciate Him and/or deeply study about Him and His eternal plans for us through His holy inspired word. It is His word that lays bare His eternal plans and goodness to us so that, as His beloved children, we can be encouraged to trust His guidance and always turn our eyes upon Him. This can be especially enhanced through deliberately and deeply engaging in self-study of His word in a bid to appreciate the treasures of His wisdom and knowledge, lest anyone deceives us with modern wisely-crafted philosophies.

Scripture - Colossians 2: 3-4 ".....In Him lie hidden all the treasures of wisdom and knowledge. I'm telling you this so that no one will deceive you with well-crafted arguments...."

Most of my studies have been largely attained through self-study – this includes my professional studies in courses like CFA-1 (CFA, Institute); Securities and Investments (CISI, UK); Islamic Financial System (IOU, India); but also in foreign languages like French and Spanish; among other professional fields. This has since then informed me to treat my students in this way so that they earn for themselves invaluable and sustainable knowledge and competences, but also be able to create and/or share knowledge with other in class (including me), as they present term papers.

A deeper study of the Pauline Epistle to the Colossians (for this analysis – Col. 2:1-5) has very crucial lessons for us on self-study. It is quite imperative to note that Colossians was an Epistle, at times referred to as "Paul's Reaction to Heresies" given the fact that the Church in Colossae had lots of heresy which Paul was addressing and they were fatally threatening the existence of the Church. This Epistle was also one of those branded, "Paul's Prison Letters", wrote from a prison in Rome. He was actually in a house kept under close guard – normally chained to a soldier but, unlike other prisoners, Paul was given special rights and privileges such as ability to freely write letters and also opportunity of meeting any visitors he wanted to see.

Laodicea was located a few miles northeast of Colossae; and like the church at Colossae, the Laodicean Church was probably founded by one of Paul's converts while Paul was ministering in Ephesus. It was a wealthy center of trade and commerce, with wide spread false teaching as a result. The problem that Paul was combatting in the Colossian church was Knowledge. This heresy (teaching against Biblical doctrine) undermined Christianity in several basic ways. It insisted that some important secret knowledge was hidden from most believers; Paul, however, emphasized that Christ provides all the knowledge we need and He does so freely to all those who worship Him. Aspects of heresy (hidden knowledge) became fashionable in the 2nd Century, and they sounded attractive to many but such teachings would seduce a church that didn't know Christian teachings well and had not deeply devoted to self-study of the Word of God. We can only combat false teachings by becoming thoroughly acquainted with God's word through personal study and sound Bible teaching. Christian faith provides a growth track into knowledge of the truth, and this helps to guard against being deceived by lies or well-crafted arguments.

There is an all-time apparent contradiction when many simplistic minds hide their lack of passion and quest for God's treasures and knowledge as revealed in many worldly sources but subjectively and literally interpreting this Scripture in Deuteronomy 29:29, which scripture these people force to allude to "hidden knowledge".

24. WHEN THE ROLL IS CALLED UP YONDER (SDAH 216)

1) When the trumpet of the Lord shall sound, and time shall be no more,
And the morning breaks, eternal, bright and fair;
When the saved of earth shall gather over on the other shore,
And the roll is called up yonder, I'll be there.

Chorus
When the roll, is called up yonder,
When the roll, is called up yonder,
When the roll, is called up yonder,
When the roll is called up yonder I'll be there.

2) On that bright and cloudless morning when the dead in Christ shall rise,
And the glory of His resurrection share;
When His chosen ones shall gather to their home beyond the skies,
And the roll is called up yonder, I'll be there.

3) Let us labor for the Master from the dawn till setting sun,
Let us talk of all His wondrous love and care;
Then when all of life is over, and our work on earth is done,
And the roll is called up yonder, I'll be there.

This wonderful hymn was composed by James Milton Black (1856 – 1938). He was an American Methodist gospel song writer with close to 1,500 songs to his name and also known to have edited a dozen song books. Black trained in voice and the organ, conducted singing schools, and was an active layman in his home church in Williamsport, Pennsylvania. Of his many songs, just one remains in popular use, and it is this hymn in question.

James Black recounts that, one day, he met a fourteen year old girl called Bessie who was poorly clad, and the child of a community drunkard. She accepted Black's invitation to attend the Sunday school, and joined the young people's society. But one evening, when members answered the roll call by repeating Scripture texts, she failed to respond. Song writer Black recalls speaking of what a sad thing it would be, when our names are called from the Lamb's Book of Life, if anyone should be absent. And he later said, 'O God, when my own name is called up yonder, may I be there to respond!'

When Black returned home that evening, he wrote the song inspired by this incident; it then emerged that Bessie had been absent because she was seriously ill, and she died shortly after. Black spoke of the above incident at her funeral service, and his song was first sung publicly at that time. Reportedly, it had a great impact on those gathered.

The fact that this song was inspired by an actual roll call at a youth meeting can also be used in drawing a parallel to a heavenly roll call, based on what the Bible says about the Book of Life mentioned in the book of Revelation (Rev. 13:8; 20:15; 21:27). Whether or not these refer to a real book with pages, it is clear that the Lord keeps accurate records of what takes place on earth; not only is there a Book of Life, but other books recording the conduct of all living (Rev. 20:12). It is worth remembering that nothing said, done, or thought, can escape the watchful eye of the Lord.

Balance Sheet Of Life

Simply put, a Balance sheet is used to establish the difference and/or relationship between credits and debits of a given business account. It is an instrument that is used to establish (measure) the financial health of a given corporate body or entity. In relation to human life:
Our Birth is our opening balance!
Our Death is our closing balance!
Our prejudiced views are our liabilities!
Our creative ideas are our assets!
The Heart is our current asset!
The Soul is our fixed asset!
The Brain is our fixed deposit!
Thinking is our current account!
Our Achievements are our capital!
Our Character and morals, our stock-in-trade!
Our friends are our general reserves!
Our Values and behaviors are our goodwill!
Patience is our interest earned!
Our Children are our bonus issues!
Our Education is our brand and patent!
Knowledge is our investment!
Experience is our premium account (bonus or awards)!

The aim is to tally the Balance sheet accurately. The goal is to get the Best presented accounts.

The most destructive habit is worry!

The greatest joy is giving!

God is our Auditor!

The choice and use of a financial tool in relation to this song is largely because there is a significant parallel between the Heavenly Roll and the Life's balance sheet that can help us better scrutinize our life's worth and also point us to the final judgment. This helps us link our present life to our future heavenly hope since Bible texts like (Prov. 11:4; Matthew 7:22; 1 John 4:17; etc) remind us of the reality of the judgment day so that as we do whatever we do right now, we should keep in mind that one day we shall stand at the judgment table of God to account for all we did or didn't do.

25. TELL IT TO JESUS (C.H 573)

1)   Are you weary, are you heavy hearted?
       Tell it to Jesus, tell it to Jesus.
       Are you grieving over joys departed?
       Tell it to Jesus alone.

Chorus
Tell it to Jesus, tell it to Jesus,
He is a Friend that's well known.
You've no other such a friend or brother,
Tell it to Jesus alone.

2)   Do the tears flow down your cheeks unbidden?
       Tell it to Jesus, tell it to Jesus.
       Have you sins that to men's eyes are hidden?
       Tell it to Jesus alone.

3)   Do you fear the gath'ring clouds of sorrow?
       Tell it to Jesus, tell it to Jesus.
       Are you anxious what shall be tomorrow?
       Tell it to Jesus alone.

4)   Are you troubled at the thought of dying?
       Tell it to Jesus, tell it to Jesus.
       For Christ's coming kingdom are you sighing?
       Tell it to Jesus alone.

This extremely repetitious hymn was composed by a minister of the United Brethren Church called Edmund Simon Lorenz (1854 – 1942); born in Ohio, he pursued studies in Divinity and music at the University of Liepzig, Germany. At 20 years of age, he served as music editor of the first United Brethren Hymnal; and for two years he was president of Lebanon Valley College, Pennsylvania. His health broke and during the period of recuperation he resolved to concentrate on music – hence establishing a very successful music publishers company called 'Lorenz and Company' which published two periodicals, and other church music and organ magazines. Besides, he composed a couple of gospel songs, hymn tunes and other books.

In 1876, Lorenz composed this repetitious hymn in question, originally being in German, but it was translated into English by an ordained minister of the Congregational Church called Jeremiah Eames Rankin (1828 – 1904) four years later in 1880.

We might complain that how can a little song, have a repetition of a four-word phrase 24 times?! This extreme repetition of that phrase has given the song its title, "Tell It to Jesus".

The crucial question that should help us put all this repetition in perspective is, "Do I 'tell it all to Jesus'?" Simply put, do we pray about the things that are troubling us? Many a times, we spend way too much time worrying, or fretfully struggling first, before we think to bring our need to the Lord!

God Knows Everything ...
A story is told of a man who took his cloth to the tailor and asked him to fix the little opening near the pocket. The tailor turned the cloth inside out and then began to tear the pocket with his hands; he exclaimed and rudely told the tailor, "I said you should sew not tear! You are tearing my cloth." But he replied, "I know!"

Those two words sank into the man like a heavy stone sinks in water, and he couldn't talk again. He reasoned, "He's the tailor, and I'm just a customer. Even though I couldn't relate tearing with sewing but the tailor says 'I know". God is saying "I know"; He hears our complaints such as: Father, I need a job, it has been long since I left school......"I know"
Father, my fiancée has abandoned me.................."I know"
I have no money to pay for my rent…......."I know"
I was rejected and abused..................."I know"

So many times when the Lord is fixing us, He starts by 'tearing' us – tearing our confidence in ourselves; tearing all our philosophies; tearing our pride and fake humility; tearing the things we call dear and giving us the truly dear things in life. The only requirement is wisdom – wisdom to know when it is the Lord and when it isn't Him. It is worth noting that the devil tears to kill but God tears to fix (the old to give you the new). Besides, God's tearing fire only refines His own; and His tearing approach only yields the fruit of righteousness. God maintains in Jeremiah 29:11 that "For I know the thoughts that I think towards you, says the Lord, thoughts of peace, and not of evil, to give you a future and a hope". And this is the basic reason as to why we ought to tell it to Jesus, because He know what we needs, and He is 'Omniscient'. But telling Him signifies confidence and trust in Him and His loving care for us. It also shows intimacy with our gracious Father who will always give us an opportunity to personally address to Him all our petitions, lest He gives us 'what we don't need' just because of His generosity.

26. SITTING AT THE FEET OF JESUS (C.H 618)

This edifying hymn text was written by K. C. Minter, and the tune was composed by J. W. Davis. It first appeared in a hymnal edited by Robert C. Welch in 1963 titled "Abiding Hymns". This song pictures the Christian sitting at the feet of Jesus and hearing His word as did Mary in Luke 10:39.

This song emphasizes some crucial divine resources that can be enjoyed by a Christian who sits at Jesus's feet, these include:

Stanza 1 talks about sitting at His feet: being at the feet of Jesus symbolizes the idea of reverent submission to Him. It is by taking our place at the feet of Jesus, spiritually speaking, that we can watch and pray lest we enter into temptation. This shows that to keep us safe all the way, we should trust in His grace and power.

Stanza 2 talks about listening at His feet: Mary was sitting at Jesus's feet to listen to Him, and Jesus wants us to listen to His word today as it is found in the inspired scriptures. The reason we need to listen is so that we can hear His commands to obey them. It is by listening to and obeying the words of Jesus that we gain true wisdom, because He is our wisdom.

Stanza 3 talks about seeking the feet of Jesus: even though we cannot literally sit at Jesus's feet as people who lived when He walked on earth did, we must still seek to learn of Him and to do His will. It is only by seeking the feet of Jesus that we can claim the exceeding great and precious promises that He has made to us. One of these promises is that by seeking Him we can have the fullness of His grace.

Stanza 4 talks about looking for hope at the feet of Jesus: someday the toils of life will be over and the dead in Christ will rest from their labors. This will take place when our race on earth is run and we have finished the course. It is the hope of the righteous that the evening shadows that bring death will find them peacefully resting in their graves awaiting their resurrection to life when they will be ushered into the presence of God where they can literally sit at Jesus's feet and dwell in the house of the Lord forever.

The Old Professor and his former Students

A popular and also educative story is told of a group of alumni (former university students), highly established in their careers, who agreed to pay a visit to their old professor. Their conversation soon turned into complaints about stress and intrigue in work and life.

Offering his guests coffee, the professor went to the kitchen and brought a large pot of coffee with an assortment of cups (of every size and kind), some expensive, some exquisite and so on. He then told them to help themselves to the coffee. When all of them had a cup of coffee in hand, he said: "If you noticed, all the nice looking expensive cups were taken up, leaving behind the plain and cheap ones. While it is very normal for you to want only the best for yourselves, that is the source of your problems and stress. Be assured that the cup itself adds no quality to the coffee; in most cases it is just more expensive and in some cases even hides what we drink. What all of you really wanted was coffee, not the cup, but you consciously went for the best cups…and then you began eyeing each other's cups.

Please take note, life is the coffee; the jobs, money and position in society are the cups. They are just tools to hold and contain life, and the type of cups we have do not define nor change the quality of life we live. Sometimes by concentrating only on the cup, we fail to enjoy the coffee God has provided us. God brews the coffee, not the cups….so, please enjoy the coffee!"

The happiest people don't have the best of everything but they make the best of everything. This environment of the professor literally sitting down his former students to remind them of the basics of living a simple and successful life reminds me of the crucial job that Jesus, if permitted by our choices, can do daily in our lives. If we can humbly sit on His feet daily (at least morning and evening) through our household and congregational worship services, he is very willing to teach in the most basic of ways He would wish we conduct our lives daily so as to glorify His name and live peaceful lives. As highlighted in this Minter-Davis hymn, sitting at the feet of Jesus suggests reverent submission to His authority and guidance, attentively listening and seeking to learn of Him (and His meekness), and above all, looking forward to His glorious return – which is perfectly branded as the 'blessed hope of all times' (Titus 2:13).

27. I WOULD RATHER HAVE JESUS (SDAH 327)

1)   I'd rather have Jesus than silver or gold,
       I'd rather be His than have riches untold;
       I'd rather have Jesus than houses or lands,
       I'd rather be led by His nail-pierced hand.

Chorus
Than to be the king of a vast domain
And be held in sin's dread sway.
I'd rather have Jesus than anything
This world affords today.

2)   I'd rather have Jesus than men's applause,
       I'd rather be faithful to His dear cause;
       I'd rather have Jesus than worldwide fame,
       I'd rather be true to His holy name.

3)   He's fairer than lilies of rarest bloom,
       He's sweeter than honey from out the comb;
       He's all that my hungering spirit needs,
       I'd rather have Jesus and let Him lead.

This popular hymn was composed by two hymn writers, both being inspired by absolutely different circumstances and also in different geographical locations: Mrs Rhea F. Miller (1894 – 1966); and George Beverly Shea (1909 …..), born to a Wesleyan Methodist minister. Beverly Shea showed keen interest in music at the age of 5, and he would watch his mother play the piano, which saw he later pick melodies on the keyboard. Due to tonsil infection, Beverly kept out of school for some years; this, his mother took it as an advantage to teach him musical instruments and he also sang bass. This saw him win a couple of musical competitions that really put him in a puzzle of choices: whether to pursue the secular line of music and popularity or to fulfil his pledge to God by continuing in ministry.

From childhood, his mother would always leave little notes in the way of: poems, quotations, essays around the house for her children to read. But for Beverly's communiques, she would place them on the piano or on his violin case. One Sunday morning in 1939, at the age of 23, George Beverly Shea had a hard decision to make. He could accept an offer in a secular singing position in New York City with a great salary and wide popularity; or he could continue singing in churches and work on Christian radio programs. While sitting at a family piano, he started to prepare a special hymn for the church service. On the piano, he found a poem by Mrs Rhea F Miller (as usual, left there by his mother); he immediately began to compose the music for the poem, and as Beverly was playing it on the family piano, his mother came in from the kitchen where she had overhead and made gestures of approval to the musical piece. Beverly Shea used the song that same morning in his father's church service. He also used those words to direct his life, and has shared this song with the wider Christian community world over.

How Mighty is Your God!?
Scripture – Ephesians 3:20 (NLT) "Now all glory to God, who is able, through His mighty power at work within us, to accomplish infinitely more than we might ask or think. Glory to Him in the church and in Christ Jesus through all generations forever and ever! Amen." This scripture is also called a "doxology" – a prayer of praise to God as composed by Apostle Paul.

In life, we have all encountered goliaths of problems, and get tempted to think that we have reached the end of the game. This has normally seen us run to human beings for help, especially those 'highly-connected personalities' that we know. But many such personalities have also soon or later ended in an extremely desperate situation, hence the Psalmist's caution against relying on human being for any kind of help. Nonetheless, a simple interaction with some biblical figures like Noah, Elijah, Joseph, Daniel, Paul, among other; would point us to a superior being whose power can be relied upon for eternity. If one could be privileged to ask those biblical heavy weights how mighty their God was, one would hear them say, "Our God is mighty enough to open prison gates wide open; to renders lions into pillows to Daniel in their own den; to interpret the king's dream when all the renown advisors had failed; to protect the three Hebrew slaves form the scorching fire; to lift Joseph from hatred, intrigue, captivity to royalty"

This same God is mighty enough today for you to get your dream job without using unconventional methods; to bring the right people in your life; and above all, to help you live a Christ-like kind of lifestyle and be a sermon to the world.

But all these are premised on the way we trust Him and pray to Him – what we pray for is shaped by how we might perceive God to be. We are often tempted to limit what He can do in our lives. As we plan anything big in our lives, we should appreciate that our God is absolutely mighty – hence "Almighty God". He is more than mighty to render us victorious in this sinful world so that we can ultimately inherit His kingdom.

28. TRUST AND OBEY (SDAH 590)

1) When we walk with the Lord in the light of His Word,
What a glory He sheds on our way!
While we do His good will, He abides with us still,
And with all who will trust and obey.

Refrain
Trust and obey, for there's no other way
To be happy in Jesus, but to trust and obey.

2) Not a shadow can rise, not a cloud in the skies,
But His smile quickly drives it away;
Not a doubt or a fear, not a sigh or a tear,
Can abide while we trust and obey.

3) Not a burden we bear, not a sorrow we share,
But our toil He doth richly repay;
Not a grief or a loss, not a frown or a cross,
But is blessed if we trust and obey.

4) But we never can prove the delights of His love
Until all on the altar we lay;
For the favor He shows, for the joy He bestows,
Are for them who will trust and obey.

5) Then in fellowship sweet we will sit at His feet.
Or we'll walk by His side in the way.
What He says we will do, where He sends we will go;
Never fear, only trust and obey.

John H Sammis (1846 – 1919) gave up his life as a businessman and part-time YMCA worker to study for the ministry. He was later ordained a Presbyterian minister in 1880 and served in various places but later taught at the Bible Institute of Los Angeles

Daniel B Towner (1850 – 1919) was music director for several popular churches and schools; he published several music books and wrote music for a couple of golden hymns.

In 1887, following an evangelistic campaign held by Dwight L Moody, a young man stood to share his story in an after-service testimony meeting. As he was speaking, it became clear to many that he knew little about the Bible of conventional Christian doctrines; his closing statement, however, spoke volumes to seasoned and new believers alike; "I'm not quite sure – but I'm going to trust and I'm going to obey".

Daniel Towner was so struck by the power of those simple words that he quickly jotted them down, then delivered them to John Sammis, who developed the words (lyrics) for this now well-known hymn, "Trust and Obey". This song has since then become a favorite for hymn singers especially among Christians in the world at large.

Are we Walking Alone??

Scripture Deuteronomy 7:9 (NLT) "Understand, therefore, that the Lord your God is indeed God. He is the faithful God who keeps His covenant for a thousand generations and lavishes His unfailing love on those who love Him and obey His commands." Besides, Moses adds on another crucial affirmation of God's steadfastness in Deut. 32:4 (NLT) "He is the Rock; His deeds are perfect. Everything He does is just and fair. He is a faithful God who does no wrong; how just and upright He is". Chapter 32 is termed to be 'The Song of Moses' which he recited publicly to the assembly of Israel. It was believed that Moses was not only a great prophet but also a song leader – after three sermons, he changed the form of his message to singing. This song in Chapter 32 reminds people of their mistakes, warns them to avoid repetition of those mistakes, and offer the hope that comes only in trusting God. This was Moses' testimony after his long experience working with God.

Despite being a sportsman (and a son to an International football celebrity), I'm not a fan of football but I love Liverpool FC's (a football team in Premier League in the U.K) popular slogan stating, "You can never walk alone". That is a heavy statement in the spiritual context, of course, not in the football perspective. But in the real secular world, it has been reliably proven that one should expect to walk alone, despite the fact that governments and other authorities are put in place to ensure that one doesn't walk alone (without being protected by laws, policies, regulations, etc).

Greenland Bank was a huge local Ugandan bank in the 1990s but it was liquidated just after 7 and a half year of operation on 1st April 1999. This saw the dreams of many stakeholders including the proprietor Dr. Suleiman Kiggundu (a former Bank of Uganda governor and an outstanding international economist) perish; which actually saw him end up in jail. It begun with UGX 1 Billion deposits as opposed to UGX 78 Billion and assets worth UGX 88 Billion at its closure. This, coupled to 400 workers; its Tanzanian subsidiary that had TZ Shs 5.7 Billion deposits; worth TZ Shs 6.8 Billion asset; with more than 100,000 clients/savers in all.

The examples of poor corporate governance systems, manipulating financials and unethical practices in the investment/financial markets world, can truly show that possibly we are really walking alone without anyone caring. For instance, the Enron and Worldcom giant corporations: Enron by 2001 had USD 60 Billion with stakes in natural gas, electric, and water companies. But no one seemed to care about shareholders' interests as the company was doctoring its financials, and management appropriating to themselves annual huge bonuses as if the firm was really profitable. Executives, Board members, auditors, regulators, etc didn't give mind about what was really going on. Many of these guys actually sold their stakes and left shareholders in trouble.

Do you feel afraid when your finances, marriage, career, ministry, spiritual life is collapsing before your eyes?? Remember that you are not alone, there is a God who has proved to be faithful once you trust and obey Him during your relationship with Him while walking together. This affirmation and trust forms the basis of Prophet Moses' composition of his remarkable song (as already highlighted) in Deut. 32:1ff. Besides, this same background significantly contributed to the Sammis-Towner song in question "When we walk with Lord, in the light of His word…….." we are therefore admonished to "Trust and Obey, for there is no other way, to be happy in Jesus…..but to trust and obey". Simply put, our loving Lord can never let us walk alone in the real sense of the word, unlike the simplistic talk in the secular world that is hardly accompanied by real action and commitment on the part of many authorities.

29. LORD, I WANT TO BE A CHRISTIAN (SDAH 319)

1)   Lord I want to be a Christian in my heart, in my heart;
       Lord I want to be a Christian in my heart

Chorus
In my heart, in my heart,
Lord I want to be a Christian in my heart

4)   Lord I want to be like Jesus in my heart, in my heart;
       Lord I want to be like Jesus in my heart

The Negro spiritual was adapted (both words and music) by Fredrick J. Work (1879 – 1942). Tough its inspiration dates back more than 260 years and is linked to the Virginia ministry of Davies, it was specially highlighted by Miles Fisher Mark in 1953. It grew out of a slave-master relationship during the mid-18th Century when slave trade was so prevalent even in Christian communities. Despite the fact that most Negro spirituals can hardly be traced back to their original stories of composition, this one has at least a link that can bless us with such valuable resources for our contemporary lives. A slave of Hanover, Virginia went up to William Davies (a Presbyterian minister) in 1756 with this noble plea, "I come to you, sir, that you may tell me some good things about Jesus Christ and my duty to God, for I'm resolved not to live anymore as I have done". Simply put, the slave was saying that, "Lord, I want to be a Christian in my heart". Miles throws more light on the song by suggesting that the quiet dignity of the song's tune, devoid of the wild abandon of some of the Negro songs and the fact that a person had to seek membership in the Christian community, qualifies it as a spiritual from a Presbyterian background.

Research indicates that the Negro Spirituals sprung up from the Deep South of the United States; and they were musical tools used to express the sufferings and oppressions of the American Negro. Characterized to be rhythmic in music, these songs contained largely a message of hope to be found in God's deliverance of His people; the sufferer finds the solutions and ultimate hope in God – who would exchange his tattered clothing for a white robe and would deliver from death through a fiery chariot. In fact, those other Blacks who rejected the message of Hope of the Negro Spirituals that emphasized divine solution to their misery, developed another musical form called "Rhythms and

Blues" to express their suffering and despair. Unlike secular R & B songs and other upbeat Negro spirituals, this hymn is an example of a Negro spiritual that is a simple quiet prayer to live as an authentic and genuine Christian.

Genuine Christian Living

Scripture Psalms 15:1ff and 1Timothy 3:1ff. There is something very interesting in these Chapters of different Books by different writers but absolutely the same message that calls for genuine Christian living. Whereas Psalms 15 (also call it song) is attributed to King David under the theme "Guidelines for living a blameless life" and written between the time of Moses approx. 1440 B.C and the Babylonian captivity 586 BC (the whole Book of Psalms); Paul's epistle to Timothy was written approx. A.D 64. And among the numerous Christian living resource that are so pertinent for our contemporary lifestyles that we can draw from both these scriptures and also the Negro spiritual, these are:

a)   The highlighted virtues of walking uprightly, working righteousness, and speaking the truth suggests "Integrity". Integrity means possessing soundness and honesty; William Lawrence once said that 'integrity is the integration of one's life around his core values'. This reminds of a popular story about a prominent pastor who could always preach about integrity and godliness in his parishioners' daily life. One day, one parishioner (a retail shop owner) where the pastor normally bought his groceries intentionally and temptingly gave a lot more balance for the food items that he had bought and thanked him for having bought from him. This saw the pastor battle with his thoughts wondering whether he should disregard this error from the shop owner and count as God's providence for His own in times of financial distress but finally He yielded to God's voice and asked this guy why he had made a mistake of giving him much more balance than he had to. The shop owner openly told him that it was not a mistake but he wanted to prove whether the pastor integrated this virtue of integrity in his daily life as he has always been emphasizing it in other people's lives.

b)   Guarding his tongue, not doing evil to his neighbor and not taking reproach against his friends signifies "credibility". Credibility is the quality or power of inspiring belief or trustworthy. It has a lot to do with reliability, and capability of being believed in whatever one does. This reminds me of a popular tale about an old English actor called Macread, who due to his massive popularity in comedy and theatre that his performance that were largely based on fictions and, of course, falsehood moved huge audiences. A commentator, one time, asked him how he manages to move and control crowds with his performances, he is believed to have said this, "You know, for me I try to act out falsehood appear as if it were the reality and my viewers have come to love and accept it the way I put it across; but the Christians, we have the real truth and inspired realities have failed to sell them to the world in an appealing manner. They don't live out what they preach and proclaim the truth as if it weren't really the universal truth; and that why many have failed to buy into what they say".

c)   Honoring those who fear God, swearing to one's heart, and not putting one money usury alludes to 'Accountability'. Accountability refers to being subject to obligation and giving report for one is responsible of; explaining and being answerable to others. This also emphasizes an important element in our lives (finances); I'm a financial economist, and my major scholarly works are on "Financial systems" since these significantly affect financial decisions and transaction in an economy. Of recent, I developed an interest in Islamic finance (a composition of Economics, Banking and Finance), which is definitely a misnomer of this glorious and divine guidance to how financing and investment should be done since it was the divine inspired way of doing business from the beginning as it is expressed in Exodus 22:25; Leviticus 25:34-36; Psalms 15:5; and also in this 3rd Chapter of 1Timothy. This financial system spell out that interest/ usury is the source of all evil and selfishness that is greatly characterized of the conventional financial system, and this has led to numerous financial crises world over from the 1930s Great Depression (which is believed to be the mother of all modern financial crises that all economies have experiences in the recent history).

30. O FOR A FAITH (C.H 245)

1. Though pressed by many a foe,
   That will not tremble on the brink
   Of any earthly woe,

2. That will not murmur nor complain
   Beneath the chast'ning rod,
   But in the hour of grief or pain
   Will lean upon its God.

3. A faith that shines more bright and clear
   When tempests rage without,
   That, when in danger, knows no fear,
   In darkness feels no doubt,

4. That bears unmoved the world's dread frown,
   Nor heeds its scornful smile,
   That seas of trouble cannot drown,
   Nor Satan's arts beguile,

5. A faith that keeps the narrow way
   Till life's last hour is fled
   And with a pure and heav'nly ray
   Lights up a dying bed.

6. Lord, give us such a faith as this,
   And then, whate'er may come,
   We'll taste e'en here the hallowed bliss
   Of an eternal home.

This dedication hymn was authored by William Hiley Bathurst (1796 – 1877). He was born in Bristol, England to Rt. Hon. Charles Bragge Bathurst once a Member of Parliament for Bristol. He was educated at Winchester, and Christ Church, Oxford, graduating B.A. in 1818. From 1820 to 1852, he held the Rectory of Barwick-in-Elmet, near Leeds. He resigned from the Rectory in the latter year, through his inability to reconcile his doctrinal views with the Book of Common Prayer. He retired into private life, and died at Lydney Park, Gloucestershire in 1877. He did a couple of publications but he was also quite beloved to his parishioners that his biographer, speaking of these years of ministerial service, wrote: "Faithfully devoting himself to the spiritual welfare of his parishioners, he greatly endeared himself to them all by his eminent piety, his great simplicity of character, his tender love, and his abundant generosity." This hymn was initially titled "The Power of Faith" and it was based on the disciples' request to Christ in Luke 17:5 to, "To increase our faith"; and this request came right after Christ's lessons about forgiveness and faith that they felt so challenged. The disciples' request was quite genuine since they wanted the faith necessary for such radical forgiveness. But Jesus didn't directly answer their question because the amount of faith is not as important as its genuineness. It is worth noting that faith is the complete trust and loyalty to God that results in the willingness to do his will. Faith is not something that we use to put on a show to others but it is a complete and humble obedience to God's will, readiness to do whatever he calls us to do. The amount of faith is not as crucial as the right kind of faith and that is faith in our all-powerful God.

This saw William Bathurst pen these remarkable words and they make a lot of valuable sense to this generation which is deeply infested with unbelief, relativism, simplicity of faith and individualism. He wrote: O, for a faith that will not shrink though pressed by every foe that will not tremble on the brink of any earthly woe! A faith that keeps the narrow way till life's last hour is fled, and with a pure and heavenly ray lights up a dying bed. Lord, give me such a faith as this, and then, whatever may come, I will taste, even here, the hallowed bliss of an eternal home.

Problems: God's Blessing Wrappers

One day, a frog fell into a hole/ditch and tried to get out but failed. Later, when his peers (fellow frogs) were passing by, they found it stuck and tried to help it out but finally failed. Then, they left it to solve its own problem all alone – as it was getting comfortable and quite resigned in the hole where it had been trapped, it suddenly heard a loud and fatal noise of a trailer approaching the hole. For fear of death, and possibly having no other option, it did all in its capacity to push itself from the hole in a bid to save its life. Later in the evening, as its peers (other frogs) had gone to the beach for recreation, they found it at the beach just relaxing and enjoy the cool breezes. They were filled with wonder and asked it how it was finally able to rescue itself from the hole yet collectively they had failed to salvage it from danger. Simply put, God permits us to be exposed to hardships in life so that we can exercise and/or grow in faith and ultimately aim at achieving the higher goal of living a life that is Christ-like and worth our calling.

God has never given His people free things (it was only Adam who was given free things and consequently he freely gave them away to the adversary). Normally, God's blessings and treasures come to His people, well packaged in a wrapper called "Problems" – whenever problems come, it is an indicator that in them, God has sent to His people a blessing/gift that they need to appreciate, manage well and also look for ways how they can unwrap it and get the beauty that is hidden therein. Where there is a problem/challenge/ discomfort, there as well is a blessing. During famine/hunger, there is a blessing of producing in abundance to take advantage of the prevalent demand and scarcity of food. It would only take a strong faith in God for His people to begin appreciating this fact of life and embrace all challenges, problems, and adversities in faith, keeping in mind that it is God's approval that opportunities and blessings come their way well wrapped in 'problems'.

31 WORK, FOR THE NIGHT IS COMING (SDAH 375)

(1) Work, for the night is coming,
Work through the morning hours;
Work while the dew is sparkling,
Work 'mid springing flowers;
Work when the day grows brighter,
Work in the glowing sun;
Work, for the night is coming,
When man's work is done.

(2) Work, for the night is coming,
Work through the sunny noon;
Fill brightest hours with labor,
Rest comes sure and soon.
Give every flying minute,
Something to keep in store;
Work, for the night is coming,
When man works no more.

(3) Work, for the night is coming,
Under the sunset skies;
While their bright tints are glowing,
Work, for daylight flies.
Work till the last beam fadeth,
Fadeth to shine no more;
Work, while the night is darkening,
When man's work is o'er.

This challenging hymn was composed by a young lady, Annie Louisa Walker (1836 – 1907). She was born in Staffordshire, England but migrated to Canada at the age of 17 years. She always wrote poems and sent them to a Canadian newspaper, and also did the same with this hymn text. She wrote novels, children plays, magazine articles and hymns which were published by various publishing houses. In 1883, she married Harry Coghill (a wealthy English merchant) and later returned to England where she served as a governess and book reviewer.

In 1854, Louisa Walker, an 18 year old young lady realized that even for her the daylight was fading and she reminded us to work for the night is coming when we won't be able to work for the Lord anymore. This hymn was based on the passage in John 9:4 where Christ was addressing His disciples, "I must work the works of Him who sent me while it is day; the night is coming when no one can work". Over the years, the hymn has reminded us that our days upon this earth are numbered because of death or because Jesus could come again at any moment. And so we should be challenged to prioritize the work of the Lord while we have the health and the freedom to do so. For the time to do this is getting shorter for each of us.

In this announcement, Christ is speaking figuratively of the time when our earthly labours come to an end. "Man goes out to his work and to his labour until the evening" (Ps. 104:23). No matter how long we live, our day of opportunity to serve the Lord here will soon be over. We need to make good use of the days allotted to us before our clocks wind up.

The Stanford University story

A popular story is told (though some critics refute its authenticity, my interest is the life applications resources from it) of a lady in faded grey dress and her husband, dressed in a home-spun suit who walked in timidly without an appointment into Harvard University President's outer office.
The Secretary could tell in a moment that such backwoods, country hicks had no business at Harvard and probably didn't even deserve to be in Harvard.
"We want to see the President" the man said softly.
"He'll be busy all day", the secretary snapped.
"We'll wait", the lady replied. For hours the secretary ignored them, hoping that the couple would finally become discouraged and go away. They didn't and the secretary grew frustrated and finally decided to disturb the President.

"Maybe if you see them for a few minutes, they'll leave", she said to him. The President, harsh faced and with dignity, marched toward the couple. The lady told him, "We had a son who attended Harvard for one year; he loved Harvard, he was happy here; but about a year ago, he was accidentally killed. My husband and I would like to erect a memorial to him, somewhere on this campus".
The President was not moved…....he was instead shocked." Madam, we can't put up a statue for every person who attended Harvard and died. If we did, this prestigious place would look like a cemetery!" he said angrily.

"Oh no, we don't want to erect a statue. We thought we would like to give a building to Harvard", the lady labored to explain. Then the President rolled his eyes, he glanced at the gingham dress and the simple suit, and he exclaimed, "A building! Do you have any earthly idea how much a building costs? We have over seven and a half million dollars in the physical buildings here at Harvard". For a moment, the lady was silent. The President was pleased that maybe he could (get the monkey off his back) get rid of them now. The lady turned to her husband and said quietly, "Is that all it costs to start a university? Why don't we just establish our own? Then, her husband nodded but the President's face wilted in confusion and puzzlement.

Mr. and Mrs. Leland Stanford got up and walked away, traveling to Palo Alto, California where they established the University that bears their name.... Stanford University, a memorial to a son that Harvard no longer cared about. Leland and Jane Stanford founded this university in 1885 but it opened its doors in 1891 as a memorial of their only child Leland Stanford, Junior.

Most of the time we judge people by their outer appearance, which can be misleading. And in this impression, we tend to treat people badly by thinking that they can do nothing for us. Thus we tend to lose our potential good relationships. In life, we seldom get people with whom we want to share and grow our thought process but because of our inner amplified ego we miss them forever. In a nut shell, we need, therefore, to work to be a blessing to as many as we can because the night (as Jesus said) is coming when we can work no more and then we shall regret the invaluable time we wasted in our lives.

32. HEIR OF THE KINGDOM (SDAH 594)

1) Heir of the kingdom, O why do you slumber?
Why are you sleeping so near thy blest home?
Wake thee, arouse thee, and gird on thine armor,
Speed for the moments are hurrying on.

2) Heir of the kingdom, say, why do you linger?
How can you tarry in sight of the prize?
Up, and adorn thee, the Savior is coming;
Haste to receive Him descend the skies.

The authorship of this hymn is anonymous and only known to God but that doesn't hinder us from exploring its resourceful lessons to us today. It seems to have been inspired by James 2:5 (NLT) "Listen to me, dear brothers and sisters. Hasn't God chosen the poor in this world to be rich in faith? Are not they who will inherit the kingdom that he promised to those who love him?"

This beautiful song portrays a pilgrim who is on the way to meet the chariot of the king but falls asleep, at the same time, he is unarmed and so unprepared. But the author encourages us all as pilgrims to raise our eyes to Jesus who is coming soon but also to flee this world since its glory vanishes very soon. The composer really exhibited a fervent belief in the imminent Second Advent of our Lord Jesus Christ, and advise us not to behave like the church in Sardis which had the likeness of being alive yet they were almost long dead. But as heirs of the Kingdom, we ought to be wide awake and not to be carried away by either worldly cares or apparent goodness in it.

The Message to the Dead

1 Samuel 16:7 (NLT) "But the Lord said to Samuel, 'Don't judge by his appearance or height, for I have rejected him. The Lord doesn't see things the way you see them. People judge by outward appearance, but the Lord looks at the heart"

Revelation 3:1ff (NLT) "Write to the angel of the church of Sardis......I know all the things you do, and that you have a reputation for being alive – but you are dead. Wake up! Strengthen what little remains......"

Qualities of a Living Church (Real Conversion) include the following: a prayerful life; a self-less life; a spirit of wide-spread evangelism. The church may be dead even when all programs are going on well but as long as its members are, (or the church as a corporate body is) lacking in prayerful life then it is a dead church. Besides, if the congregation is so self-centered, inward looking and deficient in selfless life for ministry to its community then it is socially irrelevant and a disgrace to Christ who commissioned the church to go and do wide-spread evangelism.

No one could send a message to a dead creature. Though the church of Sardis seemed dead, it still had signs of life. Consequently, Jesus Christ was rebuking and warning it lest it absolutely loses the little element of life that was remaining in its stores. In secular terms, Sardis was a wealthy city and its riches were in two locations: on the mountain top and also on the valley below. Its problem was spiritual death not heresy – in spite of its reputation for being active, Sardis was infested with sin. Its deeds were evil, clothes soiled with wickedness. The spirit had no kind words or any commendations for this church that looked so good on the outside but so corrupt on the inside (Rev. 3:6). Even though Christ called it a dead church, he also affirmed a handful of faithful believers (Rev. 3:4). This reminds me of a popular story of a certain man who went to a drinking bar in a bid to relax his troubled mind. In the process of drinking there was a beautiful lady who was hired to entertain the revelers with music performances. This guy was so moved by both the beauty of this woman and also the sweetness of her voice that he resolved to propose to her to take her to his home that night. Soon, her performance ended and this guy didn't want any other reveler to snatch the beautiful musician from him, so he hastily approached her and submitted his proposal to which the lady swiftly accepted. Later they were at the guy's home that night, the man so expectant that he didn't want anything to distract him in the course of his enjoyment – the lady seeing his impatience, she told him that he should permit him to prepare herself for the long awaited activity. This saw the lady beginning to undress and turning to the normal her: removing the artificial eyes, nose, teeth, breasts, hips, nails – until she remained almost deformed and a skeleton, with a vampire voice. The guy was held speeches, desperate and disillusioned that he didn't know what to do and what not to do, but that was the reality of the apparently beautiful lady.

This was the nature of the church of Sardis and it is the same reality (nature) that we have as Christians of this generation – we have the likeness of being alive (beautiful) on the outside but when actually we are long dead just like that beautiful musician in the story above. But Christ counsels us to "Go back to what we heard and believed at first; hold to it firmly. Repent and turn to him again. But that if we don't wake up, he will come suddenly, as unexpected as a thief". As Christ reminded the church of Sardis, we need to wake up from spiritual superficiality (shallowness) and lethargy (fatigue) because we are the heirs of the kingdom.

33. O FOR THAT FLAME OF LIVING FIRE (C.H 210)

This hymn was composed in 1831 by William Hiley Bathurst (1796 – 1877). He was born at Clevedale and his father was a Member of Parliament for Bristol. He was noted to be very controversial in acts such as changing his name, his objection to the doctrine of baptism but he also wrote several books and more than 200 hymns. The writing of this hymn seems to have been inspired by the disciples' experience of tongues like as fire (Acts 2:3). Furthermore, Bathurst combines this experience of fire and the Holy Ghost with various saints of the Lord: beginning with all the patriarchs, to Apostle Paul, to Prophet Elijah, to Prophet Moses, to Job the man of God. He winds up the poetic narrative with an appeal that we, in this end times, also plead to God so that He can remember those olden times of his great men and revive that spirit within us; we pledge our souls to God so that He can pour His mighty power on us to accomplish his work.

The hymn is a revival and also evangelistic-oriented song that is primarily intended to incite a genuine revival in us, and also energize us for evangelism. Stanza 2 highlights that the power that was given to Apostle Paul, of old, is no longer existent in this indifferent generation – hence, the rationale for claiming that flame of living fire to achieve God's missionary objective. The singling out of Apostle Paul is due to his outstanding contribution to the furtherance of the gospel in the way of: writing the largest number of Epistles, (Books in the Bible); establishing the largest number of churches; experiencing the nastiest persecutions among his contemporaries (Apostles); among other features related to evangelism. We should claim such power and be proactive in using it but not just sit and watch things happen.

Through evangelism, the church grows and then it acquires the capacity to change the habits and lifestyles of its community and the world at large. C.S Lewis (a popular Christian author), in his popular publication titled, "Mere Christianity" argues that the church's sole purpose is to bring people to become (render them into) 'little Christ'. He adds that if this is not done, then, 'cathedrals, clergy, missions, Bibles, and sermons' are just inconsequential or less important in the real sense.

The Quest for Own Balloon

One day, a group of 50 people attended a seminar and the speaker through an illustration gave out balloons to each one of them. He then asked each one to write his/her name on the balloon with a marker pen for identity, and later all balloons were collected and put in another room. The speaker ordered these delegates to enter into that room and promised a reward to anyone who would retrieve his/her balloon within five minutes. Suddenly, everyone was frantically searching for their names, pushing and colliding with each other, they could trade insults and the room was characterized by total chaos within the next five minutes, and at the end no one could find his/her balloon. Then, each one was asked to randomly collect a balloon and give it to the person whose name was written on it, and within five minutes everyone had his/her balloon. The facilitator began, "This is exactly what is happening in our lives; everyone is frantically looking for happiness all around, not knowing where it is. Our happiness lies in the happiness of others. Just help them find their happiness and you will get your own happiness too. Let go of self, and this is one of the purposes of human life….. We need to learn how to put a smile on someone's face, and we will also smile in due season". This is actually the bottom line of evangelism – helping other get the joy of Jesus' salvation and consequently better their lives, which in turn will give you the same joy but also you will have contributed to bringing peace, sanity, godliness and a crime-free society.

34. I WILL FOLLOW THEE, MY SAVIOR (SDAH 623)

This hymn was composed by James Lawson Elginburg in 1886. The second half of each stanza emphasizes the encouraging thought that the Saviour endured the same difficulties that we do, and triumphed over them.

Lawson's beautiful song is actually a pledge and/or commitment that should be made by any mature Christian who has had an experience in Jesus' redemptive power and His goodness in our daily lives. He helps us to promise that: "I will follow you, my savior, wherever my lot may be; where you go, I will follow – Yes, my Lord I will follow you". In Stanza 5, Lawson inspires us and gives us sound reasons as to why we should really count of Christ's leadership and guidance because, just like any competent and reliable role-model and Christian leader, Jesus inspires us to go through the path that he himself has tried out and completed. The composer informs that: "Though Jordan's rolling billows, cold and deep, You lead me – you have crossed the waves before me, and I still will follow you".

James Elginburg creates an impression that for every good thing we want to have, there must a kind of cost to be paid for it so as to later enjoy: this can be enhanced by the old English adage, "No gains without pain". Therefore, Christ had to undergo excruciating suffering so as to procure for us freedom in Him; but also every Christian is obliged to follow through Christ's examples of going through the pain – just as Jesus one time told Peter, along with other Apostles that they would have to partake of the cup of suffering so that they can really be His followers.

The Story of the Japanese with Fish

A popular story is told of how the Japanese have always loved eating fish but this has often come with its package of constraints. It is said that the waters which are near Japan are not conducive for aquaculture (healthy living of fish) given the nature of the water bodies and other scientific realities. This made the Japanese desperate of accessing this delicacy (basically for those who frequently travel to other regions of the world and they enjoy this relish). As prospective consumers of fish progressively demanded for this delicacy, merchants devised a mechanism of procuring their clients fish but, records have it that they had to build huge water vessels which could go to far off places with good water that accommodates life for fish (and aquaculture in general). This saw vessels travel hundreds of miles in a bid to access fish but the challenge that arose was that, by the time these vessels returned to Japan, with their fish in containers, almost all the fish had either gone bad or was not palatable as fresh fish tastes because they were dead. Consumers began demanding for better tasting fish (possibly that they had tasted elsewhere); this saw merchants devise build containers (tanks) were they could pack thousands of fish in a water-tight containers so as to preserve their life, and eventually taste good given the fact that they were still alive. What they had not anticipated was that fish would become desperate and inactive since they would be confined and/or packed in a container with less or no free movement that would sustain a healthy life – all the same, they felt imprisoned, which significantly affected their lives. Still, the consumers complained of sub-standard quality of fish taste and so, they demanded for better tasting fish varieties.

Later, merchants realized that, in a bid to carry the fish alive and be able to taste nice, they had to make the fish active all throughout the long journey to Japan. How did they get this tick? Merchants had to build bigger containers for fish, but in a special way, they resolved to drop a little shark in each container which would intimidate, frighten and render the fish restless and very active because they will be running for their dear lives all along the navigation period. Finally, they got it very right and as soon as they reached Japan, every consumer of fish was very satisfied and it is said that up to now, Japanese enjoy palatable fish.

In life, we also need such little sharks in our comfortable lives so that we can strive to achieve the God-given potential, efficiency, productivity and creativity that He destined us, before the foundation of the earth. It is, at times, God's approval and/or goodness that challenges should come our way so that we can refocus, aim higher, fight/ walk with faith in the midst of adversities to live out His image in us. This can include opportunities and social challenges that require resources from us, sickness, hatred/intrigue from family and society, among other personal challenges so that all these can serve to nurture and incentivize the deliberate growth of our faith and confidence in our God. This is because whenever we enjoy our comfortable lives, our capacities are dulled, deactivated, and hindered from attaining our destined potential/ altitude in life. That is why God permits that: the cost of living drastically increases; many church/social projects spring up which require money; drought and hunger arise so that we can fully appreciate the beauty in agriculture but also devise modern mechanism of agricultural production (basically in this part of the world, whereby agriculture is our mainstay yet millions are dying of hunger and malnutrition).

The commitment and consistence of these fishermen inspires us as well, as Christians to pledge to follow our Lord Jesus Christ wherever our lot may be; where He goes, we shall follow Him as our Lord and role model. This is the message of the little known James Lawson Elginburg's hymn, who bio data is very hard to come by but whose hymn is much more popular and resourceful than even the need for the scanty information on his life.

35. CALLED TO THE FEAST (C.H 537)

This challenging hymn was composed by a minister of the United Brethren Church called Edmund Simon Lorenz (1854 – 1942); born in Ohio, he pursued studies in Divinity and music at the University of Liepzig, Germany. At 20 years of age, he served as music editor of the first United Brethren Hymnal; and for two years he was president of Lebanon Valley College, Pennsylvania. His health broke down and during the period of recuperation he resolved to concentrate on music – hence establishing a very successful music publishers company called 'Lorenz and Company' which published two periodicals, and other church music and organ magazines. Besides, he composed a couple of gospel songs, hymn tunes and other books.

This particular hymn seems to have been inspired by Christ's discourse on the Great Feast in Luke 14:15-24 (NLT) "Hearing this, a man sitting at the table with Jesus exclaimed, 'What a blessing I will be to attend a banquet in the Kingdom of God!' Jesus replied with this story. 'A man prepared a great feast and sent out many invitations................but they all began giving excuses........I have just bought a field..........I have just bought five pairs of oxen...........I now have a wife, so I can't come........"Lorenz further appears to have been inspired by Matthew 25:31- 46 which talks about the Final Judgment, "But when the Son of man comes in His glory, and all the angels with him.......he will separate the sheep from the goats........." Jesus used sheep and goats to picture the division between believers and unbelievers – sheep and goats often gazed together but were separated when it came time to shear sheep. Besides, there is another link to Christ' discourse in Matthew 24:1ff (His teachings on the Mount of Olives) focusing on the Future and His return. Theologians and Bible scholars believe that Matthew 24:1ff is the amplification and/or what was fully explained in the Apocalyptic Book of John the Revelator whereby he was giving a full account of what we happen slightly before Christ returns to take His own. The Book of Revelation gives the nitty-gritty of details that God wanted His people to know lest they are also taken by surprise regarding the day of Christ's return.

Rev. Edmund Lorenz's song reminds us that we have been honorably invited to the greatest feast ever organized in the history of humanity so that we can fellowship with God's people across the globe. In Jesus' story, many people turned down the invitation to the banquet because the timing was inconvenient. We are not any different because many a times we have either rejected or delayed responding to God's gracious invitation and our excuses may sound reasonable – work duties, family responsibilities, financial needs, academics, pride. Nonetheless, God's invitation is the most important event in anyone's life, no matter how inconvenient the timing may be. So, the rhetoric question that everyone ought to ask oneself is 'how will it be when the King returns?' Lorenz gives us more Biblical glimpses of how the King with his crown of victory and the glory of the Only One crucified ever since the foundations of the earth – the earth filled with the greatest terror ever witnessed….and the question comes again, "which side will you be on that day?"

This hymn reminds me of some encouraging words that John in his advanced age passed on to the Christian church at that time, which was struggling with persecution and more looming hatred (animosity) from both the Jewish community that had rejected Christ Jesus and also the wide pagan world that was threatening to almost devour the young and budding Christian church. These words are found in 1 John 5:4, "For every child of God defeats this evil world, and we achieve this victory through our Faith. And who can win this battle against the world? Only those who believe that Jesus is the Son of God."

The Great Disappointment at the Feast

A story is told of a gifted Soloist who was invited to sing at the wedding of a very wealthy couple. She was thrilled by the call to such a luxurious feast and this was her special day. She was especially excited because she and her husband were invited to the reception at one of the most extravagant locations in the city. It was a place that she would never have been able to afford to attend otherwise. Following the wedding, with great expectations, she and her husband came to the reception location, a restaurant high above the city skyline. When they arrived at the door, the receptionist asked for their names but their names weren't on the list, surprisingly. She replied, "But I am the soloist". The receptionist said that made no difference, their names weren't on the list. Then they were ushered to a freight elevator which took them back down to the main floor. On the way down the soloist remembered that the invitation included an RSVP which she had forgotten to return. Her name wasn't in the book, so she wasn't allowed to enter the reception gala. What a disappointment they must have faced!!

36. ANGRY WORDS, OH LET THEM NEVER (C.H 591)

Angry words! O let them never
From the tongue unbridled slip;
May the heart's best impulse ever
Check them ere they soil the lip.

Refrain:
"Love one another," thus saith the Savior;
("Love each other, love each other,")
Children, obey the Father's blest command.
('Tis the Father's blest command.)
"Love one another," thus saith the Savior;
("Love each other, love each other;")
Children, obey His blest command.
('Tis His blest command.)

Love is much too pure and holy,
Friendship is too sacred far,
For a moment's reckless folly
Thus to desolate and mar.

Angry words are lightly spoken,
Bitt'rest tho'ts are rashly stirred,
Brightest links of life are broken
By a single angry word.

This lovely hymn was composed by Dr. Palmer Horatio Richmond (1834 – 1907). He is remarked to have authored several works on the theory of music; and he was an editor of some musical editions of hymnbooks. Besides, he contributed numerous tunes, some of which have attained to great popularity, and his publications include "Songs of Love for the Bible School"; and "Book of Anthems" whose combined sales have so far exceeded one million copies. Later in life, around 1880, the University of Chicago conferred on him a Doctorate in Music.

Stanza 1 deals with the self-control that is necessary to control the tongue or anything in life, keeping in mind that every sin we commit involves to some degree our self-control. We need self-control (Gal. 5:22-23, 2 Pet. 1:5). This song begins by reminding us of the resolve we ought to have to ensure that we do not sin with our words by speaking in anger. Eph. 4:26 tells us to not sin in our anger. Many proverbs warn against the dangers of an uncontrolled tongue and the blessings of mastering it. Prov 15:1-2, Prov. 21:23, "Whoever guards his mouth and tongue keeps his soul from troubles."

Stanza 2 – describes motives that will help us to control our tongues – Christian love and friendship. Love is the attitude that will govern what we say and how we say it. Jesus said the greatest command was to love God and the second greatest was to love your neighbor as yourself (Matt. 22:37-39).

Stanza 3 - describes the damage that angry words and a loose tongue can do. We are again reminded of James 3:6-12 which describes the damage the tongue can do. King Solomon said, "In the multitude of words, sin is not lacking, but he who restrains his lips is wise." (Prov. 10:19). But also in Prov. 17:9, "He who covers a transgression seeks love, but he who repeats a matter separates friends."

Chorus – Love one another, thus saith the Savior – John 13:34-35, 15:12, 14:15 – if you love Me keep my commandments. Matt. 22:37-39. 1 John 5:3, "This is the love of God, that we keep His commandments."

Fight the Right Battle

During Christ's arrest, Peter could not stand it anymore since he had watched his Lord's anguish in the garden of Gethsemane, sweating blood. He had witnessed a group of soldiers come to arrest his Lord. So, he took out his sword and slashed off the high priest's servant ear. We all do appreciate Peter's frustration, had it have been you, you might even have done something more deadly. We might commend him for his heroism and bravery, but in reality, Jesus didn't do that at all. He simply told Peter t put his sword away, and Peter could not understand what had happened to his Lord. Like most of us, Peter always seems to be doing the wrong thing at the wrong time. Sleeping when he ought to have been awake and praying, talking when he should have been silently listening, boasting when he ought to have been fearful, and now fighting when he should have retreated and/or surrendered. He normally viewed things upside down – he failed to see that he was fighting the wrong enemy! It is imperative to note that our enemies are not the flesh and blood as the Bible says, but principalities and powers – which can't be defeated by ordinary measures. Many a times we take things into our own hands and try to assist God, in a bid to help Him a little. And often times we forget to pull out the most powerful weapon in our arsenal, which is prayer, and use it in these times of battle. Brethren, your enemy is not that brother in your church or family or community that you are fighting, your enemy is not your neighbor who is trying to shift your landmark or disorganize you. Your enemy is not that taxi conductor who possibly insulted you, neither is he that sister who differs in biblical understanding and perspective as you do. We all have a common enemy and that is the devil. As Christians, we are too quick to protest, complain and at times to throw angry words to our brothers and sisters in the face of any misunderstanding but Dr. Palmers is admonishing us that angry words! O let them never from the tongue unbridled slip; may the heart's best impulse ever check them ere they soil the lip. Besides, this counsel forms that biggest part of King Solomon's wise sayings in Proverbs so that Christians can respond with love but not with insulting words.

37. WE HAVE THIS HOPE (SDAH 214)

1) We have this hope that burns within our heart,
Hope in the coming of the Lord.
We have this faith that Christ alone imparts,
Faith in the promise of His Word.
We believe the time is here,
When the nations far and near
Shall awake, and shout and sing
Hallelujah! Christ is King!
We have this hope that burns within our heart,
Hope in the coming of the Lord.

2) We are united in Jesus Christ our Lord.
We are united in His love.
Love for the waiting people of the world,
People who need our Savior's love.
Soon the heav'ns will open wide,
Christ will come to claim His bride,
All the universe will sing
Hallelujah! Christ is King!
We have this hope this faith, and God's great love,
We are united in Christ.

This beautiful, simple and advent hope hymn was composed in 1962 and completed in 1995 by a 21st Century Seventh-Day Adventist prolific hymn writer called Dr. Wayne H. Hooper (1920 – 2007). He is one of the seven children of Thomas Jefferson Hooper, once a publishing secretary of the Arkansas Conference of the SDA Church, but also a regular camp meeting song leader and music teacher. He comes from a fundamentally musical family (background), whereby the others could sing while their mother, Ethel, would play the piano. His musical legacy ranges from teaching it, being a soloist on radio programs, song leader, owned a music publishing house, and music evangelist in various ministries up to being ordained a gospel ministry. Besides all that, he was the executive secretary of the committee that produced the Seventh-Day Adventist Hymnal in 1985. He has a multitude of publications under his name including: six arrangements for 'Male Voices', numerous solo songs, three volumes of 'Sing a Bible Verse' for kindergarten and primary Sabbath school. He served on music committee for the General Conference (GC) sessions and youth congresses of the SDA Church. This colorful profile saw Andrews University award him an honorary Doctorate in Music in 1986. Later in 1988, he along with Edward White coauthored the "Companion to Seventh-Day Adventist Hymnal".

In 1962, as a member of the King's Heralds Quartet (part of the Voice of Prophecy radio broadcast), he was asked to serve on a special committee appointed to prepare music for the quadrennial session of the General Conference of the SDA Church to be held in San Francisco. He informs that Charles Keymer (Chairman of the music committee) advised him to try to compose a theme song for them to consider. One day, as he was driving from Glendale, California to La Sierra College to see his son, he started to think about the theme that was chosen, "We Have This Hope". After a prayerful moment for the Holy Sprirt to guide him in composing the right words and music that would be a blessing to the delegates at the General Conference session, this was perfected by God in just half an hour. He further informs that this song coming to him while driving was an indicator of God's direct intervention and he branded the song a 'gift from God'. This theme song was not only used in 1962 GC session, but it was also used in 1966 GC session held in Detroit, Michigan; also GC session in 1975 in Vienna, Austria. Besides, this same hymn was used in GC session of 1995 in Utrecht, Netherlands – this time round, Hooper added second stanza, thanks to the theme chosen for that session, "United in Christ".

Scripture – Titus 2:11-13 (KJV) "For the grace of God that bringeth salvation has appeared to all men, Teaching us that denying ungodliness and worldly lust, we should live soberly, righteously and godly, in this present world. Looking for that blessed hope and glorious appearing of the great God and our Savior Jesus Christ".

The Two Prisoners in a Foreign Land

A popular and inspirational story is told of two young men who emigrated to a foreign land in search for employment. On reaching there, they struggled with life in a foreign country just like many people do, opting for any simple job at their disposal. Life proved to be quite complicated to these folks that one of them later resolved to robbery for survival in that competitive environment. This saw this foreigner being arrested, and the law in land had prescribed a death penalty for such a crime, if committed by a foreigner. His friend was so moved and desperate for his counterpart's life and he wondered what he would tell to the friend's family on his return home. Later on, this culprit made a strange request to the prison authorities to permit him go back home (homeland) so that he can bid farewell to his family and relative, informing them that he is due to execution at the stated date. He added that his friend (countryman) would stand in for him during his absence until he returns, and that in the event that this offender doesn't return – the friend would be killed in his behalf. Outlandishly, the longtime friend had okayed such request and proposal given the love and trust he had in his friend that ultimately he would return. The prison authority, in a unique decision, granted these guys' request and the offender was permitted to go fulfil his wish but the execution date was in the following two weeks. Bidding farewell and assuring his friend who is now imprisoned on his behalf, he began his controversial journey that was filled with missed hopes from different parties. As usual, days began flying from day one to a week, but daily the prison authorities would come to check on this imprisoned friend – wondering what kind of 'weird' love he had for a friend, what strange trust he had in him, how his hope was premised on troubled grounds, and finally how he was daily heading for execution on behalf of his culpable friend. But he would always affirm them, "I know he is coming! I know he is coming! I have complete trust in him!" This strange hope in an apparently convicted friend beat the understanding of all the prison authorities. Soon, the days were completed and the culprit was nowhere to be seen; on this execution day, prison warders would visit this imprisoned friend every after an hour to assure him that this time round he can't escape execution due to his irrational decision and hopes. But he would always affirm them with the same words which resounded the same hopes he had in his friend, regardless of what had become of him. Just a few minutes to the execution place, suddenly, this culprit arrives and surrenders himself to the prison authorities. They were held speechless, flabbergasted, overawed, overwhelmed, and filled with terror given this happening; no one could ever imagine that any sensible culprit could ever do such a thing. But above all, hardly could anyone believe the strange type of hope and trust that this imprisoned friend had in his counterpart.

This story fits perfectly in the Pauline writings to Titus (who he addresses as 'his true son in the faith that they share' Titus 1:4), but it is equally in harmony with Dr. Hooper's remarkable message to this world that is largely filled with hopelessness in regard to Christ's return. The Apostle Paul, just like Dr. Hooper, emphasizes two aspects of Christian living that are so important today. We should live in this evil world while we look forward with hope. Both aspects of living and looking forward are crucial to our Christian sanity in this present evil age. The living is made bearable because we live for God – seeking to build His kingdom with whatever endowments He has given us. As we live and look forward, we anticipate three great benefits of Christ's return: Christ's personal presence – fellowshipping with Him eternally; redemption from our sinful nature – the end of the great battle between evil and good; and restoration of creation – we over-anticipate a return to the initial creation order and the real image of God in humanity.

38. ANYWHERE WITH JESUS (C.H 589)

1)   Anywhere with Jesus I can safely go,
       Anywhere He leads me in this world below;
       Anywhere without Him dearest joys would fade;
       Anywhere with Jesus I am not afraid.

Chorus
Anywhere, anywhere!
Fear I cannot know;
Anywhere with Jesus I can safely go.

2)   Anywhere with Jesus I am not alone;
       Other friends may fail me, He is still my own;
       Tho' His hand may lead me over dreary ways,
       Anywhere with Jesus is a house of praise.

3)   Anywhere with Jesus, over land and sea,
       Telling souls in darkness of salvation free;
       Ready as He summons me to go or stay,
       Anywhere with Jesus when He points the way.

4)   Anywhere with Jesus I can go to sleep,
       When the dark'ning shadows round about me creep,
       Knowing I shall waken nevermore to roam;
       Anywhere with Jesus will be home, sweet home.

This repetitive hymn was composed by Jessie H. Brown Pounds (1861 – 1921). Born in Cleveland, Ohio, at a tender age of 15, she began writing articles for weekly magazines. It is believed that, in her lifetime, she wrote more than 400 gospel songs, words for cantatas, and at least nine books.

This particular hymn is a product of many heads (authors) and also written backward including Jessie, Helen Cadbury, and the legendary Daniel B. Towner, which I believe was such a wonderful thing for us as hymn lovers.

In 1866, Daniel Towner was working with evangelist Dwight L. Moody in some meetings in New York. One evening, Mr. Moody preached a powerful sermon, picturing Christ as the Captain of our lives, saying that we could therefore go anywhere with Him, confident that the Lord would see us through. In emphasis, he illustrated this with reference to the three Hebrews cast into a fiery furnace, then Daniel in a den of lions (Daniel chapters 3 and 6), and related other passages. Inspired by the message, Daniel Towner (whose niche was largely in composing tunes but not poems/ words) thought to himself, "There ought to be a song written with that theme." He quickly sat down and composed a melody, trying to put into the notes something of how he felt. He sent the tune to a hymn writer named Jesse Brown Pounds, who lived in Cleveland. (Jesse Brown was married to Rev. John Pounds) Towner told her that he wanted the words to say, "Anywhere with Jesus."

It is quite imperative to note that Stanzas 1, 2 and 5 were written by Jessie Pounds, and stanzas 3 and 4 were added by Helen Cadbury Alexander (1877 – 1969) about thirty years later. Records have it that Helen Cadbury, was an heir to the immense Cadbury Chocolate fortune, but turned her back on wealth and social standing to be a humble servant of Christ.

In this song, the term "Anywhere!" is repeated at least twenty-seven times (which in literature, is normally deliberate and significant in that it is used for emphasis and creating a special interest in something). Besides, it is pertinent to realize that some are called of God to minister to their families, in their community, and in their local church; while others are called to go to distant places, even to other lands, and serve among those with a dramatically different culture like missionaries. Thus, as Disciples of Christ (heralds of good tidings), we ought to be prepared to go anywhere and do any work the Master assigns to us. This is based on the Lord's personal declaration (which actually inspires the Church's mission) that, "………Go ye therefore, and teach all nations, baptizing them in the name of the Father, and of the Son, and of the Holy Spirit,………Lo, I am with you always, even to the end of the age" (Matt. 28:18-20).

When we meekly accept God's leadership and guidance in life without many questions, he deliberately destines us for victory in Christ Jesus, just like the Apostle Paul rightly puts it in his Epistle to the Corinthian church then, but also to the global Christendom. In 1 Corinthians 10:31 (NLT) "So whether you eat or drink, or whatever you do, do it all for the glory of God." Thus, our actions must be motivated by God's love so that all we do will be for His glory. Keep this as a guiding principle by asking, "Is this action glorifying?" or "How can I honor God through my action?"

Can a Christian Drink Alcohol?

1 Corinthians 10:31 (NLT) "So, whether you eat or drink, or whatever you do, do it all for the glory of God".

A popular story is told that when a certain European Airline was initially launched, an educated Christian gentlemen was travelling in the first class section. An air hostess approached him with a complimentary drink, which was alcoholic, but the man politely refused the offer. The air hostess returned, this time with a drink on a platter, designed to appeal and impress. However, the Christian man again politely refused, explaining that he doesn't drink alcohol. The lady was so concerned and informed the manager, who approached the man with another platter, this time designed with flowers. He questioned, 'Is there something wrong with our service, sir? Please enjoy the drink, it is a complimentary offer." The man replied, "I am a Christian and I do not drink alcohol?" The manager still insisted that the Christian takes the drink. Then the man proposed that the manager should give the drink to the pilot first. The manager stated, "How can the pilot drink alcohol, he is on duty! And if he drinks there are all chances for the plane to crash." The Christian passenger, with tears in his eyes replied, "I'm a Christian and I'm on always on duty in order to protect my faith and if I drink alcohol I will crash my whole life here and hereafter – I'm 100% on duty".

This is a huge challenge to us all that we should accept God's leadership wherever He, out of infinite love and wisdom, guides us to go – we should honor Him through our actions and establish a solid faith in Him and His promises. For you, it may not be an alcohol but extramarital or premarital relationships, controlling your anger and emotions, dressing code, tithe and offerings, attitude towards people, relativizing biblical truths, among other crucial matters of life. We ought to humbly accept His guidance in life and exhibit maturity in faith and growth in grace despite everything including being in a foreign land where practically no one supposedly knows your Christian affiliations.

39. JOY TO THE WORLD
(SDAH 50)   A & M 27)

1) Joy to the world, the Lord is come!
Let earth receive her King;
Let every heart prepare Him room,
And Heaven and nature sing,
And Heaven and nature sing,
And Heaven, and Heaven, and nature sing.

2) Joy to the world, the Savior reigns!
Let men their songs employ;
While fields and floods, rocks, hills and plains
Repeat the sounding joy,
Repeat the sounding joy,
Repeat, repeat, the sounding joy.

3) No more let sins and sorrows grow,
Nor thorns infest the ground;
He comes to make His blessings flow
Far as the curse is found,
Far as the curse is found,
Far as, far as, the curse is found.

4) He rules the world with truth and grace,
And makes the nations prove
The glories of His righteousness,
And wonders of His love,
And wonders of His love,
And wonders, wonders, of His love.

This joyful hymn was composed by the legendary Isaac Watts (1674 – 1748); born to Dissenting parents - people who refused to accept the authority and practices of the Church of England. As a boy, he sang hymns outside prison walls to encourage his father, who had been arrested for his non-conformist beliefs. Isaac showed promise as a poet at a very young age. As he grew, he became increasingly unhappy with the hymns that he sang in church each week. Watts saw that the hymns thus reflected little or nothing of the New Testament, and set out to remedy that error. His earlier hymns reinterpreted the psalms in the light of the Christian faith.

In 1719, he published a book of hymns entitled, "The Psalms of David Imitated in the Language of the New Testament". One of those hymns was "Joy to the World," based loosely on Psalm 98, which says, "Make a joyful noise to the Lord, all the earth; break forth into joyous song and sing praises" (Psalm 98:4). That psalm looks forward to the day when the Lord will come to judge the world in righteousness. In this hymn, Watts reinterpreted the psalm to rejoice in the coming of the Christ as our Lord and savior.

Some music scholars and commentators argue that the hymn contains musical phrases from two selections from Handel's Messiah–"Lift Up Your Heads," and "Comfort Ye." The first two lines of the melody beautifully match the opening words of the text, with a descending scale representing the Lord coming down from heaven, and then ascending notes that seem to depict earth reaching up arms of welcome to the King.

The words of the hymn are a paraphrase of the latter part of Psalm 98, that Watts called "The Messiah's Coming and Kingdom." Though it is traditionally sung at the Christmas season, the psalm actually concerns Christ's second coming, when He will return to set up His earthly reign.

This hymn has nothing to do with: shepherds, a manger, wise men, angels, or any other character or element that the contemporary world normally associates it with the Christmas story simply because Isaac Watts did not write it to be a Christmas song.

"Shout joyfully to the Lord, all the earth; break forth in song, rejoice, and sing praises….Let the rivers clap their hands; let the hills be joyful together before the Lord, for He is coming to judge the earth. With righteousness He shall judge the world, and the peoples with equity" (Ps. 98:4, 8-9).

My Daughter's Favorite Psalm 98

Many of what are termed as "The Psalms of David" have their original authors, including David himself among others; and it is believed that this was the hymn book of the people of God in those times. On the contrary, this particular hymn/ psalm 98 was authored by an anonymous writer (apparently only known to God), which may not be such a big problem as long as the psalm exists and has lots of spiritual resources for us. This is one of the favorite psalms of my gorgeous daughter, and normally after we hold our singing sessions but before we go into our adult bible study, she along with her young brother do recite this psalm which enriches the whole worship atmosphere, given the metaphors (symbols) that are contained therein.

This was a song of joy and victory; because our mighty God is victorious over evil, all those who follow Him will be victorious with Him when He judges the earth. It is a hymn/psalm of praise anticipating the coming God to rule His people – Jesus fulfilled this anticipation when He came to save all people from all their sins; and he will come again to judge the world. It is worth noting that God is perfectly loving and perfectly just; He is merciful when he punishes and he overlooks no sin when he loves. Praise him for his promise to save you and to return again for us.

Psalms 98:1ff "Sing a new song to the Lord for He has done wonderful deeds. His right hand has won a mighty victory, His holy arm has shown his saving power. The Lord has announced His victory, and he has revealed his righteousness to every nation. He has remembered His promise to love and be faithful to Israel…………..let the sea and everything in it shout praise……….let the earth and all living things join in……………let the river clap their hands…………and hills sing out their songs of joy before the Lord………"

Given my background in Literature (French language, not English language which is quite shallow and largely called a thief in foreign language study given the fact that most of what people call English is not actually English but originated from French, Spanish, Arabic, German, etc), the use of those metaphors (figure of speech, symbols, representations, allegories, images, and animated figures like "the arm and hand of God; the sea shouting praise; the river clapping hands; the hills singing out; etc..) is so crucial and central to our understanding and putting the message in a unique and elevated context and perspective. I truly respect the author of this Psalm along with other sacred writings because of the use of a special kind of language that would only be expected from philosophers and literary writers.

40. LET HIM IN (SDAH 125)

1) There's a Stranger at the door: let Him in;
   He has been there oft before: let Him in.
   Let Him in, ere He is gone;
   Let Him in, the Holy One,
   Jesus Christ the Father's Son: let Him in!

2) Now admit the heav'nly Guest: let Him in;
   He will make for you a feast: let Him in.
   He will speak your sins forgiv'n,
   And when earth-ties all are riv'n,
   He will take you home to heav'n: let Him in!

This appealing and also repetitive hymn was composed by a Methodist clergyman, Jonathan Burtch Atchinson (1840 – 1882), a veteran of the American Civil war, who served various churches in New York and Michigan. Atchinson composed many gospel songs but this particular hymn, which makes an urgent invitation with a whole fifteen repetitions of the phase "Let Him in" is the most popular among them all.

The song is based on the gracious plea of the Saviour to the church at Laodicea, as recorded in the book of Revelation: "Behold, I stand at the door and knock. If anyone hears My voice and opens the door, I will come in to him and dine [feast] with him, and he with Me" (Rev. 3:20)

The song's major application to evangelistic appeal is grounded on reasons that, though the passage is addressed to a church, the Lord recognizes that any repentance and change that takes place must first of all occur at the individual level. That's why the appeal is made, "If anyone…"

Several instructive, and solemn thoughts are brought out in the song. "Let Him in e'er He is gone," for example, and "if you wait He will depart. As the Lord declares in Genesis, "My Spirit shall not strive with man forever" (Gen. 6:3). God is gracious, but the gracious invitation to turn to Him and be saved will not be extended indefinitely. "Behold, now is the accepted time; now is the day of salvation" (II Cor. 6:2).

It has always been God's initiative to save His fallen human beings, and this spans from before creation but humanity has progressively been declining God's offer for eternal life. This is freely given (God's gift); humanity has never done anything to try to reconcile itself to God. God's redemptive grace has always taken the initiative to reach out to humankind.

The Church is God's initiatives and plans to save/redeem man from sin; and so, God has authority over whatever goes on because he is in charge. God's church has systems, and it must be organized in whatever it does just as He is organized in all His undertakings. Through His church, God patiently pleads to us the sinners to heed to His gracious invitation and let Him in so that we can enjoy His forgiveness and peace with God.

Steve Jobs' Last Words

As an illustration of how this world is just vanity in the face of Christ's goodness and invitation to prepare our lives for a better life after this mortal one, we shall take the words of Steve Jobs (the genius who invented Apple computer, iPod, iTunes, etc). These are supposedly the last words of Steve Jobs, though many critics and analysts have come out to reject them as lies (that Steve Jobs never uttered these statements), but for me I'm basically interested in the gist of the narrative despite the attacks on the authenticity of the text. And below are the last remorseful words:

I reached the pinnacle of success in the business world (and this was also affirmed by his rival Bill Gates who invented The Microsoft Computers). In others' eyes, my life is an epitome of success. However, aside from work, I have little joy; in the end, wealth is only a fact of life that I'm accustomed to. At this moment, lying on the sick bed and recalling my whole life, I realize that all the recognition and wealth that I took so much pride in, have paled and become meaningless in the face of impeding death.

In the darkness, I look at the green lights from the life supporting machines and hear the humming mechanical sounds, I can feel the breath of the god of death drawing closer. Now I know, when we have accumulated sufficient wealth to last our lifetime, we should pursue other matters that are unrelated to wealth.... perhaps relationships, art/ music, a dream from younger days. Non-stop pursuing of wealth will only turn a person into a twisted being, just like me. God gave us the sense to let us feel the love in everyone's heart not the illusions brought about by wealth. The wealth I have won in my life I can't bring with me; what I can bring is only the memories precipitated by love. That's the true riches which will follow you, accompany you, giving you strength and light to go on. Love can travel a thousand miles; life has no limits, go anywhere you want to and reach the heights you want since it is all in your heart and your hands. The most expensive bed is the 'sick bed'; material things lost can be found but there is one thing that can never be found when lost: "life". "When a person goes into the operating room, he will realize that there is one book that he has yet to finish reading – 'Book of Healthy life". Whichever stage in life we are at right now, with time we will face the day when the curtain comes down; the treasure of love for your family, love for your spouse, love for your friends…. treat yourself well, cherish others. As we grow old, we realize that our happiness does not come from material things of this world, in fact having brothers, sisters and friends to chat with, talk with, laugh with, sing songs with……that brings happiness.

Lastly, the most important thing in life is to heed to Christ's invitation in the way of letting Him into the doors of our lives so that He can give us the assurance for a better life here and hereafter. But above all, He procures us that promised peace which surpasses all human understanding and worldly measures. This is the bottom line of Atchinson's golden hymn that has for more than two and half centuries been so instrumental at reminding the world of Christ's long-suffering patience lest anyone perishes with the devil – that is why He persistently keeps knocking on the doors of our hearts.

41. SWEET BY AND BY (SDAH 428)

1) There's a land that is fairer than day,
   And by faith we can see it afar;
   For the Father waits over the way
   To prepare us a dwelling place there.

Chorus
In the sweet   by and by,
   (in the sweet)   (by and by)
We shall meet on that beautiful shore;
                    (by and by)
In the sweet   by and by,
   (in the sweet)   (by and by)
We shall meet on that beautiful shore.

2) We shall sing on that beautiful shore
   The melodious songs of the blessed;
   And our spirits shall sorrow no more,
   Not a sigh for the blessing of rest.

3) To our bountiful Father above,
   We will offer our tribute of praise
   For the glorious gift of His love
   And the blessings that hallow our days.

This joyous hymn was composed by Sanford Fillmore Bennett (1836 – 1898) along with his very good friend Joseph Philbrick Webster (1819 – 1875). Bennett, a musician and compassionate pharmacist, was one whose many gifts led him into several different careers. He'd been a published poet for about twenty years, by the time he supplied the text for this song. He had served as Superintendent of Schools in Richmond, Illinois, for a couple of years, then became the associate editor of the Elkhorn Independent newspaper, in Wisconsin. After service in the Civil Way, he operated a drugstore, then studied medicine and worked as a medical doctor for twenty-two years!

Records have it that musician Joseph Webster had a chronic problem and he was subject to bouts of emotional depression, but his good friend, Sanford Bennett, knew how to help him at such times. Before he finished medical training and became a physician, Sanford Bennett was a town druggist, and one day in 1868, Webster entered his establishment, carrying his violin. Without a word of greeting, he walked over to the old stove that heated the place, and stood with his back to Bennett. This strange behavior prompted Sanford to ask his comrade what on earth was going on in his life, but Webster miserably replied that, "It's no matter. It will be all right by and by"

Dwelling on that last phrase, Sanford Bennett got an idea (possibly a prescription) that had often helped his friend in times of distress. He found that if he could suggest an interesting theme for a new piece of music, it would help to bring Webster out of his dark moods. So, he proposed, "Sweet by and by! Would that not make a good hymn?" This saw the musician answer with less vigor, "Maybe it would".

Bennett started working at his desk on a short poem, and when he handed the lines of verse to Webster, he could see a spark of life come into his friend's eyes. Taking up his violin, he alternately played and jotted down notes of music; the creation of the song, words and music, took only thirty minutes. Finally, the two men called over a couple of colleagues, and they sang the hymn "Sweet By and By" for the first time. Someone just entering the store stood listening to the impromptu quartet, with tears in his eyes he exclaimed afterward, "That hymn is immortal!"

This hymn was largely intended to be an emergency comfort and help for one who was struggling, assuring him that there was a fairer day coming when "our spirits shall sorrow no more."; as embedded in God's promise (Rev. 21:4). We can hardly conceive of the beautiful singing in which we'll participate in heaven, "the melodious songs of the blessed". The singing around the throne of God is mentioned several times which will be so melodious and filled with harmony, contrary to the current disorganized and discordant kind of singing in the secular world but also even in many churches in the contemporary world. This particular hymn reminds me of the funeral/vigil service of Mrs. Nyanzi Deborah (a beloved church member in my local church), where this beautiful hymn was used to deliberately console the bereaved family and other mourners. Thanks to its invaluable resources that point us to our heavenly home which will be devoid of sorrows, death, disappointments but filled with peace, love and blessings only. Besides, this hymn and its writers' life stories helps us to focus on some crucial life points that can serve to inspire and/or guide our contemporary lives.

Life Points (Try to change how you approach life)

a) Try to stay within your comfort zone (the serenity prayer). This will render life simple, better and scale down on tensions and pressures of the world.

b) Drop things that don't bear productive fruits in your life (like gossip). These would only bring you more sorrow and further complicate life.

c) Exercise regularly so as to live a healthy life.

d) Take time to relax and do things you enjoy, such as music, sports, travelling. This will increase the quality of life both physical and spiritual.

e) Today, we have a problem of choice overload; there are very many things that we find it hard to make a rational choice. Learn to appreciate things that you need in life and those that you don't need.

f) "You miss 100% of the shots you don't take" Wayne Gretzky

g) "Never let the odds keep you from doing what you know in your heart you were meant to do" Jackson Brown, Jr

h) Life is the most difficult exam. Many people fail because they try to copy others, not realizing that everyone has a different question paper.

i) Your smile is your logo, your personality is your business card, and how you live others feeling after having an experience with you becomes your trademark

j) "Success lies in the ability to know what you don't need in life!"

k) "Those who fight to live, live to fight another day"

l) "In a world filled with despair, we must still dare to dream. And in a world filled with distrust, we must still dare to believe" Michael Jackson

42. THERE'LL BE NO DARK VALLEY (SDAH 208)

1) There'll be no dark valley when Jesus comes,
   There'll be no dark valley when Jesus comes;
   There'll be no dark valley when Jesus comes
   To gather His loved ones home.

Chorus
To gather His loved ones home,
To gather His loved ones home;
There'll be no dark valley when Jesus comes
To gather His loved ones home.

2) There'll be no more sorrow when Jesus comes,
   There'll be no more sorrow when Jesus comes;
   But a glorious morrow when Jesus comes
   To gather His loved ones home.

3) There'll be no more weeping when Jesus comes,
   There'll be no more weeping when Jesus comes;
   But a blessèd reaping when Jesus comes
   To gather His loved ones home.

4) There'll be songs of greeting when Jesus comes,
   There'll be songs of greeting when Jesus comes;
   And a joyful meeting when Jesus comes
   To gather His loved ones home.

This magnificent hymn was composed by William Orcutt Cushing (1823 – 1902), who was born to Unitarian parents in Massachusetts. At the age of 18 years, Cushing decided to prepare for ministry and later pastored several churches in New York. He was so loved by his church members. He was noted as extremely generous that one day he gave out USD 1000 he had in life to a blind girl to help her get an education. After the death of his wife in 1870, who had been very ill for years, he suffered a stroke and was forced to retire from active ministry. But he offered this prayer "Lord, still give me something to do for you". His prayer was answered, for he was inspired to write more than 300 hymns and gospel songs, which included this hymn in question composed in 1896, but also the hymn, "When He cometh".

Some records have it that though this hymn's text is credited to Cushing, in reality he provided only an idea of the theme to Ira David Sankey (1840 – 1908), who wrote both words and music; that Cushing only provided the first line.

This song sounds like a traditional Spiritual, which uses repetitions effectively to emphasize the truth that is derived from Revelation 21:4.

In the natural world, valleys can often be beautiful, and appealing, but as a metaphor they are sometimes used to represent life's darker perils. This can be enhanced by Psalm 23, where David declares, "Yea, though I walk through the valley of the shadow of death, I will fear no evil, for You [Lord] are with me" (vs. 4). In all, what made the difference for David was the presence and loving care of God, his "Shepherd".

Now, as we live in a highly competitive and egocentric world, which is characterized by scarcity of even the basic resources; economies – particularly corporate bodies and governments are all financially distressed to the point of closure and/or collapse. The cost of living is very high and progressively escalating, this, compounded by other macroeconomic woes like high levels of unemployment and underemployment, sky-rocketing inflation, drought and famine, crime rate on the rise, and other social vices are cropping up. This has seen the whole world face the realities of a dark valley, both in the spiritual and secular world; this forms part of what inspired the message that God gave the hymn writer to comfort the people of God in the midst of such challenges.

The Beauty in Dark Valleys (Failure)
Much as dark valleys (hardships, failure and challenges) are always viewed in a negative perspective and possibly no one in life would wish to ever encounter them; by God's grace, if we determine to have a change of outlook, we can see a world of beauty and blessings in them. This will, in fact, enliven our daily toil and help us appreciate them the same way the following personalities (William O. Cushing, Apostle Paul, Winston Churchill, and Prophet Moses) viewed them in faith and used them as spring boards to their achievement in life.

Scripture – Philippians 1:12 "But I want you to know that the things which happened to me, have actually turned out for the furtherance of the gospel.."

The apostle Paul planned to go to Rome to preach the gospel as a free man but instead he was taken there as a prisoner. It looked as if he had failed to achieve his noble ambition; in his place of confinement, he witnessed with such determination that all the palace guards heard the gospel, and from his prison he wrote most of his outstanding Epistles. That's why he could write to the

Christians in Philippe that, "everything had turned out for the furtherance/ advancement of the gospel".

Twice, the great Statesman, Winston Churchill failed to win an elected office during the 1920s; he had little political influence all through the bigger part of 1930s but he kept investing in his political and social capital. Later on in 1940s, he became the Prime Minister of England, and today he is acclaimed as a great hero in global history books.

Moses spent 40 years in royalty but also studying intellectual, military and leadership courses in the best universities in Egypt (the first civilized community/ country in the world) all preparing him for being a mighty Pharaoh of the strongest nation then. This was coupled to another 40 years as a shepherd in the Midian wilderness (present day Saudi Arabia), where God was training him in crucial lessons of humility and Christ-like service, which were opposed to his earlier discipline/ education in his first 40 years that would have catalyzed self-centeredness. By the way, these years in the desert were so incremental to godliness globally because not only was he gaining a preparation for the great work before him (the next 40 years of the delivering God's people from the Egyptian bondage), but also during this time, under the guidance of the Holy Spirit, he wrote the biblical books of Genesis and Job – which would be read with the deepest interest by the people of God until the close of time. And finally, another 40 years leading the Hebrew captives to the Promised Land; worth noting is that the first 80 years were so instrumental to his calling/ ultimate vocation and purpose in life ie to lead the Hebrews to Canaan.

When one's well laid plan fails and/or are frustrated just like the personalities highlighted above (William Cushing, Apostle Paul, Winston Churchill, and Moses), it is high time one analyzed his/her failure and take appropriate actions. If one blundered, he/she should correct one's mistake but if it was due to circumstances beyond one's control, there is need to ask God to teach us what He wants of us. In this way, a dark valley (failure or challenge) would become a great stepping stone to success!

43. WHEN HE COMETH (SDA 218)

1) When He cometh, when He cometh
   To make up His jewels,
   All His jewels, precious jewels,
   His loved and His own.

Refrain
Like the stars of the morning,
His brightness adorning,
They shall shine in their beauty,
Bright gems for His crown.

2) He will gather, He will gather
   The gems for His kingdom;
   All the pure ones, all the bright ones,
   His loved and His own.

3) Little children, little children,
   Who love their Redeemer,
   Are the jewels, precious jewels,
   His loved and His own.

This children's hymn was composed by Pastor William Orcutt Cushing (1823 – 1902); born to Unitarian parents in Massachusetts. At the age of 18 years, Cushing decided to prepare for ministry, he later pastored several churches in New York; he was so beloved by his flock and extremely generous that one day he gave out USD 1000 he had in his life to a blind girl to help her get an education. After the death of his wife in 1870, who had been very ill for years, he suffered a stroke and was forced to retire from active ministry. But he offered this prayer "Lord, still give me something to do for you". His prayer was answered, for he was inspired to write more than 300 hymns and gospel songs, which included this hymn in question composed in 1856, but also the hymn, "There'll be No Dark Valley".

This hymn was written specifically for the children in Cushing's church Sunday school, though there's no particular focus on children. But he Lord Jesus called His disciples "little children", and the Apostle John also speaks affectionately to Christians in his first epistle as "little children," where the context indicates he's not referring to infants. Nonetheless, the text is based on a couple of Old Testament passages, in particular, Malachi 3:16-17, "Then those who feared the LORD spoke to one another, and the LORD listened and heard them; so a book of remembrance was written before Him for those who fear the LORD and who meditate on His name. 'They shall be Mine,' says the LORD of hosts, 'on the day that I make them My jewels. And I will spare them as a man spares his own son who serves him."

Pastor Orcutt Cushing's hymn reminds me of (significantly related to) another very interesting and popular song, "I am Thinking Today" whose tune was composed by Dr. Sweney John Robson (1837 – 1899). Sweney was a pianist, violinist, music director and popular song leader in the Methodist Church in Pennsylvania, who just like Cushing, focused his hymn on the Second Coming of Christ. He often appeals to Christians to take time to think about that new world where Christ is planning to take His elect (through His grace and love) and so, we should strive to spread the gospel of the Kingdom. His song asks a weighty question of whether we shall be adorned with many stars in our crowns, which represent all those that we, by god's grace, led to Christ through evangelism.

"When He Comes" song's theme is primarily based on the Second Coming of Christ whereby He will gather His redeemed from all corners of the world. This should prepare us for that cosmic event that will be the climax of all that we have been doing in this world since the creation times. Unfortunately, this can't easily happen unless we deliberately and collectively engage in wide spread evangelism so that the whole world can be told the Gospel of the Kingdom. This reminds me of the great need for expertise in mobilizing resources, which are largely human resources that are required to fulfil this missionary objective. This inspired my analysis on Christ as the Chief resource mobilizer the world has ever witnessed, as discussed below:

Resource Mobilization in Ministry

Acts 4: 13 "The members of the Council were amazed when they saw the boldness of Peter and John, for they could see that they were ordinary men with no special training in Scripture. They also recognized them as men who had been with Jesus". The life and efficiency of the Apostles (as business partners) significantly and visibly changed given their exposure and intimate relationship the Chief Resource mobilizer.

Through my experience in Project planning, and Corporate Finance, I have come to fully appreciate how imperative resource mobilization is in the real business world. Simply put, it encompasses establishing resource/ inputs requirement for a given intervention aimed at taking advantage of an existing opportunity and/or addressing a societal challenge, but also ensuring that those inputs are available for the intervention to successfully take place. By and large, resources may include: human, physical, financial; but also spiritual and marital resources basically in Christian circles.

The greatest percentage of the Bible is about Resource mobilization (human, financial, and otherwise); and most of Christ's parables are premised on mobilizing resources.

World records have it that the greatest resource mobilizer and/or business planner in world history was Jesus; this is because He began His enterprise/ministry close to 2000 years ago and it is growing stronger and stronger by the day. Amazingly, he did it with real business people – the fishermen; He could see what other business people and/or resource mobilizers couldn't see in these socially-despised guys. People looked at Peter and other apostles (disciples) as outright failures in life but Christ made them business partners. On one day, the business acquired 120 clients, and the other day it grew to 3000 people – thanks to Christ's business acumen and also the ingenuity of His business partners. The other day, another 5000 people joined the clientele which progressively made the enterprise competitive and a threat to other existing establishments.
Christ would have initially sought for Scribes (who had strong intellects and arguments); Pharisees (who were apparently the custodians of the Holy Scriptures); rich men and the wealthy like Nicodemus, but He chose the real business men and great resource mobilizers – the fishermen. Jesus had an opportunity of using the celestial beings like angels to further His mission but He prudently resolved to use local resources (as it is a fundamental in resource mobilization discipline) like Peter and others. These fishermen would efficiently and effectively accomplish the task, and it was soon evident that these guys did a commendable and excellent job. Later, Jesus sought for the educated/ scholars like Luke, Paul; the wealthy like Nicodemus; and other key personnel just like any prudent and strategic business planner/ resource mobilizer, given the changes in resource requirements and project implementation stages. And this was largely informed by slower progress and other constraints at certain stages of the enterprise development.

Christ expects His followers to also be good in mobilizing resource for the Kingdom so that we can qualify to have multitudes of stars in our crowns in heaven as symbols of all those that we led to Christ. These resources range from direct preaching the gospel, to mobilizing other key resources that are required in the mission of the Church so that when He comes He will say "Well done diligent servant!"

44. REDEEMED, HOW I LOVE TO PROCLAIM IT (SDAH 337)

1)   Redeemed, how I love to proclaim it!
    Redeemed by the blood of the Lamb;
    Redeemed through His infinite mercy,
    His child and forever I am.

Chorus
Redeemed, redeemed,
Redeemed by the blood of the Lamb;
Redeemed, redeemed,
His child and forever I am.

2)   Redeemed, and so happy in Jesus,
    No language my rapture can tell;
    I know that the light of His presence
    With me doth continually dwell.

3)   I think of my blessed Redeemer,
    I think of Him all the day long:
    I sing, for I cannot be silent;
    His love is the theme of my song.

4)   I know I shall see in His beauty
    The King in whose law I delight,
    Who lovingly guardeth my footsteps,
    And giveth me songs in the night.

This ecstatic hymn was composed by Frances Jane 'Fanny' Crosby (1820 – 1915). She was a daughter of John and Mercy Crosby, and was born in Southeast, Putnam County, New York. She became blind at the age of six weeks from maltreatment of her eyes during a spell of sickness. When she was eight years old she moved with her parents to Ridgefield, the family remaining there four years. At the age of fifteen she entered the New York Institution for the Blind, where she received a good education. She became a teacher in the institution in 1847, and continued her work until 1858; she taught English grammar, rhetoric and American history.

The composition of this song was inspired by and/or based on the Scripture in Lamentations 3:58 (NLT) "Lord, you are my lawyer! Plead my case! For you have redeemed my life". And, this song was a successful collaboration between Fanny Crosby (wrote the hymn text) and the legendary hymn tunes composer, Kirkpatrick William James (1838 – 1921), who though a carpenter, was very good at playing a variety of musical instruments and writer of gospel songs.

The concept of redemption was common in the ancient world, in day-to-day life; and the term was used to describe what individuals did when they made purchases in the local market. Redemption is also a pervasive theme of the Bible: words such as "redeemed" and "redemption" are found over 140 times in our English Bibles. The word itself means: to deliver by paying a price.

Redemption: God's Faithfulness

A popular story is told of a couple in Armenia in 1988 which exemplified God's redemptive initiatives and how He expresses His faithfulness to us His beloved children. It is told that Samuel and Danielle sent their young son, Armand, off to school. But normally, Samuel used would always squat before his son, and this time around he did it and looked him in the eye, "Have a good day at school, and remember, no matter what, I'll always be there for you." They would always follow passionate hugging then Armand would run off to school. On this fateful day, just hours later, a powerful earthquake rocked the area, and in the midst of the chaos, Samuel and Danielle tried to discover what happened to their son but they couldn't get any information. The radio announced that there were thousands of casualties. Then, Samuel grabbed his coat and headed for the schoolyard. When he reached the area, what he saw equally brought him tears to his eyes since his son's school had been reduced to piles of debris; and other parents were standing around crying. He found his place where Armand's classroom used to be and began pulling a broken beam off the pile of rubbles. He then grabbed a rock and put it to the side and then grabbed another one. One of the parents looking on asked, "What are you doing?" Samuel responded, "Digging for my son." The man then said, "You are just going to make things worse! The building is unstable". And then, thus guy tried to pull Samuel away from his work. Samuel simply kept working. With time, parents begun leaving one by one – then a worker at the school tried to pull Samuel away again from the rubble but he looked at him and said, "Won't you help me?" The worker left and Samuel kept digging. All through the night and into the next day, Samuel continued dogging. Parents placed flowers and pictures of their children on the ruins but Samuel kept on working. He picked up a beam and pushed it out of the way when he heard a faint cry, "Help! Help!" Samuel listened but didn't hear anything again. Then he heard a lowered voice, "Papa?"

This saw Samuel begin to dig furiously, and finally he could see his son. He said with relief, "Come on out, my son!" Armand responded, "No. let the other kids come out first because I know you will get me." Then, child after child emerged until, finally, beautiful Armand appeared. Samuel took him in his arms and Armand said, "I told the other kids not to worry because you had told me that you would always be there for me!" This redemptive gesture and also act of faithfulness saw fourteen children being saved that day because one father (in the shoes of Christ) was at least faithful.

This story is but just a faint and unclear revelation of what our Redeemer, Jesus Christ did for us close to 2000 years ago did (but in reality before even the creation of this world purposed to do) in a bid to redeem the human race that had given in to the dominion and slavery of the devil. This story gives us glimpses into the faithfulness and love of our Eternal God that Moses during his dying words assured the Hebrews in Deut.33:27 of His eternal protection, redemption and faithfulness. Whether we are trapped by fallen debris of this painful world or ensnared by life's hardships and desperation, His redemptive hand will always reach out to all His lovely children. This is because naturally He is reliable, truthful and faithful to His promises.

45. SHALL WE GATHER AT THE RIVER (SDAH 432)

1) Shall we gather at the river,
Where bright angel feet have trod,
With its crystal tide forever
Flowing by the throne of God?

Refrain
Yes, we'll gather at the river,
The beautiful, the beautiful river;
Gather with the saints at the river
That flows by the throne of God.

2) On the margin of the river,
Washing up its silver spray,
We will talk and worship ever,
All the happy golden day.

3) Ere we reach the shining river,
Lay we every burden down;
Grace our spirits will deliver,
And provide a robe and crown

4) At the smiling of the river,
Mirror of the Savior's face,
Saints, whom death will never sever,
Lift their songs of saving grace.

5) Soon we'll reach the silver river,
Soon our pilgrimage will cease;
Soon our happy hearts will quiver
With the melody of peace.

It was composed by Robert Lowry (1826 – 1899); born in Philadelphia, and in his childhood he showed a great talent in music because he would play any instrument at his disposal. At 17 years, he joined the First Baptist Church and he quickly became a chorister and Sunday school teacher, he was a brilliant speaker and a thorough Bible student.

One afternoon in July 1864, when he was Pastor at Hanson Place Baptist Church, Brooklyn, New York; the weather was oppressively hot and he was lying on a lounge in a state of physical exhaustion. Following a very horrible happening in New York; when at that time a violent epidemic was raging and ravaging human lives, he heart was so troubled at watching so many mourners in the streets who had laid and others were simply going to lay their loved ones to rest as a result of this endemic. Then this question came to his mind, "At the partying of the river of death, shall we meet again at the river of life". He affirms that he was, without doubt, reminded of John the revelator's description of the heavenly city with a pure river of water of life preceding from the throne of God and of the lamb (Revelation 22:1ff). Filled with joy and assurance, Lowry quickly went to his organ and composed both the words and the music of the hymn. He further narrates that "my imagination began to take itself wings – visions of the future passed before me with startling vividness. The imagery of the apocalypse took the form of a tableau – brightest of all were the throne, the heavenly river, and the gathering of the saints….. I began to wonder why the hymn writers had said so much about the 'river of death' and so little about the 'pure water of life', clear as crystal, proceeding out of the throne of God and the Lamb". As he mused, the words began to construct themselves, coming first as a question of Christian inquiry, "Shall we gather?" Then they broke in Chorus, "Yes, we'll gather". On this question and answer the hymn developed itself.

In his advanced stages of life (age), Pastor Robert Lowry studied musical science; he amassed one of the finest musical libraries of his time; he became a professor of rhetoric and literature at Bucknell, following his honorary Doctorate in Divinity. Simply put, Lowry made good use of his advanced aged to do a lot of things which were incremental to the world up to this generation.

Elderly: Appreciating this Divine Privilege

Scripture Proverbs 20:29 "The glory of the young men is their strength, and the splendor of Old men is their gray head". Proverbs 16:31 "The silver-haired head is a crown of glory, If it is found in the way of righteousness".

Being aged/ elderly implies being: sober, temperate, sound in faith and patience, enjoying charity, sensible and respectful. This is God-given privilege that ought to be positively embraced by all. Besides, this can allude to wisdom, understanding, experimental experience in life, but also maturity (physically and mentally).

Research has it that Elderly people enjoy the following unlike youthful stage:

a) A happier outlook and appearance, due to better coping mechanisms when dealing with challenges and hardships; but also they are more comfortable being themselves;

b) The joy of having grandchildren by their side;

c) Possibility of having more time on themselves for relaxing, and more time with loved ones;

d) Ability to achieve one's long held dreams such as – a lifetime trip, authoring books, etc;

e) Capacity to serve as volunteer or charitable works with development agencies like ADRA, Red Cross Society; but also civic involvement (elections);

f) Better capacity to control one's emotions given that one has done it and seen it all;

g) Better capability to deal with social conflicts or excellent in conflict management assignments. That is why in most conflict-plagued countries, it is the aged/ former presidents that head such missions like H.E Thambo Mbeki, Mkapa, Koffi Annan, etc;

h) Higher levels of emotional intelligence – more emotionally stable and rather contented in life;

i) During old age, such inconsequential questions like "what if" would have no relevance in one's life, since at that stage one should sidelined and gracefully accepted what one failed to do in life and also pride in what one was able to attain;

j) Special treatment in civilized societies in various life situations like being given preferential treatment over the younger ones in the bus, banks, hospital, air transport, church, etc. Moses, in his instructions to the children of Israel, emphasized this social virtue in, Leviticus 19:32 "You shall rise before the gray headed and honor the presence of an old man, and fear your God: I am the Lord".

Nonetheless, old age has a couple of real challenges that need to be rationally and comprehensively understood and worked on, if possible, such as:

i) Getting closer to the end – there is need to plan for the end (retirement and/or death) urgently than ever;

ii) Costly medical care due to weakened body, coupled to escalating cost of living world over;

iii) Body significantly slowing down – body aches, progressive loss of memory, reduced energy;

iv) Likely end to career growth given that most jobs have age limits.

But by and large, I used to share the same view with my fellow young men of forcing aged folks out of employment and crucial positions when their retirement time reaches due to the prevalent unemployment and underemployment in basically Africa. I would strongly support the view that these old guys should retire gracefully and go to take care of their grandchildren, farms and possibly enjoy their wealth accumulated during youthful stage, so that we can also fill up their positions and give our contribution to the world. However, I later realized that, for instance, if aged professors retire from teaching and guiding research at the university, and positions be filled with less and/or absolutely inexperienced younger men then the education system would be in total disaster, and it would lack the experience and exposure that these guys have accumulated for decades simply waiting to pass it on to the youngsters to become efficient human resources. Besides, universities and other institutions would really lose a lot of value when these old guys are forced to retire without giving their valuable contribution thanks to their long years of experience and exposure yet for them they actually work for money as an incentive but largely service.

This reminds me of how my Kiganda culture (Uganda) highly values the Elderly in society and even in its proverbs and wise sayings, but also equally appreciate most cultures in Tanzania which even have a special way of greeting elderly people, "Shikamo Baba!". It further reminds of the wise gesture that Rehoboam did right after ascending to the throne of Israel, following his succession of his fallen father King Solomon; in 2 Chronicles 10:6 "Then Rehoboam consulted the Elders who stood before his father Solomon while he still lived, saying, "How do you advise me to answer these people?............"

46. THE GATE AJAR FOR ME (C.H 561)

This invitation hymn was composed by the wonderful Lydia Baxter (1809 - 1874); born in Petersburg, New York, as a child, Rev. Eber Tucker, a Baptist home missionary, led her and her sister to Christ. There was no Baptist church in Petersburg, but the two girls were so instrumental in establishing it there; she later married Colonel John Baxter who thereafter gave his life to Christ thanks to Lydia's influence. They later moved to New York City where they spent the rest of their lives. Baxter's home was a gathering place for evangelists, preachers, and other Christian workers who came for advice and encouragement. After 1844 Baxter became ill and was often bedridden, but visitors remarked that they still received more encouragement from her than they were able to give. When asked the secret of her cheery disposition, she replied, "I have a special armor. I have the name of Jesus."

To fill her hours in bed, Baxter became skilled at making artificial birds and flowers. She also wrote hymns and a book of devotional poems. Although she is basically remembered for her hymn "Take the Name of Jesus with You", she also authored this hymn in question.

Mrs. Lydia Baxter was an invalid for many years but her interest in the religious welfare of those around her was manifested in many ways. She wrote the hymn, "There is a gate that stands ajar" around 1871 (3 years before her death), when she was considerably past the sixty-years of age.

In Great Britain in 1873, this hymn was frequently used in an evangelistic meeting. It was sung at the watch-night service in 1873, a young lady who was present—Maggie Lindsay, of Aberdeen, Scotland, was so impressed by the hymn, and those seated by her side heard her exclaim, "O, heavenly Father, is it true that the gate is standing ajar for me? If it is so, I will go in." That night she became a disciple of the Lord Jesus. The next day she called on her pastor, the Rev. J. H. Wilson, and told him of her decision. He was greatly pleased, and advised her to tell her school companions of her experience. This saw her succeeding in leading several of them into the light; but barely a month later, on January 28, Maggie took a train for her home, but she never reached there alive. At Manuel Junction, Scotland a collision took place between a mineral train and the one on which she was riding. A number of passengers were killed, and Maggie, all crushed and broken, was found in the wreck. In one of her hands was a copy of "Sacred Songs and Solos", opened at her favorite hymn, "There is a gate that stands ajar", the page of which was stained with her heart's blood. She was carried into a cottage near the station, where she lingered a few days and was frequently heard to sing on her dying couch the chorus of the hymn so dear to her, "For me, for me! was left ajar for me!" The church minister who watched by her said the expression of her countenance could not be described as she again and again repeated the words, "Yes. For me, for me".

Christ's Evangelistic Methodology

Scripture – Proverbs 11:30 (Holy Bible) "The fruit of the righteous is a tree of life, and he that wins souls is wise". This is among the best text I have ever read on evangelism, and it is quite strange that it is neither situated in the prophetic writings in the Old Testament nor anywhere in the New Testament (whose primary focus is on evangelism/ gospel of the Kingdom). This text is situated in the Poetic Books, where one would hardly expect to find such a resourceful text on a theme as evangelism. This text alludes to and/or emphasizes that 'the winning of souls (for Christ)' – which is the applied and practical definition of evangelism is likened to or linked to wisdom (being wise) on the part of the one who does it. On the other hand, this could signify that any Christian who is not preoccupied with winning souls can be termed as "unwise" according to the 'Holy Bible' version. This should actually stimulate us to be heavily involved in evangelism, not only as Christ's great commission but also as a means of being counted among the wise.

Ellen White (1905) offers a practical guide on how to implement an effective evangelistic campaign that is purely based on Christ's proven methodology. She informs that Christ's method alone will give true success in reaching the people; this is because He mingled with men as one who desired their good……. and finally bade them to follow him. But below are the five highlighted stages in effective and holistic model of evangelism that would successfully win souls as practiced by the Chief Evangelist, Jesus Christ:

a) He mingled with people as One who desired their good through opening networks;

b)   He sympathized with people, basically those in sorrow which helped Him to form attachments;

c)   He ministered to their needs, which showed that he was greatly concerned about their welfare and subsequently led to deeper attachments and bond;

d)   After successfully combining the first three stages, Christ won His followers/ listeners' confidence, in that they could fully count on Him and also run to Him;

e)   Lastly, He bade them to become His disciples, by appealing to them to follow Him.

She further adds, "There is need of coming close to the people by personal effort. If less time were given to sermonizing, and more time were spent in personal ministry, greater results would be seen. The poor are to be relieved, the sick cared for, the sorrowing and the bereaved comforted, the ignorant instructed, the inexperienced counseled. We are to weep with those that weep, and rejoice with those that rejoice" – Ministry of Healing, pg 143.

Christ's method was particularly used by the author of this hymn (Lydia Baxter) all through her life that was characterized by largely being an invalid and bedridden person but she used that weakness to get closer to a diversity of people by personal effort and compassionate care for the sorrowing and bereaved.

47. GIVE ME THE BIBLE (SDAH 272)

1)   Give me the Bible, star of gladness gleaming,
           To cheer the wanderer lone and tempest tossed;
           No storm can hide that peaceful radiance beaming,
           Since Jesus came to seek and save the lost

Chorus
Give me the Bible holy message shining,
Thy light shall guide me in the narrow way
Precept and promise, law and love combining,
Till night shall vanish in eternal day

2)   Give me the Bible when my heart is broken,
           When sin and grief my soul with fear;
           Give me the precious words by Jesus spoken;
           Hold up faith's lamp to show my Savior near.

This resourceful hymn was composed by Priscilla Jane Owens (1829 – 1907). She spent all her entire life in Baltimore, Maryland as a public school teacher, and also Sunday school teacher for more than 50 years in the Methodist church. Besides, she wrote poetry and prose for the Methodist Recorder and the Christian Standard, but she was also the author of other popular golden hymns like "Jesus Saves".

On the other hand, the music was composed by Edmund Simon Lorenz, Ohio USA; he was a minister of the United Brethren Church who, also like Priscilla, composed several hymn tunes and gospel songs, but also published a couple of Books till his death in July 1942 aged 88 years.

The Bible (Word of God) has significantly touched many lives and positively influenced not only the spirituality but also social welfare of those who have believed in its invaluable resources for generations and world over. It is resourcefully endowed with all the solutions to personal and societal challenges that its goodness can never be depleted nor exhausted for as long as we still live on this mortal world. It has enlightened and rendered wise Christians and Atheists, religious people, politicians, economists, medical practitioners and dieticians, social scientists, philosophers, and all sorts of professions because all wisdom comes from this sacred Book.

Center of Influence

Scripture - Proverbs 22:1 (Holy Bible) "A good name is rather to be chosen than great riches, and loving favor rather than silver and gold". Besides, another scripture by King Solomon is clearly linked to the above verse is Ecclesiastes 7:1 (Holy Bible) "A good name is better than precious ointment; and the day of death than the day of one's birth"

A popular story is told of a Professor who undertook a study on 200 African-Americans who lived in slum and crime-plagued communities, and his research findings concluded that these youngsters would amount to nothing in the future.

But 20 years down the road, another professor in the same university (same faculty/school of Social Sciences) resolved to undertake a similar study to establish how these 200 guys had ended up in life given the damning conclusions of the previous study on them. After a long and tedious search for these now grown-up guys wherever the world had dispersed them, at least 180 out of the 200 guys were identified in various localities and they were still very alive and available. 150 out of the 180 identified guys had turned up to be so successful in life (very professional and reputable in their organizations and communities); the researcher, being so moved by this reality, asked them what had led to this turn-around of events. They all, individually, told him that it was the work of one lecturer/teacher who impacted their lives from youthful stage during his interactions with them. This saw the Professor mount another search on this wonderful lecturer who significantly influenced the lives of all these guys, only to find him in a nursing home (very old but surprisingly, unlike most Whites so struggle with amnesia, he was still with a very sound brain and memory). When asked what he had inculcated in these youngsters' life during their interactions, this is what he said, "I did nothing to them but simply told them that God loves them. Despite anything, God deserves the best from them".

This is the message of hope that we need to give to a world that is filled with despair, perplexity, confusion, hatred, animosity, distrust, etc. And this message can be found in God's Holy Book, the Bible

48. WATCHMEN ON THE WALL OF ZION (SDAH 601)

1)   Watchmen, on the wall of Zion, What, O tell us of the night?
       Is the daystar now arising? Will the morn soon greet our sight?
       Over your vision shine there now some rays of light?
       Over your vision shine there now some rays of light?

4)   We have found the chart and compass, And are sure the land is near;
       Onward, onward we are hasting, Soon the haven will appear;
       Let the voices sound aloud your holy cheer;
       Let the voices sound aloud your holy cheer

This cautioning hymn was composed by Frances Jane 'Fanny' Crosby (1820 – 1915); a daughter of John and Mercy Crosby, was born in Southeast, Putnam County, New York. She became blind at the age of six weeks from maltreatment of her eyes during a spell of sickness. When she was eight years old she moved with her parents to Ridgefield, the family remaining there four years. At the age of fifteen she entered the New York Institution for the Blind, where she received a good education. She became a teacher in the institution in 1847, and continued her work until 1858; she taught English grammar, rhetoric and American history.

This beautiful and resourceful song is another blessing from Fanny Crosby, and its tune "Zion" that is currently in popular use was composed by the legendary Thomas Hastings (1784 – 1872) in Washington. Thomas was also known for composing the tune to Augustus Montague Toplady's beloved hymn "Rock of Ages" that has blessed so many lives over the ages.

The first two stanzas ask crucial questions and the last two provide the answers to those questions. Besides, the language and/or vocabulary of the last 2 stanzas uses pretty much of the language of the first 2 stanzas questions! Interesting to note is the fact that metaphors change, initially from the "Citizen in a walled town" to a "Traveler on a ship bound for harbor.

The time we are living in are challenging times – times of seeking to steal and exploit subtly or violently. Many people are looking for any opportunity to take away something from another. They are looking for a time when you are not looking, not vigilant, reckless or when you are vulnerable in times of despair and hopelessness. It is evident that a call to be watchful and to hold fast is very pertinent in this contemporary world. This is because failure to watch will give opportunity to those who are always ready to take away something valuable from us including our own lives.

Watch and Hold Fast

Scripture – Revelation 3:11ff "....Behold, I come quickly: hold fast that which you have, that no man take your crown...."

The above verses in Revelations is part of the letter written by John, the Revelator to the church in Philadelphia; it is the 6th letter of the seven letters, and the 7th being that written to Laodicea. It is imperative to note that all these letters were written to real and physical congregations which actually existed in Asia Minor, a great province of the defunct Roman Empire, just above the Mediterranean Sea. It is quite interesting that all the messages to those churches also had a prophetic dimension according to proponents of the historical approach to biblical prophecy. The underlying message to all these churches was a counsel to watch and hold fast, as this is a major in Revelation Chapters 2 and 3. Besides, the fact that the names of the churches fit into the time periods of the Christian church:

a) Ephesus – this meant "desire/ loosening"; and this was the Apostolic church which later permitted corruption to creep in. hence, Christ rebuked them that "You lost your first love". Ephesus was the capital of Asia Minor, and the center of land and sea trade; one of the three most influential cities in Eastern part of Roman Empire. The temple of Artemis (the Roman goddess) was one of the ancient wonders of the world at that time. Hence, there is need to watch and hold fast lest we live in the last days of the world's history progressively lose our first love, as did the Ephesian church.

b) Smyrna – which meant "bitter"; the time of Roman persecution of those who were loyal to the apostolic teachings and doctrines. This city was 25 miles north of Ephesus, and nicknamed "Port of Asia" thanks to its excellent harbor. The church struggled against two forces: the Jewish population that was strongly opposed to Christianity, and the non-Jewish population loyal to Rome – supported emperor worship). This city was equally famous for its athletic games. Thus, we need to watch and hold fast lest the fiery persecution that is to come in the final days dulls our faith and hope in the soon coming of our Lord Jesus Christ.

c)   Pergamum – alluding to "high tower"; the time when Constantine converted to Christianity, which saw the 'church' harness and boast of state power. This city was built on a hill 1000 feet above, thus creating a natural fortress; a sophisticated city and center of Greek culture and education, with arguably the first and largest ancient library of that time. This was a center of four cults, and it only rivaled Ephesus in idol worship; the city's chief god was Asclepius (god of healing), whose symbol was a serpent. Consequently, there is need to watch and hold fast so that the prevalent idolatry (atheism) and religious superficiality doesn't overshadow true godliness across Christendom.

d)   Thyatira – which meant "sacrificing untiringly"; this time saw the historic rise of the Catholic system, and instituting the special priesthood and wide spread idolatry. This city was characterized as working people's town with many trades, and largely a secular city with no particular religion. Stanza 2 question and vocabulary is pertinent here: "Tell, O tell us, are the landmarks on our voyage all passed by? Are we nearing now the haven?.........do we truly see the heavenly kingdom near?"

e)   Sardis – which referred to "revival/ reformation"; this saw a period of reformation, though, at the end of the reformation one would expect everything to be alright but the vices of the dark ages reappear. Hence, "You have a name of being alive but you are dead…." This wealthy city was in two locations: one on a mountain and the other in the valley. This saw the birth of the Protestant movement and all its subsequent subgroupings right from the initial work of Martin Luther and his contemporaries' basis for separation from the Catholic system.

f)   Philadelphia – which meant "brotherly love"; the time of great awakening in the 18th and 19th Century. This period saw the start of missionary work, whereby missionaries were sent out to continents like Africa, but also other parts of Asia like China, etc.. In this time, the Millerite and the Advent movement came on the world stage. This city was founded by the citizens of Pergamum, and built as a frontier area and gateway to the central plateau of

Asia Minor. Residents chased away barbarian cultures from the region and brought in Greek culture and language. This brotherly love is so crucial in this era that is heavily characterized by individualism and egocentric tendencies – hence, watching and holding fast message a lot of valuable sense lest our first love grows cold.

g)   Laodicea – which means "people's opinions" (laos – people not brothers, and dicea – opinions); the present day church – in this period, people's opinions (relativism, human philosophies, evolutionistic Darwinism, etc) reign over God's word. The love of many is growing cold and the once brothers and sisters are simply people one can play around with and use as instruments for one's selfish objectives. This was the wealthiest of the seven cities, known for robust banking industry, manufacturing of wool, a medical school that produced eye ointment; but with a huge problem of water supply. With people's opinions taking the place of Holy Scriptures, there is a great need to watch and hold fast lest we also fall prey of such well-crafted human philosophies and arguments.

49. ON JORDAN'S STORMY BANKS I STAND" (SDAH 620)

1) On Jordan's stormy banks I stand,
And cast a wishful eye,
To Canaan's fair and happy land,
Where my possessions lie.

Chorus
I am bound for the promised land,
I am bound for the promised land,
O who will come and go with me?
I am bound for the promised land.

2) All o'er those wide, extended plains,
Shines one eternal day;
There God, the Son, forever reigns,
And scatters night away.

3) No chilling winds, nor pois'nous breath,
Can reach that healthful shore;
Sickness and sorrow, pain and death,
Are felt and feared no more.

4) When shall I reach that happy place,
And be forever blest?
When shall I see my Father's face,
And in His bosom rest?

This lovely hymn was composed by Samuel Stennett (1727-1795), an English Seventh-Day Baptist minister. Though he was born in Exeter, his family moved to London when he was 10 years. He was privileged to have come from a long line of church ministers, including his father who was also a Seventh-Day Baptist church pastor.

As already highlighted in the Isaac Watts' life profile, in the 18th century, university education was not easily available to Nonconformist families (those who refused to swear allegiance to the Church of England). This was also the case for Stennett, who saw himself opt for studies at the academy at Miles End and graduated with distinction. In spite of his Nonconformist religious stance, Stennett was a personal friend to the reigning monarch, King George III. Stennett was honored in 1763 with a doctor of divinity degree from King's

College, Aberdeen, for his accomplishments; but he also refused political opportunities in order to devote himself to ministry. He attained prominence amongst the Dissenting ministry and used his influence with political figures in behalf of Dissenters suffering persecution by the government.

In 1747, he served as an assistant to his father in his congregation, and assumed the position of pastor upon his father's death in 1758. He was called as pastor of the Sabbatarian Baptist Church in 1767, a congregation that had been served by his grandfather (Rev. Joseph Stennett), but declined the call. While continuing his other position, he preached to the Sabbatarian congregation every Saturday for 20 years. His grandfather had also been a prominent Dissenting hymn writer which tradition Samuel continued, although with less passionate language than had marked his grandfather's Puritan-influenced notions of Christian experience.

Generally, Samuel Stennett's list of publications include sermons, pamphlets and his 38 hymns in a book by John Rippon (an English Baptist pastor) titled "A Selection of Hymns from the Best Authors". Among those was a hymn under the heading of "Heaven Anticipated" with the title of "The Promised Land" in eight four-line stanzas. This hymn was later transformed by Rigdon M. McIntosh, (Southern musician) who altered the tune to fit the customary American evangelicals of the 19th century but he also added a refrain beginning with "I am bound for the promised land." This version has become the standard version for many hymnals since that time.

The first four stanzas focus on heaven: the singer stands on the banks of the Jordan River looking across to the "fair and happy land" of Canaan—a metaphoric mixture of images from the books of Exodus and Revelation. This implies that our true "possessions" lie in Canaan (Heaven) and not on the earthly side of Jordan. In stanza 2, he indicates that Canaan is a land of "wide extended plains" where "the eternal day" is always shining. In this land Jesus reigns. Besides, stanza 3 informs that Canaan is a spiritually healthful place to live: "No chilling winds or poisonous breath can reach that healthful shore." Therefore, "sickness and sorrow, pain and death" do not exist in Canaan.

The Biblical Pilgrimage

During the Israelites 400-year stay in the land of Egypt, they became enslaved to the Egyptians (just the way that we have been enslaved to this deadly and sinful world for close to 6000 years – according to the Biblical account of history of the world). Pharaoh, the king of Egypt, oppressed them with the nastiest cruelty and they prayed to God for deliverance from this unbearable situation. Like the Hebrews, we have also been oppressed by Satan (who took over this world's dominion from Adam), and so we need both human and divine leadership in this pilgrimage to escape from the slavery of sin. Just like during the Exodus, this heavenly pilgrimage is packed with a variety and/or a series of God's calls and responses of His people. All through the ages, God has used various human instrumentalities to lead His people to the heavenly Canaan – these patriarchs have included: judges, kings, prophets, priests, apostles, among others. The same way God led Moses is the way He wants us to the Promised Land, but He could be preparing for a special mission of leading His people in this divine journey.

Stennett's vocabulary in Stanza 4 is quite spot on and very inspirational, "Filled with delight, my raptured soul would here no longer stay, though Jordan's waves around me toil, fearless I would launch away". And then the beautiful yet Christian invitation follows in the Chorus, "I am bound to the Promised Land, I am bound to the Promised Land; O who will come and go with me? I am bound for the Promised Land"

50. HOW FAR FROM HOME? (SDAH 439)

1) How far from home? I ask, as on I bent my steps – the watchman spoke;
The long, dark night is almost gone, The morning soon will break.
Then weep no more, but speed thy flight, With Hope's bright star thy guiding ray;
Till Thou shall reach the realms of light, In everlasting day.

4) Not far from home! O blessed thought! The traveler's lonely heart to cheer;
Which oft a healing balm has brought, And dried the mourner's tear;
Then weep no more, since we shall meet Where weary footsteps never roam;
Our trials past, our joys complete, safe in our Father's home.

This advent-inspired hymn was composed by a young lady, Annie Rebekah Smith (1828 – 1855);. She was born in New Hampshire, as the third child of four children and only daughter of Samuel and Rebekah (Spalding) Smith. At a tender age of 10 years, she accepted Jesus as her Savior and joined the Adventist church and became one of the earliest American Seventh-day Adventist hymn writers. Annie Smith was the sister of the Adventist pioneer, Uriah Smith.

In 1844, she embraced the doctrine of the soon coming of Christ, at just 16 years of age; later she experienced, along with others in Christendom, the Great Disappointment of October 22, 1844. This saw her lose interest in the Adventist teachings, and later pursued her favorite occupations of studying and teaching. Between 1844 and 1855 she taught in seven district schools, while also furthering her own education in various training colleges in Massachusetts including training as a teacher in Oil Painting and French language

She later got in touch with a Sabbatarian Adventist pioneer, Joseph Bates who was a friend to Annie's mother. This sparked her interest in the Sabbatarian Adventist movement. She consequently submitted a poem to the Adventist paper known as the Review and Herald. She was recognized by James White as a talented writer. Shortly before her early death to tuberculosis at 27 years of age, she made a record of contributing close to 45 articles to the Review and Herald and to the Youth Instructor. She also composed 10 hymns in the current Seventh-day Adventist Church Hymnal including this particular hymn.

Success in Perspective

In life, we have two choices really - to survive or succeed. But it is worth noting that if we choose to succeed and prosper, and commit to focused goals then everything is possible. This is because God designed us to succeed and our best can still be in front of us. God has placed our future in our hands, and huge untapped potential is inside us since we have unlimited value and our dreams can definitely come true. We were specially and uniquely created so as to achieve whatever we put our minds to. The requirement is to: enlarge our vision; retrain our brains; increase our confidence; attract the good around us; step forward daily so as to seize the profitable opportunities in our path. But there is need to: positively engage relationships; unleash our maximum wealth; prepare for our success; believe in ourselves; plan before we do anything; avoid the negative; move outside of our comfort zones; let go of the past; and never give up. These life resources are so pertinent to our daily living here on earth because our loving God wants us to aspire for the best in life mortal life. But above all, these resources make a lot of logical sense in our pilgrimage to heaven, which Annie Smith was referring to in her song, but in particular in the legacy of her short life. That crucial advent question of "How far from home?" signifies a passionate interest in knowing where we have come from as the Church, where we are currently in relation to Christ's return, but especially what time period is remaining for us to reach eternity. Of course, this sounds to come from a Christian who is very exhausted with this horrible world and she is over-anticipating Christ's return, which Paul beautifully calls the 'Blessed Hope" when writing to Titus (a Greek who had gotten converted thanks to Paul's ministry and had become Paul's special envoy to the Island of Crete) in Titus 2:13.

51. NOT I BUT CHRIST (SDAH 570)

1) Not I, but Christ, be honored, loved, exalted;
Not I, but Christ, be seen, be known, be heard;
Not I, but Christ, In every look and action;
Not I, but Christ, in every thought and word.

2) Not I, but Christ, to gently soothe in sorrow;
Not I, but Christ, to wipe the falling tears;
Not I, but Christ, to lift the weary burden;
Not I, but Christ, to hush away all fear.

This dedication hymn was authored by Ada Anne Fitzgerald Whiddington (1855 – 1933) in 1891. She was daughter of Robert Fitzgerald in England, and Ada married Richard Whiddington. She is thought to have been associated with the Keswick Convention in the United Kingdom. Their son Richard is believed later to have become a Cavendish Professor of Physics at Cambridge University. The theme is extracted from Apostle Paul's confession in Galatians 2:20 (NLT) "My old self has been crucified with Christ. It is no longer I who live, but Christ lives in me. So I live in this earthly body by trusting in the son of God, who loved me and gave Himself for me." The hymn emphasizes that only as He dwells within us can we reveal His goodness to the world or sympathize with others and also be humble. Much as legally, God looks at us as if we had died with Christ and without any condemnation since our sins died with Him, the prime focus of Christianity is not on dying but on living. Because we have been crucified with Christ, we have also been raised with Him – hence, we are legally reconciled with God and are free to grow in Christ's likeness. We are no longer alone, for Christ lives in us, as our power for living and our hope for the future.

Jesus Christ, in Perspective
He is the first and the last; the beginning and the end;
He is the keeper of creation and creator of all;
He is the architect of the universe and the manager of all time;
He always was, always is, and always will be;
Unmoved, unchanged, undefeated and unrivaled;
He was bruised but brought healing, pierced but heals pain;
He was persecuted but brought freedom, dead but brings life, he has risen to bring power and he reigns to bring peace;

The world can't understand him, the armies can't defeat him, schools can't explain him, and leaders can't ignore him;
Herod couldn't kill him, Nero couldn't crush him, and New Age can't replace him;
He is light, he is love, he is longevity, he is the Lord, he is goodness, kindness and faithfulness;
He is God, he is holy, righteous, powerful and pure;
His ways are right, his word eternal, his will unchanged, and his mind is on us;
He is our Savior, our God, our peace, our joy, our comfort, our Lord, and he rules our lives;
I serve him because his bond is love, his yoke is easy.

The Vision of Self

After a Christian receives the vision of God (an appreciation of who God is) in contrast to who humanity is, then a servant of God ought to be endowed with the vision of self. This implies an understanding of one's sinfulness and/or spiritual status – this will serve to unearth one's insufficiency, weaknesses, and complete need for God's mercy. Whenever we encounter God, we get an opportunity to fully appreciate our sinfulness and our need for God's grace in everything that we do. This will lead to meekness and humility on the part of any Christian, which will see him/her reflect and/or apply Apostle Paul's (and also Ada Fitzgerald Whiddington) remarkable words, "Not I but Christ……….." Consequently, this will lead to God's glory suppressing one's weakness upon receiving the vision of God, and the vision of self.

52. WONDERFUL WORDS OF LIFE (SDAH 286)

1. Sing them over again to me, Wonderful words of Life;
   Let me more of their beauty see, Wonderful words of Life.
   Words of life and beauty, Teach me faith and duty:

Chorus
Beautiful words, wonderful words, Wonderful words of Life.
Beautiful words, wonderful words, Wonderful words of Life.

2. Christ, the blessed One, gives to all, Wonderful words of Life;
   Sinner, list to the loving call, Wonderful words of Life.
   All so freely given, Wooing us to Heaven:

3. Sweetly echo the gospel call, Wonderful words of Life;
   Offer pardon and peace to all, Wonderful words of Life.
   Jesus, only Savior, Sanctify forever:

This hymn was written by Philip Paul Bliss in 1874. He was born in July 1838 in Pennsylvania to religious and musical parents. At the age of 10 years, he first saw the piano. He used to work on farms and in lumber camps but he accepted Christ and joined the Baptist church at the age of 12. It is said that in 1864 he sent an original song to a Publishing company in Chicago offering it to them in exchange for a flute. Recognizing such as promising talent, this company sent him the flute and later gave him a job of holding concerts and conventions for that company. Later in life, he accepted an invitation to go to England for some meetings along with his wife Lucy but on December 29 1876, while on a trip back to Chicago where he was to sing in Moody's service, a bridge gave way and the train plunged into the icy river below and burst into flames. Reports have it that he had actually survived the fall by escaping through a window but he went back to try to rescue his wife Lucy and both lost their lives in the flames.

Bliss' composition of "Wonderful words of life" allude to wisdom that is only the gift of God to His obedient, diligent and humble children in a bid to help them make rational and spiritual choices that are required in daily lifestyle. These crucial words seem to have been inspired by King Solomon's (the all-time wisest man on earth) remarks on wisdom titled 'The Benefits of Wisdom' in Proverbs 2:1ff (NLT) "My child………..tune your ears to wisdom, and concentrate on understanding………… search for them as you would for silver; seek them like hidden treasure………." It is imperative to note that wisdom comes in two ways: it is a God-given gift and also the result of an energetic search. But the starting point is God and His revealed Word, which is the source of knowledge and understanding. Wisdom can be likened to an education in the broader perspective of life. And this will require us to make a clinical analysis of what education is and what it is not.

Christian Education (Holistic Perspective)

This submission is derived from my close 10 years' experience both as an educationist at majorly high school and university levels but also as Director of the Education Department at SDA Church Najjanankumbi District (composed of now 19 local churches in Kampala, Uganda). Under this ministry, we have endeavored to design and promote a holistic approach to education, which has seen us also pioneer a couple of initiatives that were aimed achieving each of these ten (10) constituents of what we believe can be the model concept of Christian education. This concept was further linked to and/or complemented by Aggarwal (2014) who defines 'Education' as the producing of a well-balanced personality, who is:

a) Culturally …..refined (the best model is being inter-culturally cultured);

b) Spiritually …upright (whereby parents are the primary Shepherds in home church)

c) Mentally …..alter (with dynamic and quick decision-making)

d) Physically …. Strong (capacity to take on any manual work)

e) Socially …….sound (excellent interpersonal skills and easily adaptable)

f) Morally …….. upright (moral – principles of right and wrong in behavior)

g) Emotionally …..stable (with excellent emotional intelligence and self-control)

h) Ethically …….. Efficient (principles of right and wrong in a society and/or profession).

i) Vocationally ……self-sufficient (well-equipped with a vocational skill or trade).

j) Internationally ……liberal (being inclusive, open-minded, accommodative)

Education/ human capital investment (development) has a positive externality to the society, given the spill-over advantages or benefits from the individual who has attained it to the whole society.

In a certain African community, there is a very crucial saying that alludes to how invaluable and indispensable education is (but above all, keeping a record of such educational experiences in a way of a publication and/or storage device is to any given society). Loosely translated, it goes, "In any given African society, when an elderly person dies, it could be likened to a huge laboratory and/or library of valuable resources in the Western world that has been set ablaze and/or destroyed to ashes". This is because, all the invaluable skills and experiences, of which the world doesn't have a copy would perish for good and be wasted never to be replaced

There are three important aspects of Education that should be deliberately and systemically addressed so as to ensure that education truly becomes the software of development in any given society. These include: access to the requisite learning resources; the quality of the learning/educational resources given the level of societal advancement; and the relevance of those skills and/or educational experiences to the contemporary societal opportunities and challenges.

Steps in Acquisition of Wisdom:
The first thing in the quest of wisdom in 'Silence'.
The second is 'Listening'
The third is 'Memory'
The fourth is 'Practice'
And finally, the fifth is 'Teaching'.
In conclusion, the pathway to wisdom and/or education is strenuous. When we are on the path, we discover that true wisdom is God's and that He will guide us and reward or sincere and persistent search as indicated in Proverbs 2:1ff. God gives wisdom and victory to the godly but not to those wandering through life or acting irresponsibly with His gifts and resources. We gain wisdom through a constant process of growing including: trusting and honoring God; realizing that the Bible reveals God's wisdom to us; making lifelong series of right choices and avoid moral pitfalls; and lastly, learning from our errors and recover.

53. PASS ME NOT O GENTLE (SDAH 569)

1.   Pass me not, O gentle Savior, Hear my humble cry;
       While on others Thou art calling, Do not pass me by.

Chorus
Savior, Savior, Hear my humble cry;
While on others Thou art calling,
Do not pass me by.

2.   Let me at a throne of mercy, Find a sweet relief;
       Kneeling there in deep contrition, Help my unbelief.

3.   Trusting only in Thy merit, Would I seek Thy face;
       Heal my wounded, broken spirit, Save me by Thy grace.

4.   Thou the Spring of all my comfort, More than life to me,
       Whom I have on earth beside Thee? Whom in Heav'n but Thee?

This hymn was composed in 1868 by Fanny Crosby (1820 – 1915); it was inspired by her visit to one of New York's prison in that year whereby she appealed to the convicts to accept Christ as their personal Saviour. It is said that she was interrupted by one prisoner who claimed, "Good Lord, don't pass me by"; and in this same place, Crosby was with another great musician who had actually composed many tunes to Crosby's poems. William Howard Doane suggested to Crosby to compose a hymn with the title "Pass Me Not, O Gentle Saviour". She took a deep thought about the incident and the spiritual resources that this hymn would portend, then she wrote the words to the now popular hymn which rendered it a real prayer from this encounter in her personal experience. This hymn was further inspired and/or amplified by the experience of Jesus when healing the blind beggar in Mark 10:46ff who pleaded with him. This equally fits so well Crosby's nature of being blind from childhood that she could better understand this blind man's plea to Christ literally not to pass by him without restoring his sight.

Scripture – Luke 18:38 (NLT) "So, he began shouting, 'Jesus, son of David have mercy on me."

Much as the hymn emphasizes calling on God in prayer (lest He passes by us without responding to our requests), I would wish to orient the life application resources to being called by God's name. This is partly because I have already exhausted two hymns on prayer, but also the beauty of being called by God's name.

Called By His Name

Scripture – 2 Chronicle 7:14 (NLT) "Then if my people who are called by my name will humble themselves and pray and seek my face and turn from their wicked ways, I will hear from heaven and I will forgive their sins and restore their land"

In many cultures, naming members is an important element in social traditions and cultural heritage given the significance of particular names used and what occasions the naming process or event. For instance, in my Kiganda culture (Central Uganda) there are at least 56 clans and each clan has its unique names that identifies its members, each name has a cultural significance. That's why of old, before modern technology of DNA tests, clan leaders would occasionally organize ceremonies aimed at establishing whether the children that mothers affirm (claim) to be part of that clan are really clan members. And in their traditional technology they would finally succeed in that initiative.

In the same vein, even God is desirous of identifying His people and subsequently naming them (give them His special name) so that they can fully be His own people, so beloved to Him, separated and anointed. They should follow His instruction and God has special blessings for them. God wants His name to be mingled with my name so as to cement our relationship, to partake of His glory, nobility and power. Sharing His name with us is aimed at proving that He protects, provides us and so that we can trust Him. Ultimately, He wants to become the ruler and governor of our lives. That is why the Hebrews used to name their kids (with significant and consequential meanings):

Zedekiah ---- God is my righteousness;

Isaiah -------- God is our salvation;

Amos --------- God is the burden-breaker;

And this precisely explains why God had to change Abram and Sarai's names, and added on a significant "H" on their name which comes from His own name "YHW";

Abram -------- Abraham

Sarai --------- Sarah

It was in a bid to make His people partake of His name, godliness and consequently be His own. This further explains why most Hebrew names have an "H" that signifies a relationship with God. But below is a selective analysis of God's names as identified by the Hebrews which are so consequential to our being and also relationship with His people:

a) Erohim ....God is the creator of the universe; and also God of love. Some translations have 'Erohim' as "to swear" because when He says something, He doesn't have a change of mind. This can be further evidenced in Psalms 110:4 "The Lord made a solemn promise and He won't take it back....."

b) Jehovah ....God of justice. And so, Erohim and Jehovah ie God of love and God of justice show that in God's government, love and justice go hand in hand. To expound on this reality, Genesis 3:1ff, this account gives the genesis of the theology of love with justice; but the belief of love without justice is absolutely defective in all aspects.

c) El Shaddai ...... God who calls His people back from wandering, darkness and destruction to His glorious light and peace.

d) El Elion .... God who is higher than everything, God who possesses in that when one becomes His own, He owns their fears, problems and challenges.

e) Adonai .... God, the Master. This highlights a Master-servant relationship between God and His people, but which is based on exploitative tendencies that are so characterized of the worldly employer-employee relationship but purely on a self-sacrificing love. In fact, the church is a church only and only when it acknowledges the authority of God.

54. ASK NOT TO BE EXCUSED (C.H 513)

1) Ask not to be excused, There's earnest work to do; Stand ready to be used,
Where God may station you. His invitation kind to thee has oft been given;
Accept, and thou shalt find, Tis sweet to work for heaven.

Chorus
Come, O come, Ask not to be excused; Come, O come, Stand ready to be used.
Ask not to be excused, This answer today, may be given;
Thou hast my love abused, Thou art excused from heaven.

2) Ask not to be excused, The Master calls today; Too long hast thou refused;
Now hasten to obey. The harvest fields are white, The laborers are few;
Let this be thy delight, The Master's work to do.

This challenging hymn was authored by the SDA Church prolific hymn writer, Franklin Edison Belden (1858 – 1945). Belden was so talented that he could write a new song within an hour; while the preacher was reading the morning scripture, he would then slip out and write a new hymn based on the text, which he and his wife would stand and sing. After the service he would give a copy to the preacher. By 20 years, Belden was already writing hymns and he wrote several hundred hymns during his lifetime.

This particular hymn seems to have been inspired by Christ's discourse with the Samaritan woman at the well, which scenario also inspired the composition of another hymn that I also discuss in this Book, "Fill My Cup Lord". Jesus condemns giving excuses regarding ministry, as expressed in John 4:35 (NKJV) "Do you not say, 'There are still four months and then comes the harvest?' Behold, I say to you, lift up your eyes and look at the fields, for they are already white for harvest!" Sometimes Christians excuse themselves from witnessing by saying that their family or friends are not ready to believe. Jesus, however, makes it clear that around us a continual harvest waits to be reaped. Don't let Jesus find you making excuses. We ought to be always on the look-out for anyone within our circles who is ready to hear God's word but also we should be ready to do anything in our capacity that is incremental to God's mission (ministry).

For this reason, I deem it necessary to share with you some crucial things that courageous people who have a will power do that are so applicable to our spiritual and ministerial lives but also to our secular lifestyles (as developed by Forbes.com).

The 16 Things Mentally Strong People Do

a)   They move on – they don't waste time feeling sorry for themselves;
b)   They keep control – they don't give away their power;
c)   They embrace change – welcome challenges and face uncertainty head on;
d)   They stay happy – don't complain and don't waste energy on things they can't control;
e)   They are kind – fair and unafraid to speak up. They don't worry about pleasing others;
f)   They are willing to take calculated risks – make risk-benefits analysis before taking action;
g)   They invest their energy in the present – don't dwell on the past;
h)   They accept full responsibility for their past behavior – don't make the same mistakes over and over;
i)   They celebrate other people's success – they don't resent that success;
j)   They are willing to fail – they don't give up after failing and they see every failure as a chance to improve;
k)   They are prepared to work and succeed on their own merit – they don't feel the world owes them anything;
l)   They have staying power – they don't expect immediate results;
m)   They evaluate their core beliefs – and modify as needed;
n)   They think productively – replace negative thoughts with productive ones;
o)   They tolerate discomfort – accept their feelings without being controlled by them;
p)   They reflect on their progress daily – take time to consider their achievements and where they are going;

55. COME TO THE SAVIOR MAKE NO DELAY (C.H 1155)

This invitational hymn was composed by George Frederick Root (1820 – 1895). Though he was born in Sheffield, Massachusetts, his father moved to North Reading when the boy was six years old, and he spent his entire youth there. He was always fond of music, not singing at all as a boy, but played upon every kind of instrument. Though his relatives and friends despised music, his ambition to become a successful musician was strongly supported by his mother. A most important event to him was meeting Dr. Lowell Mason and being accepted as a bass singer in the celebrated Bowdoin Street choir. Dr. Root authored about seventy-five books, nearly two hundred songs in sheet form, and many popular gospel songs. He occupies a prominent place in the musical history of the U.S.A While teaching in New York State Institution for the Blind, he continued his summer work with the celebrated Mason and Webb in Teachers' Classes. Up to the year 1849, he had written just little music (only a few hymn tunes) while in Boston. At the Institution, there was a young lady, a former pupil, but now a teacher who had shown some poetic talent. He asked her to help him with the words. He would suggest in prose and she would put it into rhyme; she did it so well that it seldom needed any alteration. This lady was the now famous Fanny Crosby (he did a great job in promoting Crosby's career in Christian music). He used to work in a team with other principal teachers and also celebrated contributors to hymnology such as: Messrs. Mason, Webb, Root, Hastings, and Bradbury. Dr. Root was the author of about 75 books, close to 200 songs, and many popular gospel songs.

This beautiful hymn is a humble invitation to all humanity to come to Jesus without making any delay because our Savior is patiently waiting for any one can heed to his gracious calling. In his appeal, Dr. Root makes reference to Matthew 11:28 where Christ Himself pleaded with all those who are weary and heavy-laden by loads of earthly care to come and find for themselves rest from the fatal storms of this world. He also makes a ground-breaking declaration that everyone on earth can easily have their sins pardoned totally since Christ took over the burden of guilt and sin (through a ransom he paid at Calvary) that we inherited from our ancestor Adam.

Making Bad People Good

Scripture; 1 Peter 2:24, "Jesus bore our sins…that we, having died to sins might live for righteousness.".

A prison psychiatrist exclaimed, "I can cure a person's madness but not his badness. The only way to make bad people 'good' is to expose them to the gospel of kindness".

Even Charles Darwin, the originator of the evolutionistic thinking admitted this; he wrote to a certain Evangelist, "Your services have done more for our village in a few months than all our efforts for many years. We have not been able to reclaim a single drunkard, but through your services I don't know that there is a drunkard left in the village!" It is said that later, Darwin visited a certain part of South America and he was greeted by horrific scenes beyond description which included high crime rate, promiscuity, permissiveness among children, drunkenness, and indifference. But on returning thereafter a missionary had worked among the people in that community, he was amazed at the change. He acknowledged that the gospel doesn't only declare people right with God but it also transforms lives. He was so moved by what he saw, he resolved to contribute money to the mission until his death. Later reports indicate that Darwin was eventually impressed by the goodness of the gospel and he was considering returning to Christian roots (faith). However, it is not conclusive whether he finally yielded to Christ's gracious invitation completely to renounce his defective movement that created the evolutionistic philosophy of earth's creation account.

Frederick Roots' hymn reveals how Christ's loving invitation has the potential to render bad people (drug addicts, murderers, robbers, egocentric, pride, promiscuous folks) into good people before the sight of God but also very incremental citizens in any given society. The songs assures us that Christ exceedingly loves us despise our criminal and evil records since it is the sick and sinful children of God that made Him leave the glory in heaven.

Besides sin, the Christian church is one of the greatest global equalizers of all time since it has the potential of bringing people of varying social status, educational attainments, income classes, spirituality into one family that is guided by God's word.

This hymn, along with another similar one titled, "Have you been to Jesus?" authored by Hoffman are favorites at funeral services. These hymns are basically sung by drunkards, drug addicts, social outcasts, and the like because of their theme (a fundamental Christian belief) that we all sinned and fell short of God's glory. Thus, given that fact that sin is a global equalizer regardless of social status and religious orientation, we all ought to come to the Savior without any delay because He truly loves us sinners and those burdened by guilt. This is why Dr. Root together with Hoffman, and also guided by the Pauline writings in Roman 3:1ff affirm that no one is righteous because we all sinned. It is only the precious blood of Jesus, our Savior that can cleanse us of all iniquities and folly. Much as many 'sinner' groups love this hymn due to its equalizing element and also the invitation that goes to the whole world, they should, along with all of us, yield or heed Jesus' gracious appeal and His longsuffering. We should not simply enjoy the reality and atmosphere that, after all, we are all sinners and so no one should look at my sinfulness.

56. LOVINGLY, TENDERLY CALLING (C.H 572)

This divine hymn was composed by Ogden William Augustine (1841 – 1897). Though he was born in Ohio, his family moved to Indiana in 1847. From childhood, Ogden showed musical talent, and in his lifetime he published 98 tunes, 9 hymn texts and 18 songbooks. He was a great teacher of music and conducted large choirs at various conventions in USA and Canada. He was also the composer of another popular and beautiful hymn, "Seeking the Lost" which has a similar theme as this hymn.

The hymn "Lovingly, Tenderly Calling" brings in a picture of a shepherd who is courteously pleading to us to get back to the fold (due to his undying love despite our wickedness, indifference and lack of regard to his goodness so that we can procure eternal and divine rest for our troubled souls regardless of our stages in life (be it young or old). This appeal reminds me of one of David's all-time best - Psalms 23 - that has brought a lot of peace to people's lives across generations and across religious orientations – this is because Christians, and some Non-Christians have been enormously blessed with this Psalms 23 and they hold it dearly as their own emblem world-over. Below is an analysis of various terms as used in Psalms 23, along with their amplification, application and fitting in the contemporary context and perspective which all emphasize God's qualities in relation to His children which gives us a lot of hope and courage to face uncertainty, hardships and challenges with courage and boldness, by God's grace.

The Psalms 23 Redefined
The Lord is my Shepherd …that's Relationship!;
I shall not want…..that's Supply!;
He maketh me to lie down in green pastures …that's Rest!;
He leadeth me besides the still waters….that's Refreshment!;
He restoreth my soul…..that's Healing!;
He leadeth me in the paths of righteousness….that's Guidance!;
For His name sake…..that's Purpose!;
Yea, though I walk through the valley of the shadow of death….that's Testing!;
I will fear no evil….that's Protection!;

For thou hart with me…..that's Faithfulness!
They rod and thy staff, they comfort me…..that's Discipline!;
Thou prepares a table before me in the presence of mine enemies…..that's Hope!;
Thou annointest my head with oil….that's Consecration!;
My cup runneth over….that's Abundance!;
Surely goodness and mercy shall follow me all the days of my life…..that's Blessing!;
And I will dwell in the house of the Lord……that's Security!
Forever……….that's Eternity!
In describing the Lord as a shepherd, David wrote out of his own experience given that he had spent his early years caring for sheep (1 Samuel 16:10ff). Sheep are completely dependent for provision, guidance and protection. The New Testament addresses Christ as a good Shepherd (John 10:11) and as the great Shepherd (Hebrews 13:20); thanks to the goodness of the shepherd, we are not frightened but obedient followers – wise enough to follow the one who will lead us in the right places. This alludes to discipleship qualities on the part of Christians.

Our shepherd knows the "green fields and peaceful streams" that will restore us. We will reach these places only by following him obediently. Rebelling against the Shepherd's leading is actually rebelling against our own best interest. Death casts a frightening shadow over us because we are entirely helpless in its presence; we can struggle with our enemies such as pain, suffering, disease, injury but strength and courage cannot overcome death. Only one person can walk with us through death's dark valley and bring us safely to the other side – the God of life, our Shepherd.
The Shepherd calls us for our own good, therefore, let us obey and follow as He lovingly and tenderly calls us today. This was Ogden's primary message that has blessed hymn singers for more than one and a half centuries ago and it still sounds to us now as if it was just composed yesterday.

57. IT MAY BE AT MORN (SDAH 207)

1)   It may be at morn, when the day is awaking,
        When sunlight through darkness and shadow is breaking,
        That Jesus will come in the fullness of glory, To receive from the world His own.

Refrain
O Lord Jesus, how long, how long,   Ere we shout the song?
Christ returneth, Hallelujah!   Hallelujah! Amen, Hallelujah! Amen

2)   It may be at midday, it may be, it may be at twilight
        It may be, perchance, that the blackness of midnight
        Will burst into the light in the blaze of His glory, When Jesus receives His own.

This advent hymn was authored by H.L Turner (who is arguably believed to have been Colonel Henry Lathrop Turner (1845 – 1915), who evidently lived in anticipation of the second advent of the Lord Jesus Christ. He is believed to have been a prominent citizen of Chicago and enjoyed different professions in the course of his life (a soldier, banker, and a poet). He was a man of many talents destined for prominence. Born in Ohio in 1845, he began college in his early teens and hurriedly finished his degree before he came of age for service in the civil war. He became Lieutenant at 20 years of age. After the war he turned to Journalism. He later tried real estate and banking and became one of the most prominent money lending men in the booming industrial city in Chicago.

Scripture - Matthew 24:36 "However, no one knows the day or hour when these things will happen, not even the angels in heavens or the Son himself – only the Father knows". It is good that we don't know exactly when Christ will return; if we knew the precise date, we might be tempted to be lazy in our work for Christ. Worse yet, we might plan to keep sinning and then turn to God right at the end. As we prepare for heaven, we must remember that there is work to do here. And we must keep on doing it until death or until we see the real cosmic return of our glorious Lord.

The song centers our attention on that day and hour when Jesus will come back. There has been lots of skepticism regarding His return and lots of errors/theories on this biblical doctrine but someday "Christ Returns".

Stanza 1: Christ will return to receive His own, and this is the most prominent promise not only of the New Testament times but of all times since we had an experience of sin and death.

Stanza 2: We don't know when Christ will come back, and His coming is pictured as a thief in the night as Paul illustrates in 1 Thessalonians 5:1ff.
Stanza 3: At Christ's coming, He will be glorified with His saints and angels.
Stanza 4: We should be prepared for the time when He will return. Some will be privileged to be alive and others dead when He comes.
Chorus: There is use of words/vocabulary that joyfully looks forward to the time of His return.

Choosing from one of Colonel Turner's life professions, I would wish to expound on music and its contribution to mental, physical but also social development of an individual and society at large. There is need to deliberately establish its effect on an individual's and societal growth and resilience.

Music Basics

Globally, music has been instrumental in rallying morale among people such as the army, at the funeral, sports, etc. Besides, music has served as a repository (store) of values and cultures in many societies. Furthermore, it has been used to keep harmony among people – it is actually advised to sing a hymn/song before and during the sermon to gather people's attention.

Music is the universal language that everyone understands regardless of their ethnic background or origin, including babies. Rhythm is one of the principle universal laws that everyone must obey regardless of natural differences amongst humans. That is why everything that is done on earth has a rhythm ie moving, eating, blinking, laughing, breathing, and even crying; they all follow a certain pattern that is musically referred to as a 'rhythm'.

Harmonious music contributes 60% in the growth of mental faculty (brain) of a child. It is worth noting that this should be done between 7 months in the womb (fetus) and the first 3 years on earth since human physiological development research has it that almost 85% of a person's growth takes place up to 3 years. Therefore, exposing children (or better enough, involving them in godly and good music activities) significantly enhances the mental development. This reminds me of my daughter's (Gracia Namuli) experience who broke into a popular 'Baby Jesus' song when she was traveling in Taxi (Matatu) with her mum at just 10 months of age. The passengers were held in shock thinking that the baby had something wrong, probably an unfamiliar spirit over her – little did they know that she began getting accustomed to music when still in the womb. Actually, by the time she was born, she could easily connect to many things that we used to do while she was still in the womb, majorly music-related experiences.

Hymns are a distillation of the experience of grace and relationship between God and humanity in various circumstances; and it is in such experience that theology and doctrine meet human situations. These are a fertilization of God at work, and men circumstances that finally produce hymns. All these hymns have a cultural and aesthetic forms and heritage, and are largely a distillation of doctrine and theology synthesizing human life. These are a product of people's encounter with God's grace. Music has a powerful influence in lifting the hearts to God and we should endeavor, in our songs of praise, to approach as nearly as possible to the harmony of the heavenly choirs. Thus, the proper training of the voice is an important feature in education and should not be neglected. Singing, as a part of religious service, is as much an act of worship as is prayer. Thus, the spiritual experiences of Christian song writers become the prayers and Christian lifestyles of the worshippers as they sing in the contemporary generation.

58. A SHELTER IN THE TIME OF STORM
(SDAH 476)

1) The Lord's our Rock, in Him we hide,
A shelter in the time of storm;
Secure whatever ill betide,
A shelter in the time of storm.

Chorus
Mighty Rock in a weary land,
Cooling shade on the burning sand;
Faithful guide for the pilgrim band –
A shelter in the time of storm.

2) A shade by day, defense by night,
A shelter in the time of storm;
No fears alarm, no foes affright,
A shelter in the time of storm.

3) The raging floods may round us beat,
A shelter in the time of storm;
We find in God a safe retreat,
A shelter in the time of storm.

4) O Rock divine, O Refuge dear,
A shelter in the time of storm;
Be Thou our helper ever near,
A Shelter in the time of storm.

This hymn of solace was composed by Pastor Vernon John Charlesworth (1839 – 1915). He wrote a couple of gospel songs but this particular hymn is the only one in common use today. Charlesworth served as a co-pastor of the old Surrey Chapel, and five years later, he was appointed headmaster of Charles Spurgeon's Stockwell Orphanage.

In 1880, Pastor Vernon wrote the text of this beautiful hymn and in 1885, Ira Sankey (a guru in composing tunes in that generation) saw the hymn printed in a small London paper called The Postman. It was being sung by the fishermen in the north coast of England, to what Sankey called "a weird minor tune." This prompted him to write the more pleasant melody, and also added the refrain himself. It is said that Sankey had given the song the title, "My God is the Rock of My Refugee" which was a direct reference to Psalms 94:22 but later the title was revisited to what we currently have in most hymnbooks.

By and large, Charlesworth's hymn celebrates our safety and security in Christ, and the Word of God, especially the Psalms and other Biblical resources remind us of the Almighty's protecting care and His being our Rock in whom we hide.

The twin images of a storm, and a sheltering rock, are used frequently in Scripture to depict the trials and troubles of the believer's life, and the protecting care of the Lord. It's not surprising that many of these appear in the book of Psalms, which is a book representing the devotional and musical life of the saints; and it was also the hymn book of Israel, and the early Christian church.

It is worth noting that the Lord Jesus Christ is described as a rock, and as the foundation and chief cornerstone of the church (Eph. 2:19-20; I Pet. 2:6-7). "For no other foundation can anyone lay than that which is laid, which is Jesus Christ" (I Cor. 3:11). The Apostle Paul also says that He is the same One who aided Israel in the wilderness: "That Rock was Christ" (I Cor. 10:4). Whenever we find ourselves tossed about by the storms of life, it is a wonderful comfort to know that the Lord of the storm is with us in the midst of our challenges and desperation.

Escape from Trouble (Kendu Bay to Kisumu)

This scenario happened during one of my study adventures across Kenya, and after having travelled extensively across this country without any major problem even in some communities that were believed to have weird cultural practices. Kendu-Bay is situated in the formerly Great Nyanza Province, a place where Christianity is visibly prevalent even to an unobservant tourist. One day, as I was crossing from Kendu-Bay to Kisumu (one of the major towns and Counties in Kenya), I was really rushing to meet someone there which saw me hire a Taxi (Special hire car) lest I reach late and miss my appointment. On reaching the stage at the high way, I was practically forced by a Taxi driver to board his Taxi and not to take a Matatu, on grounds that he only needed two passengers; surprisingly no sooner had I entered, than the two guys (driver and his colleague) also entered the Taxi. On trying to inquire what happened to the second passenger, they simply told me that they were no longer interested in another passenger, that luckily enough they had gotten one on board. Our God hardly exposes us to challenges of which we have no idea of maneuvering at all (without equipping us prior to such incidents).Fortunately enough, I had been in such situations at least three times in Kampala (Uganda) whereby I could board a Matatu (Taxi as it is called in Uganda) but very soon to realize that it is manned by robbers but God has always helped me escape, by His grace, without being robbed nor harmed. Given such experiences, God had been arming me with techniques that robbers use to trap their victims, when this Kendu-Bay scenario happened, within just a moment of boarding the Taxi I had already realized that I was in deep trouble that could only require God's intervention basically because I was in a foreign land. Soon these guys noticed that I was suspicious of all their moves and they had realized that I was a foreigner since I was using a mixture of English and Swahili, they then switched to Luo (which of course I couldn't comprehend at all given my Bantu ethnic background). As the guy in the back seat would try to attack me, I was already monitoring him through the side mirror; and when he realized that, he changed his position and relocated where the side mirror couldn't capture him, which also saw me change my sitting posture, then the guy did many funny things including locking doors. Luckily enough, whenever they could try to forcefully attack me along the way where there were no vehicles passing and maybe nobody along the way, God would save me through one way or the other. Finally, I realized at some point that there was a trading center ahead, so I pretended as if the person I was rushing to meet in Kisumu had called and that he was cancelling our appointment after some negotiations, as soon as we reached the trading center I ordered them to stop so that I can clearly interact with this guy on phone. No sooner had they stopped than I jumped off the car and began negotiating how much they wanted me to give them (better in an intelligent and polite way lest they realize that I had understood their plan); actually I remained pretending on phone even during the negotiations up to 20 minutes when they had left, since they drove just 100 meters and continued monitoring me. When they realized after close to 20 minutes that I was still on phone, I believe that my God convinced them that my call was genuine and that I had not consciously intercepted their evil plans. So, I witnessed God's saving hand that day since exactly the same period there was a prominent lawyer who had been killed and his body drowned in the river, so what would have happened of me a foreigner!! In the midst of deep trouble, God protected me from evil men as my shelter in the time of storm.

59. SAFELY THROUGH ANOTHER WEEK
(SDAH 612 A & M 391)

1)   Safely through another week God has brought us on our way;
       Let us now a blessing seek, on th'approaching Sabbath day;
       Day of all the week the best, emblem of eternal rest,
       Day of all the week the best, emblem of eternal rest.

2)   While we seek supplies of grace, Through the dear Redeemer's name;
       Show Thy reconciling face, Take away our sin and shame;
       From our worldly care set free, May we rest this day in Thee;
       From our worldly care set free, May we rest this day in Thee.

3)   May Thy gospel's joyful sound conquer sinners, comfort saints;
       Make the fruits of grace abound, bring relief for all complaints;
       Thus may all our Sabbaths prove till we join the church above,
       Thus may all our Sabbaths prove till we join the church above!

This hymn was composed in 1770s by an Anglican priest, Rev. John Newton (1725 – 1807). He was born in London to a father (who was rarely at home because he was the captain of a ship), and to a mother who was a Dissenter. His mother taught him the importance of praying and filling his mind with Holy Scriptures with an objective of preparing him for ministry. Unfortunately, she died when young Newton was around 7 years. He resolved to join his father's ship at 11 years; and this marked the beginning of his moral and spiritual degeneration to the point of becoming a reckless and godless sailor blaspheming God like nothing. After a series of maritime adventures, he linked up with a West African ship that was heavily involved in slave trade (which compounded his spiritual and moral problems to the point of becoming an unscrupulous slave dealer and later almost a slave of this nasty trade himself). In 1748, through the working of God's grace, he was later found by a captain who was working under the direction of Newton's father who took him back to England; but on their way back, the ship was almost wrecked in a terrible storm. This experience, together with other pleadings from the Holy Spirit reminded him of his Christian background from his mother but he still continued with sailing for six years as captain of a slave ship (with a lot of guilt in his conscience). Later in mid-1700s, Newton abandoned the sea for another profession. He later pursued a career in ministry in the 1760s, inspired by his encounters with the Wesley brothers (Charles and John) and other Christian ministers. This saw him being ordained and appointed to Olney in Buckinghamshire; and records have him as having been a passionate preacher, faithful visitor to his flock and prayer warrior for which he wrote particular hymns. Most of his hymns were designed to promote faith and comfort Christians. He is especially remembered for his life-long and also dying words at his advanced age of 82 years, "My memory is nearly gone, but in life I remember two things – that I am a great sinner and that Jesus is a great Savior".

The hymn is believed to have been written for and also entitled "Saturday Evening", which according to Newton was the time immediately preceding the day of rest; and the inspiration seems to have come from Leviticus 23:32. This hymn first appeared in Psalms and Hymns, in 1774. Then, in 1779, it was published in Olney Hymns, the famous book by John Newton and William Cowper.

Theory of Competitive Advantage

In strategic management, there are four fundamentals of establishing an institution's Competitive advantage, which are squarely based on resources. We believe that for any institution to survive and out-compete its rivals:
- These resources should be very different from those of the competitors, and they should be immobile lest they are acquired by the competitor.
- They should add value: they should be valuable so as to create value strategies.
- These resources should be rare to get; and they should not be copied/imitated.
- There should not be substitutes that can deliver the same benefits that your resources can. This is because competitors can capitalize and develop strategies on the substitutes which has been a winning strategy world-over.

In the same vein, God designed His holy Sabbath, just like the resources discussed above, to be very different from all the six days of the week – by resting on it; blessing it and finally sanctifying it (setting it apart from the days of creation – Genesis 1:31; 2:1-3). Besides, the Sabbath adds value because it is a recreation from whole six days of toil – basically to give humankind an opportunity to reflect upon God and His creative power. This creates value strategies to Christians because it helps them to make use of this weekly rest to re-examine and evaluate their social relationships, spirituality in this evil world but also refocus their set goals for another week. Finally, according to the Bible there is no available substitute to God's holy day.

60. AMAZING LOVE: AND CAN IT BE …………..

1) And can it be that I should gain
An interest in the Savior's blood?
Died He for me, who caused His pain—
For me, who Him to death pursued?
Amazing love! How can it be,
That Thou, my God, shouldst die for me?
Amazing love! How can it be,
That Thou, my God, shouldst die for me?

2) 'Tis mystery all: th'Immortal dies:
Who can explore His strange design?
In vain the firstborn seraph tries
To sound the depths of love divine.
'Tis mercy all! Let earth adore,
Let angel minds inquire no more.
'Tis mercy all! Let earth adore;
Let angel minds inquire no more.

3) He left His Father's throne above
So free, so infinite His grace—
Emptied Himself of all but love,
And bled for Adam's helpless race:
'Tis mercy all, immense and free,
For O my God, it found out me!
'Tis mercy all, immense and free,
For O my God, it found out me!

4) Long my imprisoned spirit lay,
Fast bound in sin and nature's night;
Thine eye diffused a quickening ray—
I woke, the dungeon flamed with light;
My chains fell off, my heart was free,
I rose, went forth, and followed Thee.
My chains fell off, my heart was free,
I rose, went forth, and followed Thee.

5) Still the small inward voice I hear,
That whispers all my sins forgiven;
Still the atoning blood is near,
That quenched the wrath of hostile Heaven.
I feel the life His wounds impart;
I feel the Savior in my heart.
I feel the life His wounds impart;
I feel the Savior in my heart.

6) No condemnation now I dread;
Jesus, and all in Him, is mine;
Alive in Him, my living Head,
And clothed in righteousness divine,
Bold I approach th'eternal throne,
And claim the crown, through Christ my own.
Bold I approach th'eternal throne,
And claim the crown, through Christ my own.

This hymn was composed by Charles Wesley (1701 – 1788), who was born in Lincolnshire by a village Anglican priest who had 18 children. Wesley, his brother and George Whitefield, along with some other Christians founded the "Holy Club" which adopted habits of methodical study, prayer, devotions and fasting; besides attending communion services regularly and practicing charitable works. The adherence to such strict rules and regular methods gave the name "Methodists". He led a very controversial life in ministry to the point that once he was forbade from preaching due to his theological views, which saw him along with his brother John Wesley become itinerant preachers across England, Scotland and Wales.

The hymn in question is believed to have been written soon after Charles' conversion around May 1738, firstly appearing under the title "Free Grace". This song is a reflective study of the atonement by one who was deeply touched by the mystery and significance of the death of our Lord Jesus Christ. Charles read Martin Luther's book on Galatians and was convicted. He wrote, "At midnight I gave myself to Christ, assured that I was safe, whether sleeping or waking. I had the continual experience of His power to overcome all temptation, and I confessed with joy and surprise that He was able to do exceedingly abundantly for me above what I can ask or think.

Forgiven: Paid by the King

Scripture - Colossians 3:13, (NLV) "Make allowance for each other's faults, and forgive anyone who offends you. Remember the Lord forgave you, so you must forgive others."

A story is told of the late Czar Nicholas of Russia (Russian king) who had deployed his friend's son as treasurer for the Russian army. One day, through an impromptu visit at the army Headquarters, as all other offices were closed at midnight, one office (surprisingly the treasurer's office) had light; and on opening, the young man was laying asleep on his table. This was due to the fact that he had failed to reconcile the army's books of account since he had misappropriated or misused the army's funds in gambling (betting) that the debt was so huge for anyone to repay. As he planned to shoot himself, sudden sleep overtook him and that is when the king entered his office; given that this young man was his friend's son, he wrote down below the figure of his debt that, "I, the King of Russia will pay for the debt" in red pen and then signed. On waking up, as he was planning to resume from where he had ended before sleeping, but he was later relieved by the redemptive words from the king that he had written even without the young man's notice, and confirmed by his signature which the young man recognized very well.

Just like this young man, all are free to receive this forgiveness paid in full by accepting by faith the amazing love of Jesus Christ.

61. GUIDE ME, O THOU GREAT JEHOVAH (SDAH 538)

1) Guide me, O Thou great Jehovah,
Pilgrim through this barren land.
I am weak, but Thou art mighty;
Hold me with Thy powerful hand.
Bread of Heaven, Bread of Heaven,
Feed me till I want no more;
Feed me till I want no more.

2) Open now the crystal fountain,
Whence the healing stream doth flow;
Let the fire and cloudy pillar
Lead me all my journey through.
Strong Deliverer, strong Deliverer,
Be Thou still my Strength and Shield;
Be Thou still my Strength and Shield.

3) Lord, I trust Thy mighty power,
Wondrous are Thy works of old;
Thou deliver'st Thine from thralldom,
Who for naught themselves had sold:
Thou didst conquer, Thou didst conquer,
Sin, and Satan and the grave,
Sin, and Satan and the grave.

4) When I tread the verge of Jordan,
Bid my anxious fears subside;
Death of deaths, and hell's destruction,
Land me safe on Canaan's side.
Songs of praises, songs of praises,
I will ever give to Thee;
I will ever give to Thee.

5) Musing on my habitation,
Musing on my heav'nly home,
Fills my soul with holy longings:
Come, my Jesus, quickly come;
Vanity is all I see;
Lord, I long to be with Thee!
Lord, I long to be with Thee!

This pleading hymn was composed by William Williams (1717 – 1791), who was born in Llandovery to a wealthy farmer, who wanted William to study medicine but he dedicated himself to ministry, and was later ordained as deacon in the Established Church in 1740. Nevertheless, his evangelistic views saw him join the Calvinist Methodists, where he became an itinerant preacher travelling extensively in Wales. He was one of Wales' greatest hymn writers in the late 18th Century (known for having composed at least 800 hymns in Welsh and 100 hymns in English). He also wrote poems, tracts and periodicals. He was a layman-preacher and he ministered for 40 years travelling almost 100,000 miles, on foot or horseback.

Williams was quite concerned over the obvious lack of good hymns in Welsh, and given this challenge, he purposed to produce better songs to the point that he was later branded the "Welsh Watts" in reference to the prolific English hymn writer, Isaac Watts. Other music enthusiasts called him the "Sweet singer of Wales." It is worth noting that this hymn in question was composed in Welsh but it was translated by his friend Peter Williams; in fact, it is still sung at the beginning of outdoor sporting events in Wales. The hymn relates Christian life to the march of the Israelites through the wilderness of Sinai to the Promised Land of Canaan, under the all-knowing guidance of the Almighty God. We have the joy of knowing that God guides, protects and provides for each of us; that is majorly why we can sing songs of praise. But God created the family institution on earth as a crucial guide to responsibility and a pillar to social development and nation-building at large.

The Family: Earthly Guide to Responsibility
This is the strength of our faith and God's original plan for the manifestation of love and unity;
Foundation of society, basis of individual responsibility and the building block of character;
Starting point for generations, and the strength of nation;
The center of each life and determination of each thought patterns, and establishment of people's dreams;
Strength of courageous men and starting point for destiny;
Is the pruning ground for integrity and springboard for self-esteem;
The mirror of history and inheritance, and a starting point of excellence;
The example of order (instruction), authority and provision for experience.

Apart from religious influence, the family is the most important unit of society. The family and the home can never exert their proper influence while ignoring the biblical standards. The Bible calls for discipline and a recognition of authority; if children don't learn this at home, they will go out into society without the proper attitude towards authority and law. The only way to provide the right home for one's children is to put the Lord above them, and fully instruct then in the ways of the Lord.

The way God longs to guide His children in this earthly pilgrimage with the ultimate objective of leading them to inherit the Kingdom of God; is the same way that a family should be a guide to godliness, responsibility, morality and other crucial life values that would help its members to be socially acceptable and exhibit the basic levels of social responsibility.

62. JESUS, THOU HATH PROMISED (C.H 602)

1. Jesus, Thou hast promised
That where two or three
In Thy name have gathered,
Thou wilt present be;
And Thy word believing,
Now in pray'r we kneel;
Jesus, come and bless us;
Lord, Thyself reveal.

Chorus:
Jesus, come and bless us
While we linger here;
Jesus, come and bless us,
Be Thou ever near.

2. Jesus, Thou hast met us
Oft in seasons past,
But we need Thy presence
With us till the last;
Come, O blessed Saviour,
And Thy grace display;
Hear us and accept us;
Bless us while we pray.

3. Jesus, tune our voices
To Thy songs of praise;
Be in each petition
That to Thee we raise:
May our faith grow stronger,
And our hope more bright;
May our love be purer,
And our path more light.

This lovely hymn, and arguably our all-time favorite at family worship services, was composed by Eden Reeder Latta, (1839 -1915). He was born at Haw Patch, Indiana. Reeder Latta taught for a time in the public schools of Colesburg, Iowa and he wrote over 1,600 songs and hymns in his life-time. Records have it that he was childhood friend of William A. Ogden, a music guru of Latta's time.

This hymn is so lovely at home in that it was among the first hymns to be learnt and sung by my gorgeous daughter, Gracia Namuli, and whenever we are going to praise God before our family prayer in a brief family fellowship – this is the hymn that will always be on her lips or even on her young brother's choice. I think that it is due to the claim that Jesus has promised that where two or three in His name have gathered, Jesus will be present; and the fact that we can always count on His word, now we kneel and pray in faith; thus, Jesus come and bless us but also reveal yourself to us.

We always enjoy the 3rd Stanza: Jesus, tune our voices to your songs of praise; Be in each petition that to you we raise; May our faith grow stronger, and our hope more bright; May our love be purer and our path more light.

This hymn emphasizes fellowship and praise both at household and congregational levels, and encourages us that our loving Lord will always be with us and willing to bless our prayers/ petitions. Though primarily focused on corporate worship and prayer (both at household and congregational levels) due to its whole build-up, I'm going to orient this song to mission (evangelism). This is largely because there is a significant connection between our worship/prayer life and the passion for mission. We worship God for who He is – this ignites in us that fervent desire to respond to Christ's great commission of evangelism in a bid to joyously share the gospel of the kingdom with a desperate world that is visibly longing for a word of hope from their creator. Thus, it introduces an important aspect of consecrating ourselves as we head for mission in everything we do and all of our professional endeavors. This is basically because, everything we do and/or not do should be inspired by the ultimate goal of evangelism/ mission. This should remind us that all our initiatives must be people-centered since that is the bottom-line of our existence on earth and whatever we undertake should be inspired by that fact.

Mission Gist of the Church

The mission statement of the Christian church is derived from the great commission as given by Christ (the originator and master of the church) in Matthew 28:18ff. This is premised and/or can be summarized into one word, "People"- this is why, as a church and particularly the leadership, there is need to focus on people since the church is a people-centered entity. Leaders ought to understand people/ parishioners; work for them; mobilize people and build them for Christ's soon return not majoring in other simplistic and earthly things.

In Matthew 28:18-20, Jesus told his disciples to make more disciples as they preached, baptized, and taught. With this authority, He still commands us to tell others the Good News and make them disciples of the Kingdom. When someone is leaving or dying, his/her last words are very important (actually in Law, if it is testimony for a crime, it is called the "dying declarations" – which are held in much more higher esteem than even a living witness). Jesus left the disciples with these last words of instruction: they were under his authority, they were to make more disciples; they were to baptize and teach these new disciples to obey Christ; Christ would be with them always. Whereas in previous missions Jesus had sent his disciples only to the Jews, their mission from now on would be world-wide – since He is the Lord of the earth and his universal death empowers him to draw all nations to himself. We are to go – whether it is next door or to another country and make disciples; it is not an option but a command to all who call Jesus "Lord". We are not all evangelists in the formal sense but we have all received gifts that we can use to help fulfil the great commission; and as we obey, we have the comfort in the knowledge that Jesus is always with us.

63. TO GOD BE THE GLORY (SDAH 341)

1. To God be the glory, great things He has done;
   So loved He the world that He gave us His Son,
   Who yielded His life an atonement for sin,
   And opened the life gate that all may go in.

Refrain
Praise the Lord, praise the Lord,
Let the earth hear His voice!
Praise the Lord, praise the Lord,
Let the people rejoice!
O come to the Father, through Jesus the Son,
And give Him the glory, great things He has done.

2. O perfect redemption, the purchase of blood,
   To every believer the promise of God;
   The vilest offender who truly believes,
   That moment from Jesus a pardon receives.

3. Great things He has taught us, great things He has done,
   And great our rejoicing through Jesus the Son;
   But purer, and higher, and greater will be
   Our wonder, our transport, when Jesus we see

This worship hymn was composed by Frances Jane 'Fanny' Crosby (1820 – 1915); a daughter of John and Mercy Crosby, was born in Southeast, Putnam County, New York. It is as a writer of Sunday-school songs and gospel hymns that she is known wherever the English language is spoken, and, in fact, wherever any other language is heard. She was a champion among hymn writers (particularly women hymn writers) who were good and extraordinarily gifted with composing worship songs in a deliberate and purposed environment for worship.

It is worth noting that many composers of psalms, hymns and gospel songs wrote out of their unpleasant and nasty life experiences but not having deliberately purposed to compose such songs as worship music. Nonetheless, in a way, such songs found their place into worship services simply because of their musical structure and other considerations. For Crosby, despite her tragic background, she composed many of her worship songs in a background and/or with an objective of using it in worship service in her mind. Simply put, worship refers to having an encounter with God and appreciating His supremacy but also our inferiority. And in so doing, humanity is the actor, God is the audience and the ministers (be it pastors/ reverends/ etc or music leader) are the facilitators in the process of true worship. Among the fundamental stages in worship, there are: worshipping with our bodies (Roman 12:1ff); worshipping at our households; and, corporate/congregational worship.

The Vision of God

True worship is premised on having an encounter with God, which leads to giving a personal testimony on how God revealed Himself to you (as a response to that meeting – full of awe, glorifying and gratitude for who He is). This reminds me of Prophet Isaiah' experience during his encounter with God in Isaiah 6:1ff (which is also titled 'Isaiah's Cleansing and Call'), "It was in the year King Uzziah died that I saw the Lord. He was sitting on a lofty throne............. Holy, holy, holy is the Lord of Heaven's Armies! The whole earth id filled with His glory! .... (NLT)." It is worth noting that Isaiah was initially a palace prophet during King Uzziah's reign in BC 740s. He was entitled to a salary for his services, instructions from the king and so, he attributed his survival and well-being to king Uzziah's goodness. Simply put, from Isaiah Chapters 1 to 5, he had never encountered God nor appreciated His supremacy, provision and direction in his life because he had another master. But the beginning of Chapter 6 marks the conversion and/or encounter of Isaiah with the Almighty God, soon after the death of king Uzziah – which procured him an opportunity to personally meet God. This is actually why he glorifies Him, laments and acknowledge his sinfulness which later leads to true repentance, submission and worship. Before Isaiah could give prophetic messages partly based on king Uzziah's preferences and instructions that is why he was so judgmental and indifferent in his proclamations. But as soon as he encountered God, even his vocabulary changed and his whole outlook since he had begun a ministry under God's guidance and which was premised on understanding God but also that he himself was sinful just like other children of Israel.

Scripture – Galatians 1:1-5 "......Our God and Father, to whom be the glory forever and ever. Amen." This scripture also reveals Apostle Paul's encounter with God (as we recall that it is Christ himself who encountered Saul on his way to Damascus and later impressed on him His eternal truths. During this encounter, Paul witnessed the vision of God which led to his conversion and later in Galatian 1:1ff saw him glorify God in a special way (but beginning with clarifying on the authenticity of his apostolic calling), leading him to sideline all that was valuable to him in a bid to win Christ – the all-time invaluable choice. This same scripture inspired Crosby to compose this popular worship song in question. This song became so popular in Great Britain way before it actually received popularity in the USA, the country of its origin.

64. O DAY OF REST & GLADNESS
(SDAH 382   A & M 36)

1. O day of rest and gladness,
    O day of joy and light,
    O balm of care and sadness,
    most beautiful, most bright;
    on thee the high and lowly,
    before the eternal throne,
    sing, "Holy, holy, holy,"
    to the great Three in One.

2. On thee, at the creation,
    the light first had its birth;
    on thee for our salvation
    Christ rose from depths of earth;
    On thee our Lord victorious
    the Spirit sent from heaven,
    and thus on thee most glorious
    a triple light was given.

3. Thou art a port protected
    from storms that round us rise;
    a garden intersected
    with streams of paradise;
    thou art a cooling fountain
    in life's dry dreary sand;
    from thee, like Pisgah's mountain,
    we view our promised land.

4. Today on weary nations
    the heavenly manna falls;
    to holy convocations
    the silver trumpet calls,
    where Gospel light is glowing
    with pure and radiant beams,
    and living water flowing,
    with soul refreshing streams.

5. May we, new graces gaining
    from this our day of rest,
    attain the rest remaining
    to spirits of the blessed.
    And their our voices raising,
    to Father, Spirit, Son,
    for evermore be praising
    the blessèd Three in One

It was authored by Christopher Wordsworth (born in London in October 1807). Christopher was educated at University of Cambridge, and he won many prizes. He was ordained into Anglican ministry in 1833 and later became a Bishop of Lincoln, a position he held almost up to his death in March 1885. He is believed to have written at least 127 hymns, a Bible commentary, various books on history, classics, speeches and sermons. He was a prolific author (scholar) of different kinds of publications but this hymn is one of his all-time compositions that are still in popular use today. Little wonder because the hymn is based on an all-time biblical truth and creation memorial for all generations – the Sabbath.

This hymn was written in a bid to instil the doctrine of the Holy Sabbath. It was based on Psalms 118:24 "This is the day that the Lord has made; we shall rejoice and be glad in it". This scripture is derived from the Book of Psalms (which I already explained that it was the official hymnbook for the Hebrews at that time). Chapter 118, or simply put song 118 in the Psalms was composed by an anonymous author under the theme 'confidence in God's eternal love'- God's love is unchanging in the midst of changing situations. Frankly, there are times (days) when the last thing one wants to do is rejoice – mood is down, and situation is getting out of hand, and our sorrows or guilt is overwhelming. One can always relate to composers of psalms who often felt this way but in a special way, God gives us His holy day (the day of rest and gladness) despite our weekly toil and disappointments – His Sabbath should always revive us and help us to get a hope and encouragement as we plan to face yet another week of uncertainty.

Two Weeks of Creation

In a bid to better amplify on the uniqueness of the Sabbath (Day of Rest and Gladness), in the Bible, there are two weeks of creation:

a)   The week of the Genesis creation story that lasted for six days and God rested on the 7th day (Genesis 1:1 – 2:3; Exodus 20:11). This marked the beginning of life on earth and also creation of the created world that we now know; this saw the creation of the first Adam who was the ruler of all created beings.

b)   The final week of Jesus' life (commonly known among Christians as "the Passion Week") as recorded in the New Testament. It began with Christ's triumphal entry into Jerusalem and ended with His crucifixion. During this week, Jesus Christ, the new Adam, laid the foundation for the redemption and recreation of the human race by His sacrificial death on Calvary on Good Friday. Again He rested in the grave on Sabbath (Luke 23:54-56), and rose from death on the first day of a new week, commonly known as Easter Sunday (Matthew 28:1-8; Mark 16:1-9; Luke 24:1-5).

Both these weeks were very busy from the first day to the 6th day. However, in both accounts, God rested on the 7th day. The first week of creation was characterized by God's creative power; while the second week of creation was filled with God's redemptive power. In both accounts, the seventh-day was set apart for rest by God as an indicator that this day is one for global rest and gladness as the Anglican Bishop, Christopher Wordsworth emphasizes it in this particular hymn.

The Sabbath (day of the Lord) is the all-time memorial of God's creation and the everlasting reminder that God (and only Almighty God), not the simplistic evolution creation account nor the inconsistent Big Bang theory, created the universe and all its beauties. This Holy day is God's signature and also flagship symbol that He created the earth and heavens, and that they all belong to Him. It is imperative to note that the positioning of this seventh-day was not arbitrarily chosen or even stolen in by surprise, but it was God's design that it falls on the last (final) day of the week climaxing the weekly toil of God's people. This rest was actually the first 'public holiday' that Adam (which means humanity) celebrated, and it was meant to be celebrated for generations to come up to eternity.

65. WE'LL BUILD ON THE ROCK (SDAH 531)

1)   We'll build on the Rock, the living Rock, On Jesus the Rock of ages;
           So shall we abide the fearful shock, When loud the tempest rages.

Refrain
We'll build on the Rock, We'll build on the Rock
We'll build on the Rock, on the solid Rock, On Christ, the mighty Rock.

2)   Some build on the sinking sands of life, On visions of earthly treasure;
           Some build on the waves of sin and strife, Of fame, and worldly pleasure.

3)   O build on the rock forever sure, The firm and the true foundation;
           Its hope is the hope which shall endure, The hope of our salvation.

This challenging hymn was also authored by Franklin Edison Belden (1858 – 1945).The eldest of the five children of Stephen Belden and Sarah Harmon (the eldest sister of Ellen Harmon White – the pioneers, along with her husband, James White). He moved to Colorado in 1881, where he married Harriet MacDearmon, a woman with musical talent but the couple later moved to Battle Creek. Belden was so talented that he could write a new song within an hour; while the preacher was reading the morning scripture, he would then slip out and write a new hymn based on the text, which he and his wife would stand and sing. After the service he would give a copy to the preacher.

This Franklin Belden hymn was inspired by the remarkable words from Jesus in Matthew 7:24-25 (NKJV) "Therefore whoever hears these sayings of Mine, and does them, I will liken him to a wise a man who built his house on the rock………." These eternal words form part of the concluding discourse that many Bible students popularly refer to as "The sermon on the Mount of Olives"; which is arguably believed to be Christ's manifesto for His kingdom that was to come then. This sermon is said to one of the most, outstanding speeches that any human in history has made that truly touched its listeners' lives. The content of this sermon has not only significantly moved the lives of Christians but even non-Christian folks who have taken the care to read and study it since it introduced a whole new concept of living and belief systems. This sermon formed the basis of Belden's concept for this beautiful and easy to sing hymn. Building on the rock means hearing and responding not superficially but practicing total obedience. According to the words of Jesus, this will become the solid foundation to withstand the storms of life.

I always want to draw practical and simple life lessons from Mother Nature, and especially lifestyles from the animal kingdom. I would wish to link the resources from Belden's hymn to one of our beloved domestic birds – the hen; and, the listed virtues of the hen can be likened to the benefits that are gained from practicing total obedience to the Word of God in our daily life choices.

Ten Lessons from the Hen

She first lays enough eggs before sitting on them ……….. this is indicative of Good planning;

When she starts sitting on her eggs, she minimizes movements……….that's Discipline;

She physically loses weight while sitting on her eggs due to decreased feeding…….Sacrifice and Self-denial;

She can even sit on eggs from another hen………….. Indiscriminate and Generosity;

She sits on her eggs for 21 days, patiently waiting and even if they don't hatch she will still lay again…………………..Faith, Hope and Courage;

She detects unfertilized eggs and rolls them out………….. Sensitive and Discerning;

She abandons the rotten eggs and start caring for the hatched chicks even if it's only one………Wise, Conscious and Realistic;

No one can touch her chicks………………….Protective love;

She gathers all her chicks together……………. Unity of Purpose;

She doesn't abandon her chicks before they mature…………...Mentoring.

In conclusion, the two lives Jesus compares at the end of the sermon on the Mount have several points in common: they both build, they both hear Jesus' teachings, and they both experience the same set of circumstances in life. The difference between them is not caused by ignorance but by one ignoring what Jesus said. On the surface, their lives look similar; but the lasting structural differences will be revealed by the storms of life. This would ultimately turn out to affect even their eternal destiny.

66. GREAT IS THY FAITHFULNESS (SDAH 100)

1. "Great is Thy faithfulness," O God my Father,
   There is no shadow of turning with Thee;
   Thou changest not, Thy compassions, they fail not
   As Thou hast been Thou forever wilt be.

Chorus
"Great is Thy faithfulness!" "Great is Thy faithfulness!"
 Morning by morning new mercies I see;
All I have needed Thy hand hath provided—
 "Great is Thy faithfulness," Lord, unto me!

2. Summer and winter, and springtime and harvest,
   Sun, moon and stars in their courses above,
   Join with all nature in manifold witness
   To Thy great faithfulness, mercy and love.

3. Pardon for sin and a peace that endureth,
   Thine own dear presence to cheer and to guide;
   Strength for today and bright hope for tomorrow,
   Blessings all mine, with ten thousand beside!

This hymn was composed by Thomas Chisholm (1866 – 1960). Born in Kentucky, he authored more than 1,200 poems of which 800 were published and some were set to music by a couple of the contemporary best-known gospel song composers. He became a teacher at age 16 just after only an eighth-grade education. But he served as associate editor at Franklin Favorite and later of the Pentecostal Herald at the age of 21 years. In 1903, he was ordained a Methodist minister but due to ill health, he only served as pastor for one year, and later tried farming and life insurance agency business until his retirement in 1953 in New Jersey.

Thomas sent this hymn in 1923 to his coworker, William Runyan (a son of Methodist minister, who himself was ordained as Methodist minister at 21 years); who set it to music after a deep prayer to God that his tune would carry over its message in a worthy way. Since then, this hymn has touched many people's lives given the fact that it focuses and/or emphasizes that our Eternal God is always faithful.

Scripture – Lamentations 3:22-23 "The faithful love of the Lord never ends! His mercies never cease. Great is His faithfulness; His mercies begin afresh each morning". Jeremiah knew from personal experience about God's faithfulness. God had promised that punishment would follow disobedience, and it did. But God also had promised future restoration and blessing, and Jeremiah knew that God would keep us confident in His great promises for the future. Besides, the Lord's faithfulness and mercifulness gives us a practical example to also emulate the same grace and mercy to the world, which is heavily infested with self-centeredness, indifference and individualism. God's goodness should inspire us to manifest a Christ-like character by demonstrating mercy and sympathy to other.

Showing Sympathy

A popular story is told of a 17-year old girl, who after struggling with love relationship and other challenges of the teenage, resolved to take her own life as a resort for her exceeding anguish. This saw the parents undergo such unexplainable sorrow because they had lots of hope in their daughter. But among the many people who came to comfort and/or stand with this bereaved family, was one pastor who simply sat down in the living room next to the parents, and for a long time said nothing. He simply immersed himself in their grief, and then later, he began weeping until his tears ran dry; then, without saying a word, he got up and left. It is reported that, sometime later, the father told him how much he appreciated what the pastor had done; and that at such a time, he and his wife didn't need words, nor promises, nor counselling, nor nothing less than just expressing such raw sympathy as the pastor did. The father added, "I can't fully tell you how much your sympathy meant to us".

Social Capital

Social capital consists of positive, productive relationships that are just as valuable as money in the bank. When someone nurtures rapport with community leaders, asking them about community needs, and seeking their advice on responding to these needs, and following up with action – then one is building relationships that is technically referred to as "Social Capital". Each positive experience with people is like an investment in one's relationship; and then one's social capital continues to grow and one increases in value in people's eyes.

67. ABIDE WITH ME (SDAH 528)

1) Abide with me; fast falls the eventide;
The darkness deepens; Lord with me abide.
When other helpers fail and comforts flee,
Help of the helpless, O abide with me.

2) Swift to its close ebbs out life's little day;
Earth's joys grow dim; its glories pass away;
Change and decay in all around I see;
O Thou who changest not, abide with me.

3) Not a brief glance I beg, a passing word;
But as Thou dwell'st with Thy disciples, Lord,
Familiar, condescending, patient, free.
Come not to sojourn, but abide with me.

4) Come not in terrors, as the King of kings,
But kind and good, with healing in Thy wings,
Tears for all woes, a heart for every plea—
Come, Friend of sinners, and thus bide with me.

5) Thou on my head in early youth didst smile;
And, though rebellious and perverse meanwhile,
Thou hast not left me, oft as I left Thee,
On to the close, O Lord, abide with me.

6) I need Thy presence every passing hour.
What but Thy grace can foil the tempter's power?
Who, like Thyself, my guide and stay can be?
Through cloud and sunshine, Lord, abide with me.

7) I fear no foe, with Thee at hand to bless;
Ills have no weight, and tears no bitterness.
Where is death's sting? Where, grave, thy victory?
I triumph still, if Thou abide with me.

8) Hold Thou Thy cross before my closing eyes;
Shine through the gloom and point me to the skies.
Heaven's morning breaks, and earth's vain shadows flee;
In life, in death, O Lord, abide with me.

This gloally popular hymn was composed by an English Pastor, Henry Francis Lyte (1793 – 1889). He wrote many hymns but this particular hymn ranks as one of the finest hymns in the English language and hymnody.

Records indicate that Henry Lyte suffered from Asthma, and towards the end of his life he contracted tuberculosis. As his condition deteriorated, he reluctantly agreed to move to the south of France, in hopes that the warmer climate would help him. When he preached his last sermon, he was so weak he had to be assisted into the pulpit. In the evening of the same day he placed in the hands of his relative the text of this hymn (which was a product of earthly toil but also his intimate relationship with Christ), along with a tune he had written for it. Unfortunately, the change of climate did little help to him, soon after that incident, He died and was buried in Nice, France, just 3 months after he left England. Currently, his stirring prayer hymn lives on long after him and is now sung with a beautiful tune by William Henry Monk.

The opening lines were visibly inspired by the appeal of the couple on the road to Emmaus, who met the risen Christ, though at first they had not recognized Him. When they reached their home, they said to the Lord, "Abide with us, for it is toward evening, and the day is far spent" (Lk. 24:29). However, it's clear the author didn't have the close of day in view when he wrote, but the end of life; sunset is simply used as a metaphor for the subsiding out of "life's little day".

The abiding presence of the Lord is an assurance given to every believer. "Lo, I am with you always, even to the end of the age" (Matt. 28:20). "He Himself has said, 'I will never leave you nor forsake you'" (Heb. 13:5). Nor will this ever change, even in eternity (I Thess. 4:16-17). The song fits into the category of evening songs and is also in common usage during funerals given its allusion to the 'eventide' of life.

Alexander the Great's Death Wishes (Gist of Time)

It is said that on his death bed, he summoned his army Generals and gave them the following three wishes, which were of course in form of instructions:

a)   The best doctors should carry his coffin……..

b)   The wealth that he has amassed (money, medals, gold and other precious stones) should be scattered along the procession to the cemetery……………

c)   His hands should be let loose, so that they can hung outside the coffin for all to see!...

And below is the significance and implication of Alexander's wishes which procures us outstanding lessons to us who have witnessed the ends of all generations:

i)   "I want the best doctors to carry my coffin to demonstrate that in the face of death, even the best doctors in the world have no power to heal……"

ii)   "I want the road to my tomb to be covered with treasure so that everybody sees that material wealth acquired on earth will stay on earth………"

iii)   I want my hands to swing in the wind, so that people understand that we come to this world empty handed and we leave this world empty handed after the most precious treasure of all is exhausted, and that is: TIME.

We don't take to our grave any material wealth; Time is our most precious treasure because it is limited. We can produce more wealth but we can't produce more time. Therefore, when we give someone our time, we actually give that person a portion of our life that we will never take back since "Our time is our Life". The best present that one can give his/her family is one's time and to God, it is one's life (since life is representative of one's time).

68. I AM COMING TO THE CROSS (SDAH 307)

1)   *I am coming to the cross; I am poor and weak and blind;*
           I am counting all but dross, I shall fail salvation find

Chorus
I am trusting Lord in Thee, O Thou Lamb of Calvary;
Humbly at Thy cross I bow, save me Jesus save me now

4)   *Jesus comes! He fills my soul Perfected in Him I am;*
           I am every whit made whole Glory glory to the Lamb

This dedication hymn was composed by William McDonald, a Methodist Episcopal minister (1820 – 1901), born in Maine. For a number of years, he was editor of the "Advocate of Christian Holiness". In addition, he was a writer of biographies and religious books, but he also compiled and assisted in compiling a number of song books. At the age of 19 years, he had become a local preacher in the Methodist church and later served in various conferences. While a pastor in the city of Brooklyn, William felt the need of a hymn to aid seekers of heart purity while at the altar but it had to be something simple in expression, true to experience, and ending in the fullness of love. He was sitting in his study one day in 1870 in New York, when a line of thought came quickly into his head. He penned these thoughts on a paper, and in a short while the words of this gospel song were done.

This hymn contains words of a sinner's personal prayer expressing the decision to come to the cross to claim, receive and enjoy God's grace in its fullest. It connotes a recognition of human insufficiency that results in repentance that brings divine salvation full and free. It truly fulfils the writer's goal: a simple song for a poor sinner coming to the altar to receive Christ into the life.

But there is always a problem in our spiritual journey, and that is stagnating in spiritual growth which would pain our Savior Jesus Christ. Simply put, a Christian should have a deliberate growth in the spiritual life right after coming to the cross of Jesus. This spiritual development that is evidenced in a sinner's progressive growth in grace should be an indicator of reciprocating Christ's redemptive undertakings and power.

Growing in Grace

Scripture – 2 Peter 3:18 (NLT) "Rather, you must grow in the grace and knowledge of our Lord and Savior Jesus Christ. All glory to Him, both now and forever! Amen." Peter concludes his brief letter (second Epistle of Peter) as he began, urging his readers to grow in the grace and knowledge of the Lord and Savior Jesus Christ; that is, they were to get to know him better and better. This is the best way to discern false teaching. No matter where we are in our spiritual journey, or how mature we are in our faith, the sinful world will always challenge our faith. We still have much room for growth; everyday, we ought to draw closer to Christ so that we will be prepared to stand for truth in all circumstances.

Peter is believed to have made a record of preaching one sermon and 3000 people got baptized in one day. Below are some crucial elements of Growth in Grace:

i) Growth in Faith, which is a function of faith, love and hope;

ii) Bible study, which nourishes an individual's spiritual life and betters spiritual decision-making;

iii) Prayer, there is no other activity in life as important as that of prayer. Every other activity depends upon prayer for its best efficiency;

iv) Fellowship with God and other Christians;

v) Evangelism, which is quite outward-looking and widening the boundaries of the kingdom of God;

vi) Giving Testimony and witnessing. The biggest part of witnessing is actually not spoken but viewed and noticed by observers. That is why I love a certain Christian slogan, "Be the sermon!"

69. O PERFECT LOVE (SDAH 656   A & M 578)

O perfect Love, all human thought transcending,
Lowly we kneel in prayer before Thy throne,
That theirs may be the love which knows no ending,
Whom Thou forevermore dost join in one.

O perfect Life, be Thou their full assurance,
Of tender charity and steadfast faith,
Of patient hope and quiet, brave endurance,
With childlike trust that fears nor pain nor death.

Grant them the joy which brightens earthly sorrow;
Grant them the peace which calms all earthly strife,
And to life's day the glorious unknown morrow
That dawns upon eternal love and life.

Hear us, O Father, gracious and forgiving,
Through Jesus Christ, Thy coeternal Word,
Who, with the Holy Ghost, by all things living
Now and to endless ages art adored.

This lovely hymn was authored by Dorothy Frances Blomfield (1858 – 1932) at Finsbury Circus, London. She was initially an Anglican member, who actually married a Anglican minister – Gerald Gurney but in 1919, the couple converted to the Roman Catholic Church. From childhood, she is believed to have been a good poet, with a strong musical background.

Records have it that on one Sunday evening in 1883, the two Blomfield sisters, along with some friends were praising God in hymns at their home in Cumberland. Dorothy's sister was shortly to be married to her long time fiancé, and so the thoughts of this group of ladies turned to hymn for the wedding ceremony. Dorothy had composed the lyrics of the hymn using John Bacchus Dykes' tune, which lyrics didn't sound pleasant to her sister who complained as to why she would have a poet for a sister if she couldn't write suitable words for her favorite tune (by John Dykes – who composed a tune for the popular hymn "Holy, Holy, Holy! Lord God Almighty!"). This saw Dorothy go to a quiet place for at least 15 minutes and returned with the beautiful words to this hymn, which they all sang. It was later chosen to be the hymn for her sister's wedding and it didn't only bless worshipper on that wedding but up to now we still enjoy this lovely song, which is among the very few hymns absolutely dedicated to wedding ceremony.

Marriage: Making Your Spouse the Rarest Thing

Scripture – Isaiah 13:12 (NKJV) "I will make a man more precious than fine gold; even a man more than the golden wedge of Ophir". Actually, some Bible versions use the term 'rare' and 'precious' interchangeably. This biblical reference to 'man' alludes to both man and woman ie each partner is pledging to make his/her partner much more rare and precious than anything in the world. Ophir was known for its rare and valuable gold. It is thought to have been located on the southwestern coast of Arabia. This later turned out into a commercial center that had all tradable treasures during the biblical times. This trading environment rendered Orphil the most precious, desirable and sought after place of that time. In the marital context, marital vows should be a pledge to render one's partner much more rare and precious than any desirable thing on earth. This reminds me of one orator who make a comparison of two terms ie "wedding' and 'welding" since they both lead to bonding. He argues that the difference between them is actually what makes wedding unique: whereas for welding, bonding comes after sparks of fire which render the union permanent; for wedding, on the contrary, bonding comes first and then sparking and sparkling follows forever (according to God's design). This follows each partner rendering the other much more rare and scarce than Orphil or any other thing in this world.

This further reminds me of some indicators of rendering one's partner more rare and precious as reflected in the years that couples have spent in the marriage institution. Below are the wedding anniversaries as recognized globally (this is a selection according to the author's preference):

1st year	Paper Anniversary;
5th year	Wood Anniversary;
7th year	Bronze Anniversary (my wife and I celebrated this on 14th February 2017)
10th year	Tin Anniversary;
15th year	Crystal Anniversary;
35th year	Pearl Anniversary (my parents will be celebrating this year);
45th year	Sapphire Anniversary;
50th year	Golden Anniversary.

70. BLEST BE THE TIE THAT BINDS (C.H 608)

1) Blest be the tie that binds
    Our hearts in Christian love;
    The fellowship of kindred minds
    Is like to that above.

2) Before our Father's throne
    We pour our ardent prayers;
    Our fears, our hopes, our aims are one
    Our comforts and our cares.

3) We share each other's woes,
    Our mutual burdens bear;
    And often for each other flows
    The sympathizing tear.

4) When we asunder part,
    It gives us inward pain;
    But we shall still be joined in heart,
    And hope to meet again.

5) This glorious hope revives
    Our courage by the way;
    While each in expectation lives,
    And longs to see the day.

6) From sorrow, toil and pain,
    And sin, we shall be free,
    And perfect love and friendship reign
    Through all eternity.

This hymn was composed by Dr. John Fawcett (1740 – 1817), born in Lidget Green in England. Thanks to the ministry of G. Whitefield, he was converted at the age of sixteen, firstly in the Methodist Church but later joined the Baptist Church where he was even ordained as a minister.

In 1772, after having had a successful career in ministry at Wainsgate, York, he was invited to London to succeed the famous Dr. J. Gill as pastor of Carter's Lane, which invitation had been formally accepted. As he preached the farewell sermon at Wainsgate (already loaded his goods on a wagon for dispatching) but he had to do so before leaving, in the process the love and tears of his parishioners prevailed and he decided to stay at Wainsgate despite having to disappoint the London church. Besides, exactly twenty one years down the road, in 1793, he was again invited to become President of the Baptist Academy at Bristol but still he declined the offer.

One would be tempted to think that Fawcett had specialized in declining offers and/or disappointing others given the bond/fellowship that he used to enjoy with his people to the point that he felt he had a duty to preserve and uphold the social contract that he had subconsciously made with his people.

There are a diversity of bonds mentioned in the Bible such as the fellowship of believers, the marriage bond, among others but the term 'fellowship' refers to have a duty to live harmoniously with other believers based on love and the fact that you have made a social contract for which each party has to do its part (not disappointing each other). The major hindrance to enjoying a vital meaningful fellowship amongst Christian believers is failing to honor and/or uphold each one's part of the social contract, which leads to disappointments in all our relationships be it: marital, family, friendship, work, Christian, etc.

Disappointment: Surviving the Aftermaths

Simply put, disappointment can refer to undoing the appointment (breaching the social contract and/or commitments in our relationships); keeping in mind that all our relations (be it marital, family, church, school, neighborhood, work, etc) are premised on some unwritten agreements/ contracts that are bound by each party expecting the other part to behave responsibly in the way of fulfilling its expected role in the whole arrangement. Disappointment constitutes surprising the other party by not living according to the basic expected way and manner. In our appointments/ social contracts and/or relationships, we invest some of the most valuable resources: time, finance, trust, emotions, faith, energy, and even at times our families.

Largely, disappointments are caused by the following among different parties: over-expectation and over-anticipation, unmet needs, poverty, lack of self-awareness, personality clash, unwillingness to learn, poor life-skills (self-care, communication, etc..).

Disappointment is always short-lived but the storm that comes with/after it can be long-lived and so disastrous up to sudden death, since disappointment is a trigger but the storm is usually fatal. The storms and/or aftermath (outcomes) of disappointment can comprise the following: extreme anger, depression, shame, guilt, revenge, low self-esteem, self-blame, self-pity, self-denial.

But by and large, below are techniques and mechanisms of how one can survive the aftermaths (storms) of any given disappointment:

a) Since it can primarily be caused by the lack of self-awareness – whereby one party (A) unrealistically desires and/or expects a lot from another party (B), of which party (A) is not even worth. When one party understands itself, this will better its understanding of the other party that leads to rational expectation management systems between the two parties.

b) There is need to know one's foundation and/or family heritage – for instance, in marital affairs, if as a lady, all your aunties have had broken marital relationships, there is need to clinically scrutinize any marital counsels they give you in the face of any marital conflict, but also you ought to keep that fact/heritage in mind.

c) Let your feelings out – one should never be ashamed of expressing one's emotions since it is healthier to express emotions than suppressing them. Personally, I come from a background that find it weird for a man to express emotions like crying, being afraid, and being shocked, etc; I had been oriented in this line to the point that I had equally trained my son (Gentil, now 3 years) never to express emotions as a man. But it is of recent that I have learnt that, it is actually the strong men who do cry but weak ones suppress their emotions that leads them to become monsters because they are devoid of feelings and compassion. Medical research has actually showed that due to this fact, men die seven years earlier than women.

d) It is prudent to mourn the loss (since disappointment is a loss of relationship and/or trust). Allow oneself to go through the pain, if you don't then the pain will see its way through you; this has led many to be taken to mental rehabilitation facilities, and at the worst some have committed suicide.

e) One ought to take time and dress one's wounds since it is the natural way of healing (at times, no one may help you heal better that you can).

f) Rationalizing one's disappointment: it is at times logical to reason/rationalize, for instance, telling oneself that this is not as real and big a disaster as Tsunami, terrorist attack, flood that have ravaged hundreds of lives, not even equaled to a cancer. Then, this should give one reason to continue living, after all life is there. There is a saying, "It is not how much one runs from the rain but how much once danced in the rain"; this will brace you to learn how to cope with the challenge/ disappointment at hand instead of running away from that reality.

g) Expectation management: there is need to adjust our expectations from people regardless of how much trust we have built in them and other factors.

h) There is need to being nice to oneself during the disappointment: one ought to summon all energies to be calm and treat oneself to the best everything,

"In the midst of disappointment, we have the capacity to stand in the storm, and there are a diversity of lessons that can be learnt both in the calmness and in the storm".

i) It is imperative to keep off the company of negative people (who will always compound the crisis) but one should get in touch with good people; and this is rationale and/relevance of the church community in the lives of the disheartened, to positively influence and solace the affected person. There is need, on the part of the affected, to find people of faith to hold him/her up when down.

j) Lastly, it is very important for the disappointed person to establish and/or know one's worth (value) so that one doesn't bury oneself in self-negation and/or discount oneself to the lowest by over-bargaining with the other party, that might create a situation whereby the afflicted party can be taken for granted and hence exposing him/her to more chances of being disappointed.

71. LORD DISMISS US WITH THY BLESSINGS (SDAH 64)

1) Lord, dismiss us with thy blessing; Fill our hearts with joy and peace
Let us each, thy love possessing, Triumph in the redeeming grace.
O refresh us, O refresh us, Traveling through the wilderness.

2) Thanks we give and adoration, For thy gospel's joyfull sound.
May the fruits of thy salvation, In our hearts and lives abound;
Ever faithful, ever faithful, To the truth may we be found.

The hymn was authored by John Fawcett (January 1740 – July 1817). He was born in Yorkshire and at the age of 16 years he was converted to the Baptist church by evangelist George Whitefield (a close friend to John Newton). He was ordained as a Baptist minister in 1765. He was remembered for having published a couple of books on his own hymn compositions along with other composers. Fawcett is also the author of the popular hymn "Blest Be the Tie that Binds", which is somewhat similar to this particular hymn.

This hymn is inspired by Aaron's blessing in Numbers 6:24ff "The Lord bless you, and keep you …and give you peace."

There is an incomprehensible nature of God's blessings & providence to His people that can take any form (as long as we accept His leadership and choice for our lives). The problem is we often twist God's arm when we pray and we already have what we want in mind. This confines God and reduces His wealth of choices for us. But when we pray with faith and let Him do according to His will and promises, He will always and absolutely exceed our human expectations and limits in His generosity.

The Blind Man who gathered an Antelope

A story is told of an old blind man who asked God to provide for him what to feed his household and bless him as he goes ahead to look for food for his people. This guy went to the forest to fetch firewood and any herbs that could serve as lunch. Soon after collecting firewood and some wild herbs he packed them well for easy carrying back home. As he was leaving he requested a young man to help him lift and put the pile of firewood on his head so as to head home.

Incidentally, where he had put his pile of firewood, was also a dead antelope which confused the young man up to asking him which load the blind man was referring to (of the firewood and the antelope). This equally confused the blind man since he had not anticipated such a huge and miraculous blessing but finally he quickly resolved to tell the young man to help him lift the antelope since it was his original load he had come for. This saw him walk away with such a big blessing after taking a second thought before quickly answering to the young man's question. This illustration truly brings the nature of God's blessings and interventions in our daily lives. When we accept His goodness and we let Him do according to His generosity, we shall always realize that even our expectations and prayer request underestimate His providence and the wealth of His choices.

72. TREAD SOFTLY (SDA 479)

1) Be silent, be silent,
A whisper is heard;
Be silent, and listen,
Oh, treasure each word.

Refrain
Tread softly, tread softly,
The Master is here;
Tread softly, tread softly,
He bids us draw near.

2) Be silent, be silent,
For holy this place,
This altar that echoes,
The message os grace

3) Be silent, be silent,
Breath humbly our prayer,
A forestate of Eden
This moment we share.

4) Be silent, be silent,
His mercy record;
Be silent, be silent,
And wait on the Lord.

This devotional hymn was composed by Frances Jane 'Fanny' Crosby (1820 – 1915), a daughter of John and Mercy Crosby, and she was born in Southeast, Putnam County, New York. She became blind at the age of six weeks from maltreatment of her eyes during a spell of sickness. When she was eight years old she moved with her parents to Ridgefield, the family remaining there four years. At the age of fifteen she entered the New York Institution for the Blind, where she received a good education.

The composition of this hymn was inspired by Habakkuk 2:20 "But the Lord is in His holy temple, let all the earth be silent before Him". The Lord is in His Temple; He is real, alive, and powerful. He is truly and fully God unlike idols that have no life nor power. Idolaters command their idols to save them (like during Elijah's time) but we who worship the living God come to Him in silent awe and reverence. We acknowledge that God is in control and knows what he is doing. Idols remain silent because they cannot answer. Our living God, by contrast, speaks through His word. We should therefore approach God reverently and wait silently to hear what He has to say (because He knows everything).

In worship services, this Fanny Crosby hymn has always been largely used by some Christian denominations like the SDA Church as a 'call to worship'. The purpose of this call to worship is to gather and focus the congregation in a worshipful attitude. This can further alert worshippers that the service is soon beginning so that they can reverently prepare themselves for this worship session (service). This hymn can be likened to another one of its kind that was authored by George Frederick Root titled, "The Lord is in His Holy Temple", which was also inspired by the same scripture Habakkuk 2:20 – which is equally used as a 'call for worship' just like this Crosby hymn that we are currently studying.

Lest We Forget II

The Book of Joel was written between 835 BC and 796 BC in the Southern Kingdom of Israel. Judah during that time was enjoying economic prosperity which prompted them to forsake God. They were so busy that they were no longer interested in worshipping God; it was at this time that God raised Joel to revive Judah towards godliness and true worship .Samaria was the capital city of Judah, which comprised of 10 tribes that had seceded (broke away) from the 12 tribes of Israel during Rehoboam's reign (heir/son of Solomon). This kingdom had completely forsaken the Lord for ages; God called Joel to go and remind Judah where God had brought her from, that is, he begins by pleading to them to, "…….Mourn/ lament like a virgin bound with sackcloth for the husband of her youth……" It is so crucial for us to remember and then remind our children from where God delivered us ie bondage, suffering, addiction, ungodliness, hopelessness, etc so that they can appreciate the goodness of being godly and so as to subsequently establish a personal and intimate relationship with God as a friend and a deliverer of His people.

Unless we go back to the basics and our history in a bid to remember and refocus towards our eternal mission (objectives), we shall continue going under, with our children inclusive. This saw Joel admonish his people in Joel 2:12-13, "Now, therefore, says the Lord, Turn to me with all your heart, with fasting, with weeping, and with mourning. So rend your heart, and not your garments……….return to the Lord your God, for He is gracious and merciful, slow to anger, and of great kindness…."

BIBLIOGRAPHY & REFERENCE SECTION

PRAISE SONGS
Anne Steele (1863) *Hymns, Psalms and Poems. Charles Cordelier.* London.
Campbell, J. (1877) *Book of Psalms. Macmillan & Company.* London
Garen L. Wolf (1996) *Music of the Bible in Christian Perspective.* Salem
Harold Best and David K. Huttar (1993) *Music in Israelite Worship, in "The Complete Library of Christian Worship".* Ed. Robert E. Webber. Peabody, MA.
John W. Kleinig (1993) *The Lord's Song: The Basis, Function and Significance of Choral Music in Chronicles.* Sheffield, England.
Kenneth W. Osbeck (1985) *Devotional Warm-Ups for the Church Choir.* Grand Rapids, MI.
Lorenz, S. Edmund (1909) *Practical Church Music.* Fleming H Revell Co. New York.
Mugerwa, Paul (2015) *Gracia & Gentil: Hymn Stories For Our Contemporary Lifestyles.* Vol. 1. EPS Publishers Ltd. Kampala
Seventh-Day Adventist Elder's Handbook (2013) Ministerial Association. GC of Seventh-Day Adventists
Showalter, A. J. (1904) *The Best Gospel Songs and Their Composers.* A. J Showalter Co. Dalton.
Wayne, Hooper., and Edward, E. White (1988) *Companion to the Seventh-day Adventist Hymnal.* Review and Herald Publishing Association.
Wesley, John and Charles (1744) *Collection of Psalms and Hymns.* 3rd Ed. London.
http:// www. Pewresearch.org/fact-tank/2017/04/06/why-muslims-are-the-worlds-fastest-growing-religious-group
https://en.wikipedia.org/wiki/List_of_religious_populations

CHRISTIAN LIVING SONGS
123 Glorious Hymns Every Christian Should Know (2011)
Braun H. Myron (1982) *Companion to the Book of Hymns Supplement.* Discipleship Resources. Nashville
Ellen G. White (….) *Steps to Christ.* Ellen G. White Publications
Hasel M. Frank (2017) *The Holy Spirit & Spirituality*

Hall, J. H (1914) *Biography of Gospel Song and Hymn Writers*. New York
Jackson, S. Trevena (1915) *Fanny Crosby's Story of Ninety-four Years*. Fleming H Revell Co. New York.
John Julian (1907) *Dictionary of Hymnology*
Johnson, W., and Johnson, R. (1925) *The Book of American Negro Spirituals*. Viking Press. New York.
Mugerwa, Paul (2015) Gracia & Gentil: *Hymn Stories For Our Contemporary Lifestyles. Vol. 1*. EPS Publishers Ltd. Kampala
Sankey, D. Ira (1906) *My Life and the Story of the Gospel Hymns*. Harper & Brothers. New York
Seventh-Day Adventist Elder's Handbook (2013) Ministerial Association. GC of Seventh-Day Adventists
http://www.poetry.com/poems/861338-THE-BALANCE-SHEET-OF-LIFE (by Prateek Guru)
http://ipost.christianpost.com/post/15-famous-quotes-and-5-principles-about-prayer
https://www.stanford.edu/about/history/
https://www.linkedin.com/pulse/japanese-fish-shark-story-rohit-gupta
https://www.littlethings.com/balloon-happiness-exercise

DISCIPLESHIP SONGS

Aggarwal, J. C (2014) *Essentials of Educational Psychology. 3rd Ed*. Vikas Publishing House Pvt Ltd. India
David J. Pleins (2013) *The Evolving God: Charles Darwin on the Naturalness of Religion*. Bloomsbury Publishing PLC.
Discovering the Songs of Christmas (Pg 245 – 247)
Dudley-Smith, Timothy (1981) *A Collection of Hymns, 1961 – 1981*. Hope Publishing Co.
Ellen G. White (1995) *Education: Learning from the Master Teacher*. Review and Heralds Publishing Association
Ellen G. White (1905) *The Ministry of Healing*. Ellen G. White Publications
Fisher, M. Miles (1953) *Negro Slave Songs in the United States*. Citadel Press. New York.
Ivan Vandor (1980) *The Role of Music in the Education of Man: Orient and Occident*. The World of Music. New York

Mugerwa, Paul (2015) *Gracia & Gentil: Hymn Stories For Our Contemporary Lifestyles. Vol.1.* EPS Publishers Ltd. Kampala

Oresmus Hymnal. Hymns Ancient & Modern, Standard Edition (1875 – 1924)

Stennett Samuel (1824) *Works. 2nd Vol.* London.

Seventh-Day Adventist Elder's Handbook (2013) Ministerial Association. GC of Seventh-Day Adventists

Wayne, Hooper., and Edward, E. White (1988) *Companion to the Seventh-day Adventist Hymnal.* Review and Herald Publishing Association.

White, E. Edward (1968) *Singing with Understanding.* Signs Publishing Co. Victoria.

http://www.snopes.com/steve-jobs-deathbed-speech

WORSHIP SONGS

Adam, Fox. *English Hymns and Hymn writers.* Collins, London

Donald, W. Mckay (1969) *The People Behind Our Hymns.* Faith for Today Press. New York

Duffield W. Samuel (1888) *English Hymns: Their Authors and History. 3rd Ed.* Funk & Wagnalls. New York

Gealy, F., Lovelace, C., & et al (1970) *Companion to the Hymnal: A Handbook to the 1964 Methodist Hymnal.* Nashville, Abingdon.

Gradenwitz Peter (1949) *The Music of Israel.* W. W Norton & Co. New York.

Jensen William Reynolds (1976) *Companion to the Baptist Hymnal.* Broadman Press. Nashville.

Mugerwa, Paul (2015) *Gracia & Gentil: Hymn Stories For Our Contemporary Lifestyles. Vol. 1.* EPS Publishers Ltd. Kampala

Mugerwa, Paul (2016) *The East Africa Financial System: Towards an Optimal Regional Integration.* Mabira International Publishers. Kampala, Uganda.

Newton, John (1817) *Olney Hymns.* Hamilton. London.

Polack, G. William (1958) *The Handbook of the Lutheran Hymnal. 3rd Ed.* Concordia Publishing House.

Raymond C. Holmes (1984) *Sing a New Song! Worship Renewal for Adventists Today.* Berren Springs

Richard Paquier (1967) *Dynamics of Worship.* Philadelphia

Seventh-Day Adventist Elder's Handbook (2013) Ministerial Association. GC of

Seventh-Day Adventists
Wayne, Hooper., and Edward, E. White (1988) *Companion to the Seventh-day Adventist Hymnal.* Review and Herald Publishing Association.
http://www.angelfire.com/mo2/goodnews/debt.htm (The Russsian king story & forgiveness)

EXTRAORDINARY OCCASION SONGS
Blanchard Kathleen (1940) *Stories of Favorite Hymns.* Grand Rapids. Zondervan Publishing House.
Frost, Maurice (1962) *Historical Companion to Hymns Ancient and Modern.* William Clowes & Sons Ltd. London.
Kelly, Thomas (1820) *Hymns on Various Passages of Scripture.* Martin Keene. Dublin.
https://en.wikipedia.org/wiki/Wedding_anniversary
blog.funeralguide.co.za/last-wishes-alexander-great/
https://sites.google.com/site/.../the-three-last-wishes-of-alexander-the-great

BENEDICTION & DOXOLOGY SONGS
Bosch G. Henry (1943) *Stories of Inspiring Hymns.* Grand Rapids. Zondervan Publishing House
Haeussler, Armin (1952) *The Story of Our Hymns.* Eden Publishing House.

NB: This should be coupled to my in-depth interaction with all the Church leaders, music scholars and evangelists and worship leaders (more than 30 experts) as highlighted in the "Acknowledgement Section" of this Book. The content of this Book was enormously blessed by their experience, expertise and resourceful guidance.

www.ingramcontent.com/pod-product-compliance
Lightning Source LLC
Chambersburg PA
CBHW032149010526
44111CB00035B/1360